MY LIFE'S PILGRIMAGE

September, 1910.

THE AUTHOR.

[Frontispiece.

MY LIFE'S PILGRIMAGE

By THOS. CATLING
FORMERLY EDITOR OF "LLOYD'S WEEKLY NEWSPAPER."

INTRODUCTION BY
THE RIGHT HONOURABLE LORD BURNHAM

WITH ILLUSTRATIONS

LONDON
JOHN MURRAY, ALBEMARLE STREET
1911

BRADBURY, AGNEW, & CO. LD., PRINTERS,
LONDON AND TONBRIDGE.

TO

MY DAUGHTERS

WHO

ASSISTED IN ITS PREPARATION

I LOVINGLY

DEDICATE THIS BOOK

INTRODUCTION.

The period over which Mr. Catling's reminiscences extend has been the brightest epoch in the annals of the British Press. This, therefore, is more than a personal record. It spans an era of momentous change. Personally I can look back on considerably over half-a-century of Fleet Street. With its life and work I had been associated, as a member of the staff of the *Sunday Times*, for several years before Mr. Catling came to London, and before the establishment of the *Daily Telegraph*. How much has happened since then! The vista of the past, which this volume recalls, Mr. Catling and I amongst living journalists have known by experience. In the nature of things it can have been given to very few indeed to spend over fifty years in close association with Fleet Street and its Press—as we have been. Within the scope of "My Life's Pilgrimage" the political, social, intellectual, and material life of England has advanced by leaps and bounds. We have progressed from the tinder-box to electric light, from the stage coach to the flying machine; and journalism has reflected and kept pace with the social evolution. Its machinery, organisation, and sphere of action have improved and extended marvellously. Before the date when Mr. Catling's recollections begin, the greatest achievement in the art of printing—since Fust and Gutenberg first used type to make their impressions—was the application of steam to the printing machine, and that was the triumph of a journalist. In 1814 Mr. John Walter, of the *Times*, announced, with justifiable flourish of trumpets, that he was working his machine by steam. Here are his words: "It is done with a variety and simultaneousness of movement that not less than 1,100 sheets are impressed in one hour." Though we can nowadays print far more sheets of much larger newspapers in a minute than Mr. Walter could in an hour, this was an epoch-making advance. In the days and nights upon which I am looking back a large amount, even of newspaper printing, was done by manual machinery, the motive power being supplied by two men turning a wheel. To-day in all large establishments we have engines of extraordinary horse-power, and the type itself is set by machinery.

Mr. Catling's earliest experiences in Fleet Street coincide almost exactly with the period when the "Taxes on Knowledge," as they were rightly called, were beginning to be removed. Under the Stamp Duty of a penny a sheet, the tax of 1s. 6d. on every advertisement, and the Excise Duty on paper, journalism marched in fetters. The Advertisement Duty was repealed in 1853, the Stamp Duty in 1855, and the Paper Duty in 1861; with each of these concessions the Newspaper Press took giant strides forward. The journalistic recollections in this volume cover the epoch of what I may call telegraphic journalism. The Electric Telegraph Company was formed in 1846, and from that time onward telegraphy has been a growing force. The name of the journal to which my life has mainly been devoted is an historic embodiment of the fact that in 1855, when the *Daily Telegraph* was founded, the influence of the electric current had become a potent factor in the nation's life. It was the one touch of science that made the whole world kin. Yet the process of this mighty agency was very gradual. I was impressed with this fact a few years ago. On May 9th, 1864, a naval battle took place between the fleet of Denmark and the combined fleets of Russia and Austria. If there be anything in which the British public takes deep concern it is a sea-fight; yet here was a battle almost within earshot of our own seaboard, and the London press on the following morning published less than a quarter of a column of details, supplied by Reuter's Agency. There was no special correspondence, no graphic narrative. In 1904 and 1905, when the war raged between Russia and Japan, we devoted to naval and military conflicts, occurring 10,000 miles away, not merely columns, but pages of description and narrative telegraphed at enormous expense. The crucial event in this matter was the Franco-German war of 1870. Before the outbreak of that gigantic struggle, foreign correspondence published in the newspapers was forwarded by post. After July 15th, 1870, when war was declared, all this was altered; thenceforward from every part of the globe, reached by wire and cable, or by the ethereal waves of Wireless Telegraphy, news of importance has been transmitted by electricity.

All the associations with these changes link themselves to one spot in London—Fleet Street—

which I have known by day and by night for full sixty years. For more than four centuries this historic thoroughfare has been the home of literature. To Fleet Street the first successors of Caxton brought their printing presses from the precincts of Westminster Abbey. Shakspere's "Hamlet" was printed in 1604 in Fleet Street, and sold at a "Shoppe under Saint Dunstan's Church." Here Ben Jonson and Samuel Johnson, Boswell, Richardson, Fielding, and Goldsmith kept the lamp of literature burning. Many a time have I wondered what Fleet Street looked like to other eyes. Here in Crane Court the Royal Society had its home for seventy-two years, during a third of which period Isaac Newton was its president, the greatest of the world's natural philosophers being almost as frequent a visitor as was Dr. Johnson in later days. But journalism eventually ousted book-publishing and science. In the year 1702 the *Daily Courant* was sold by one Edward Mallett, at the King's Arms Tavern, Fleet Bridge. A little further west *The Morning Post* was started in 1772, and fifteen years later the *Times*; then came in succession the *Morning Advertiser* in 1794, the *Evening Standard* in 1827, *Punch* in 1841, *Lloyd's News* in 1842, the *Daily News* in 1846, and the *Daily Telegraph* in 1855. And thus more and more Fleet Street has become the journalistic centre. There is no such concentration in any other part of the world—remembering always that from Ludgate Circus to Temple Bar is only a third of a mile. To-day more than one hundred newspapers have their offices in this famous street—metropolitan and provincial, colonial and foreign, European, American, African

INTRODUCTION.   xi

and Asiatic, the Far West and the Far East, from California to Hong Kong, they meet journalistically in Fleet Street. Dr. Johnson one hundred and fifty years ago wrote an essay on a project for the employment of authors. "It is my practice," he says, "when I am in want of amusement, to place myself for an hour at Temple Bar, or any other narrow pass much frequented, and examine one by one the looks of the passengers, and I have commonly found, between the hours of eleven and four, that every sixth man is an author." If you went through that process to-day you might find every sixth man a journalist.

It is men that make newspapers. The most perfect machinery, the finest organisation, world-wide agencies of information, and the most lavish expenditure fail of half their effect without the gifted mind to think and the hand to write. In the period under review we have known such writers and editors as Charles Dickens, Makepeace Thackeray, Harrison Ainsworth, Douglas Jerrold, John Delane, Thornton Hunt, George Augustus Sala, Edwin Arnold, Henry Traill, Frederick Greenwood, Augustus St. John, William Howard Russell, Stirling Coyne, Alexander Cockburn, Henry Stanley (the Explorer), George Smith of Assyrian fame, Archibald Forbes, Canon Mozley, Robert Lowe, Alexander Knox, Wingrove Cook—the last four being men who wrote the *Times* leaders in its most brilliant days—Walter Besant, Fitzjames Stephen, George Henry Lewes, "George Eliot," Shirley Brooks, Mark Lemon, Clement Scott, and a host of others, now no more with us. To many readers of this "Pilgrimage" several of these will be names only;

to some of us they are mementoes of friendships that never die.

On the personal side of Mr. Catling's interesting narration I have little need to touch. It tells its own story. In presiding over a banquet which the author's colleagues gave him on his retirement in 1907, I said, "In our guest to-night we honour a noble profession, a glorious past, and a hopeful future." Here we have, as he himself tells us, a man in the main self-educated, who rises from a humble position in a provincial newspaper office, to be the editor of an influential London journal. Of no other profession can it be said, as of this, that here an honourable career is thrown open to every man of ability, without distinction of class or creed, of technical training or academic culture—a career open to talent and character. The next best thing to the possession of merit is its discovery in others. In this quality the Press has no equal. How many men to-day in the front rank of politics, literature, law and the drama, have, like Mr. Catling, owed their advancement to the "open door" of journalism! So may it ever remain.

BURNHAM.

Hall Barn,
　Beaconsfield,
　　September, 1910

AUTHOR'S APOLOGY.

WHILE resting in the solitude of Egypt's great desert some years ago, memories of the past crowded thick upon me and were jotted down. Any idea of a book was then remote, and faded entirely away on my return to the activities and duties of Fleet Street. With my retirement the outlook was changed. Knowing that I had seen fifty-three years' service on the newspaper, friends called for reminiscences. To meet that wish the compilation was commenced; facts were packed together, and recollections piled up, until confusion set in. The constant aim had been to deal with the doings of other people; keeping my personality out of the record. Whatever may be thought of the plan, it was at least a sincere effort; though it failed in effect. Some expert advice, followed by a mental review of the position, showed that an altogether different method must be adopted.

Remembering all that had been said and written of the vanity of Autobiography, I strove to avoid it; but strove in vain. The vital changes affecting the national, political, and social life of the people during the past seventy years could only be presented with the right perspective through the medium of individual experiences. Those who follow my homely record from infancy to age will see how varied and unexpected were many of the happenings by the way.

T. C.

October 25, 1910.

CONTENTS.

	PAGE
INTRODUCTION BY LORD BURNHAM	vii
AUTHOR'S APOLOGY	xiii

FIRST STAGE . . . . 1—29
    A BOY'S BEGINNING, 1838—1854.

SECOND STAGE . . . . 30—83
    THE CRAFT OF CAXTON, 1854—1866.

THIRD STAGE . . . . 84—159
    A BOUND INTO JOURNALISM, 1866—1884.

FOURTH STAGE . . . . 160—193
    THE EDITORIAL CHAIR, 1884—1890.

FIFTH STAGE . . . . 194—256
    THE OLD ORDER CHANGED, 1890—1898.

SIXTH STAGE . . . . 257—328
    THE PROFIT AND PLEASURE OF TRAVEL, 1898—1906.

SEVENTH STAGE . . . . 329—363
    RETIREMENT AND REFLECTION, 1907—1910.

AUTHOR'S ADIEU . . . . 364—365

INDEX 367

ILLUSTRATIONS.

THE AUTHOR	*Frontispiece*	
From a Photograph, September, 1910.		
ROYAL ARCH AT CAMBRIDGE, 1843 . . ⎫	*To face page* 4	
THIRD CLASS RAILWAY CARRIAGE . . ⎭		
THE AUTHOR'S FATHER	,, ,,	28
THE COMET OF 1854 . . . . ⎫	,, ,,	34
"THE IMPALEMENT" BY CHINESE JUGGLERS . ⎭		
THE AUTHOR AT SEVENTEEN . . .	,, ,,	48
DOUGLAS JERROLD . . . . ⎫		
From my Office Photograph. ⎬	,, ,,	52
HOE'S "TURTLE" OF THE FIRST ROTARY PRESS ⎭		
HYDE PARK RAILINGS THROWN DOWN . .	,, ,,	88
BROKEN BRIDGE ACROSS THE SEINE, 1871 . ⎫	,, ,,	104
RUINS AT ST. CLOUD . . . . ⎭		
TEMPLE BAR DECORATED, 1872 . . .	,, ,,	108
CAPTAIN WEBB LANDING AT CALAIS AFTER ⎫		
SWIMMING THE CHANNEL . . . ⎬	,, ,,	138
TRAM-LINE RUNNING INTO THE CHANNEL TUNNEL ⎭		
MR. GLADSTONE'S CONTRIBUTION . . .	,, ,,	198
A PROPHETIC PAGE	,, ,,	242
JOHN NORTHCOTT AND MYSELF . . .	,, ,,	274
Sketched by Alfred Bryan.		
THE AUTHOR IN THE NILE DESERT . . ⎫		
SOUDANESE WAITING FOR THE TRAIN . . ⎬	,, ,,	284
A Snapshot at Khartoum in 1900.		

L.P.

ILLUSTRATIONS.

THE GATE OF OMDURMAN . . . . *Photographed from Gunboat on the Nile.* RUINS OF THE MAHDI'S TOMB, OMDURMAN .	*To face page* 286
GEOFFREY THORN'S IDEA OF THE ALPS .	,, ,, 312
IN MINERS' DRESS FOR DESCENDING DOLCOATH	,, ,, 346

ERRATA.

Page 207, line 3, *for* " 1891 " *read* " 1881."
,, ,, ,, 8, *for* " Three months " *read* " Ten years."

MY LIFE'S PILGRIMAGE.

FIRST STAGE.

A BOY'S BEGINNING.

In My Father's Garden—Ravages of a Great Storm—Queen Victoria Drives to Cambridge—Days of the Tinder-box—The "Hungry Forties"—Arrival of the Railway—First Visit to the Theatre—Recreation and Sports—A Grim Tragedy—Fire in a Church—Scene at an Execution—Memories of School—Work on a Newspaper—Overcoming a Difficulty—Olden Customs—Holiday in London—Peeps Behind the Scenes—Lively Doings at an Election—Home Influences—In a New Office—Prince Albert and the Tower—How I Missed College.

BEYOND the fact of being my mother's first-born, there is nothing to chronicle concerning my advent on September 23rd, 1838. As environment now counts for much in the estimate of life's chances and changes, it may be recalled that a pleasant garden on the outskirts of Cambridge was my first happy hunting-ground. My father, a skilful botanist, experienced in everything relating to horticulture and floriculture, loved his garden with unceasing ardour, but had not a sufficiently keen eye for profit. Enthusiastic in the production of choice flowers and fruit, he was more mindful of gaining honour at a show than securing a good market. Though certain college contracts were helpful, he found gardening a life of struggle, made more trying by bad seasons and an uncertain demand. His labours, however, were a source of continual delight, and a few floral triumphs made him one of the happiest of men.

RAVAGES OF A GREAT STORM.

A terrific thunderstorm is the earliest incident that can be recalled. So vividly does the scene of havoc and destruction recur that, but for the undoubted evidence of dates, I could scarcely believe it happened a month before my fifth birthday. Mr. Glaisher, then an assistant at Cambridge Observatory, in describing the awful character of the storm of August 9th, 1843, said the lightning flashes followed each other with such rapidity that there seemed to be one continuous roll of thunder. Hailstones, many of them an inch or more in diameter, killed the birds in the trees, cut the harvest to pieces, and crashed through every pane of exposed glass. My father's plant houses, as well as his growing crops, were wholly destroyed in this one disastrous afternoon, involving losses which could not be made good.

QUEEN VICTORIA DRIVES TO CAMBRIDGE.

Autumn brought a gleam of brightness, my father being busily engaged with decorations for the visit of Queen Victoria. There was no railway to the University town in those days, and the young Sovereign made a triumphal progress by road. Leaving Windsor Castle at twenty minutes to eight on the morning of October 25th, the Queen drove to Slough Station, travelling by train to Paddington. Entering a carriage, the royal party proceeded across Regent's Park, through Camden Town, to Tottenham, where horses were changed. On then at the rate of fourteen miles an hour, the cortége sped by way of Waltham Cross and Ware to Buntingford. Here a brief stay was unexpectedly made at the Bell Inn, and thence with fresh horses the route was continued to Royston and Melbourne. Every town and village was ablaze with flags and banners; laurelled arches crossed the entry to each place; and when at two o'clock the travelling carriage, drawn by four bay horses, reached Cambridge, a most enthusiastic welcome awaited Her Majesty. Across Trumpington Street there stood a triumphal arch, made hollow, like the famous horse of Troy. Inside solid platforms were erected for the accommodation of favoured spectators, who were enabled to enjoy an uninterrupted view of the whole procession through openings in the wooden sides. It was from this splendid coign of vantage that my young eyes first looked down upon the great Queen, as she rode smiling beneath, with Prince Albert by her side. My father had covered the arch with wreaths of laurel and festoons of paper roses; hence my place within. I well remember the ladies being armed with scissors, with which they clipped away any leaves or decorations that threatened to mar their outlook.

DAYS OF THE TINDER-BOX.

Domestic comforts that are now within everybody's reach were unknown in my early days. The person who obtains gas to boil a kettle while dressing in the morning, by simply putting a penny in the slot, has no idea what lighting a fire meant when the tinder-box had to be relied on. Overnight it was needful to see that enough linen rag had been burnt to provide the requisite tinder. In the morning, with flint and steel, sparks were struck on to the tinder until it became sufficiently heated to ignite the phosphorus ends of what are now called "Guy Faux matches." These were placed in the grate, under pieces of crumbled turf (dried peat), which required equally careful handling and the frequent use of bellows to secure the lighting of further fuel, whether it was turf, wood, or coal. When lucifer matches came into use, they were indeed an immense boon. For illumination we had to struggle with candles, the economical rushlight being just sufficient to make darkness visible, while "dips" required frequent use of snuffers. All were ill-smelling; unpleasant to handle; a constant source of discontent; and (as Carlyle growled) involved a great waste of time. Cambridge being near the Fen district, many people suffered from ague, rheumatism, and kindred ailments. Hence in winter they abandoned all idea of ventilation, shutting themselves up as cosily as possible. Woollen wraps included close-fitting nightcaps for young and old. The warming-pan, now regarded as a curiosity, was nightly used for airing all the beds in the house.

THE "HUNGRY FORTIES."

When I read of the "hungry forties," and find the period described as one "when every form of

ROYAL ARCH AT CAMBRIDGE, 1843.

THIRD CLASS RAILWAY CARRIAGE.

[To face p. 4.

social evil was rife, and society seemed to be drifting into moral chaos," a few things come to mind. Known as a kindly guardian of the poor, my father was often appealed to by sufferers from the hard times. Even those at work lived literally from hand to mouth. Adults made less than a shilling a day; in some cases not more than two-thirds of that sum. Ground down by destitution as the people were, the only wonder is that they remained so patient. One remedy, provided by royal proclamation, was the coining of half-farthings. A recognised authority described it as " a very pretty little coin, not issued in sufficient numbers to test its convenience, especially to the poor." No tradesman was compelled to accept more than sixpennyworth of these half-farthings at a time.

It was in the "forties" that I tumbled into the Cam while fishing from a barge. Many a time since, when reading of drowning people remembering all the events of their lives, has my narrow escape come to mind. I simply recall the fact of being fully conscious, while sinking and rising in the water, yet not afraid. Coming up in a clear space between the barges I was hauled out, when a man flourished a whip as he shouted, " You young rascal, you deserve to be thrashed." The only result of my ducking was that it killed all taste for fishing at once and for ever.

ARRIVAL OF THE RAILWAY.

The introduction of the railway in 1845 excited the whole country round. As simple folk made short trips, they marvelled why the hedges seemed to "run by them"; indulging in the wildest speculations as to changes likely to follow travelling by steam. The Eastern Counties line began in a struggling way, and years elapsed before it made any advance either in respect to comfort or speed. Some trains took between four and five hours to cover the fifty-seven miles between Cambridge and London, naturally exciting ridicule. Queen Victoria's first trip in July, 1847, led to much talk. The company, having no suitable saloon carriage, arranged to borrow one from the London and North-Western line. In the *Times* my father was greatly amused to find a paragraph stating that, in order to avoid leaving the metals, this carriage had been sent by way of Peterborough (a distance of two hundred and ten miles) to Tottenham Station, from which the Queen was to start. By special command the royal train was not allowed to exceed a speed of thirty-five miles per hour at any time. The visit was in association with the installation of Prince Albert as Chancellor of the University. At the election he had received 953 votes against 837 given to Lord Powis. Madame Bunsen, in describing the brilliant scenes of that glorious summer day, said, " I think I never saw so many children before in one morning. I felt so much moved at the spectacle of such a mass of life collected together and animated by one feeling, and that a joyous one, that I was at a loss to conceive 'how any woman's sides can bear the beating of so strong a throb' as must attend the consciousness of being the object of that excitement, and the centre of attraction to all those eyes." The Queen was saved from regarding the proceedings— the reception, presentation, and reading of the Address—too seriously by a sense of humour, for she wrote in her diary " Albert went through it all admirably—almost absurd, however, as it was for us!"

FIRST VISIT TO THE THEATRE.

Just after my tenth birthday came what can confidently be set down as one of the greatest treats of my boyhood—the first visit to a theatre. Macbeth, as played in vociferous fashion by Mr. Melville, filled me with wonder. The defiance and fight at the close can be distinctly recalled. Of the pantomime which followed I have only a vague recollection of certain accidents. One half of Card Castle, from which the piece took its name, fell down with a great crash; a little later a fire broke out on the stage; a third mishap befell Harlequin. He took his flying leap before the window had been opened, and must have been badly bruised by his violent contact with the scenery.

RECREATION AND SPORTS.

Our boyish games were few; there was no football; we gambled freely with marbles, and raced wildly about over "rounders." Still, diversions were not wanting, the greatest being afforded by the arrival of a circus. Outdoor equestrian displays divided the honours with the antique procession of javelin men which twice a year accompanied the judges to the Assize Courts. Wombwell's Show of animals was glorious. To see an elephant dispose of sixteen half-quarter loaves in thirty-two mouthfuls was a real object lesson in natural history. On one occasion I walked to the Huntingdon road to see a procession marshalled up to parade the town. A small green branch was in my hand. Suddenly an elephant moved towards me, quickening its pace as I began to run. "Drop it," shouted one of the keepers, an order quickly obeyed. The animal only wanted the branch, but I never forgot being thus chased by an elephant. I remember the visit of Tom Thumb, being taken to see that remarkable mannikin at the Town Hall; also sitting on my father's shoulder to watch the entry of Van Amburg into his cage of lions. Banvard's panorama of the Mississippi and Missouri rivers, with its glowing pictures of Indian life, buffalo hunting, prairie fires and rising American cities, made a lasting impression. When an American named Sands imitated a fly by walking head downwards across a flat ceiling, the feat was voted more curious than entertaining. It provoked much discussion as to the means by which the appliances attached to his boots were made to act as suckers. A harvest home when the ride in an open cart was followed by a dish of furmenty, washed down with syllabub, was one of the charms of autumn. Plough Monday, with its Mumps, like Jack-in-the-Green on May Day, had become too much associated with rowdyism. Lamenting the loss of these rural recreations, Washington Irving drew too largely on his imagination when he wrote, "I value any custom that tends to infuse poetical feeling into the common people and to sweeten and soften the rudeness of rustic manners without destroying their simplicity." With the increasing growth of the drink habit these old sports developed into an intolerable nuisance.

A GRIM TRAGEDY.

Ever since the time of Cain, who "did the first murder," the world has been deeply moved by its tragedies. Boy as I was in 1848, the excitement created by the killing of Mr. Jermy and his son at Stanfield Hall, in Norfolk, comes readily to mind; and a paper of the time which has been preserved shows how thoroughly the demand for news was met. The prologue of the tragic story goes back to the dawn of the nineteenth century, when Mary Blomfield, a farmer's daughter, being deceived by a gentleman admirer, brought an action for breach of promise. Recovering large damages she married Mr. Rush, a well-to-do farmer, who was content to acknowledge and receive her two-year old son. There were no children of the marriage, so the boy received a good education. Having taken the name of James Blomfield Rush, he at the age of twenty-four made a start for himself. Some three or four years later he married well, but henceforward had a troubled life. A wheat stack on his farm having been burned, a prosecution for incendiarism was started but abandoned. In 1830 the introduction of machines into Norfolk greatly roused the agricultural labourers. During a riot a number of machines were destroyed, Rush being arrested for aiding in the rescue of one of his men. For this the magistrates bound him over to keep the peace. Having rented a farm attached to Stanfield Hall, he was sent as agent to buy the adjoining Pot Ash Farm for Mr. Jermy, at the price of £3,500. Rush bought it in his own name for £3,750, and then coolly asked Mr. Jermy to lend him the money. The transaction was carried through on a mortgage.

Soon after Mr. Rush, senior, was found dead, with his own gun lying beside him. Young Rush's wife also died, leaving him with nine children. Henceforward, he was always in pecuniary difficulty. Auctioneering, farming, and agency work alike failed to provide enough for his needs. His troubles grew greater in 1847, when his mother died, litigation being followed by bankruptcy. Meeting a young woman named Emily Sandford, Rush promised her marriage, and kept her for a time in London, she passing as his niece. Afterwards she was taken to his home at Pot Ash Farm, and lived with him more or less openly. He evaded payment of rent, but the claim for interest on the mortgage hung over his head. A time was fixed for payment, which expired on November 30th, 1848. Two days before this date, while sitting at tea with Emily Sandford, Rush said he had been thinking a good deal about the story of Robert Bruce in a tale he had just read. While he was in hiding, Bruce watched a spider as it swung backwards and forwards with a view of reaching the side of his cave. Six times the insect tried and failed; on the seventh it succeeded. On seeing this Bruce said he had tried several times to assert his and his country's rights, but he would follow the example of the spider and try once more. Rush in a very excited manner said, "I have tried several times; I have been out five or six times, and the next time, perhaps, I shall be successful." Emily Sandford in alarm asked what he meant, when he replied, "I shall like you better if you do not ask me any more." An hour or two later Rush went out, and that night Mr. Jermy and his son Jermy Jermy were shot dead by a masked assassin in their own home, Mrs. Jermy and a servant being also wounded. Rush, it was afterwards proved, returned to his house, locked himself in his room for some time, and told Emily Sandford, "If any inquiry is made, you will say I was not out more than ten minutes."

The trial took place at the Assizes, occupying six days. Mr. Baron Rolfe presided, with a strenuous earnestness that would astonish easy-going judges of to-day, sitting from nine in the morning till after seven at night—more than sixty hours in all.

Among the various curious incidents was the adjournment of the Court for a quarter of an hour one morning while Emily Sandford left the witness-box to go out and suckle her baby. At the close the jury took less than five minutes to decide on their verdict of "Guilty." Rush's bravado never left him. On the scaffold, as the rope was placed round his neck, he said to the hangman, "This does not go easy; put the thing a little higher. Take your time; don't be in a hurry." Emily Sandford, with her child, was sent out to Australia, under the protection of her brother, who was accidentally drowned while landing from the ship. Left thus alone, the poor woman struggled on for a while, and some years later there came news that she had ended her life by taking poison.

FIRE IN A CHURCH.

Cambridge had another thrill on the morning of Sunday, November 12th, 1849, when St. Michael's

Church was found to be on fire. The means then in use for fighting the flames will cause a smile to-day. An old-fashioned hand-engine—a clumsy, bumping, clattering machine, that with much labour threw a stream about the force of a good garden-hose—was with much shouting hauled to the scene. Though the engine was on the spot, the only available water was in the Cam, nearly a quarter of a mile away. So the leathern fire-buckets, of which every college possessed a set, were brought out, and a double row of men was formed from the engine to the river. Up to his armpits in the water stood a man who rapidly filled the buckets, which were then passed from hand to hand, emptied into the engine, and returned along the opposite line. While this went on hour after hour two or three other like engines were brought up and worked by undergraduates toiling willingly alongside the townsmen. The firemen managed the hose so skilfully that the church, though much damaged, was saved from destruction.

SCENE AT AN EXECUTION.

Doubtless the continued talk over the gruesome details of the Stanfield Hall crime was the main cause of my boyish interest in a double hanging which took place at Cambridge some short time after. It arose from no special ferocity of disposition, but was rather an outcome of the light in which public executions were then regarded. Horror was swallowed up by the idea of the spectacle affording excuse for a holiday and providing matter enough to talk about for a whole month. Hence the crowds which gathered to witness the hanging of Elias Lucas and his sister-in-law, Mary Reeder. The wife of the male prisoner had died from arsenic poisoning. Down to their last moment both the husband and sister denied the murder ; but no doubt was entertained as to their guilt. No place in the whole country was probably better suited for making a public show of the hangman's work than Cambridge County Gaol. The gate looked out towards the Castle Hill, over a hundred feet high, which formed a natural amphitheatre capable of accommodating many thousands of sightseers. They came from all the surrounding neighbourhood ; special trains were run, and every kind of vehicle brought into requisition. The governor of the gaol being one of my father's friends, I had ready access to the scene, and remember reaching the foot of the hill before seven in the morning, though the execution was not to take place until noon. So minutely did I survey the setting up and testing of the gallows, that on returning home it was an easy task for me to make a working model, drop and all, and scare my little sister by hanging one of her dolls. When the fatal hour arrived I was in a favourable spot, high up, my young eyes watching every movement of the hangman as he placed the ropes round the necks of the unhappy culprits, and then kicked aside the beam that supported the trap on which they stood.

MEMORIES OF SCHOOL.

School days can never be forgotten. My first lessons were derived from an ancient dame, whose chief difficulty was to keep boys and girls apart in her humble cottage. She praised and encouraged my progress with arithmetic; giving me also credit for being a fairly docile pupil. Both reports pleased my good mother. Of the routine and lessons of a large national school to which I went later no deep impression remains; albeit the headmaster did not spare the rod. On one occasion, after the mid-day interval the boys did not return to school, but remained playing outside. The master's anger rose, till he seized a cane, and, standing at the entrance, thrashed each boy to his seat. Real education I only received for a short period at a private academy. A fairly large schoolroom was built on an upper floor, overlooking a good playground. In a central position on one side stood a desk, so raised that from his chair the master could note everything that was going on around. Nothing seemed to escape his eager eyes, and many were the surprises amongst the boys in consequence. He was a most unusual compound of kindliness and severity, but I look back upon his rule with feelings of warm admiration. Absolute silence and close attention to any lessons in progress were imperative requirements; and woe betide any boy, little or big, who, either from carelessness or a wilful disposition, set these demands at defiance. Late-comers stood no chance whatever. One bell sounded the note of preparation, and at the second ringing all had to make their way upstairs and settle in their places. Then the master entered, and the chief usher went round to see that every boy's hands and nails were clean. The subjects taught were fewer than is the custom now, but the master and his assistants displayed the greatest patience in seeing that the pupils were well-grounded in them. We had good practice in reading aloud, and special care was taken with our writing—close observation being kept that our fingers were straight in holding the pen. As to spelling correctly, that was an ever-present necessity, the master ranking it with honesty. "No credit is due to you for being honest," he was wont to say, "but to be otherwise is a shame and disgrace." In this way we were taught to spell without reward, though many marks were taken off for any failure. Old methods of arithmetic were in vogue, and we filled huge slates and manifold pages with the working of rule of three and long division sums, before getting to practice, fractions, and higher lessons. The brightest afternoon in all the week was one devoted to dictation. It was looked upon as recreation, yet it helped to quicken many faculties, and led up to results which have again and again stood me in good stead. The master read aloud a lengthy passage from some entertaining book, which was taken down word for word in longhand on slates. Directly the reading ended, the passage was written out in rough copybooks; these being handed in for examination and marking. The books were then given out again; the boys who had blundered had to make their own corrections from a perfect copy; and finally all rewrote the dictated passage in more permanent books—further marks being awarded for the style and finish of the handwriting. For reading aloud the one book used was the Bible, the Psalms being always selected. Directly the last Psalm was finished we turned back to the first, and began them over again. In my own experience the monotony of this proceeding had a most unhappy effect—the Psalms became so uninteresting, not to say repellent, that all through life I have failed to appreciate properly the beauty of those grand Eastern compositions. Matters were made worse by one of the common punishments being the compulsory learning of ten, twenty, or even a hundred verses of the Bible. The Psalms proved such a light task, that ten or more of the longest verses of Isaiah came to be chosen. There was no escape, the offender being kept in after school hours until he could repeat the passage given him to learn. This plan had one beneficial result, in that it helped most of us to what Shakspere calls " a good sprag memory." Although my stay here was all too brief, I acquired a grounding in English grammar. One biggish boy came to the school with a bad character, to see if the master could do anything with him. On his committing some offence he was laid face downwards over a double desk and thrashed with a severity that would now surely lead to the master's imprisonment. Yet this master in hours of relaxation was a companion with the boys, and it may be said gave his life for them. Injuring his spine by throwing up a ball in the cricket field, he was ever after a cripple, and died at the age of thirty-five.

WORK ON A NEWSPAPER.

My father's business continuing to decline, something had to be done. I was a tall slim lad, with a growing appetite, and there were two younger children. So it came about that before my twelfth birthday I went to the *Cambridge Chronicle* for just the wage which Charles Dickens received on beginning life in similar circumstances. A newspaper afforded no soft places in those days, though there was abundant variety. As the time for going to press arrived, pressure increased in all departments. The paper was printed one side at a time, the motive power of the machine being supplied by a couple of sturdy navvies turning a wheel. One of the compositors stroked the sheets singly on to a large upper cylinder; my duty was to "take off" each one as it came through the machine. When the completed papers appeared, the first issues were folded, packed into wrappers, and taken in washing baskets through the churchyard of Trinity to the neighbouring post office. Albeit the entire issue did not quite reach two thousand, the work went on through the whole of Friday night. After the post had been supplied there were parcels to prepare for newsagents, and then more single copies for town subscribers. These were delivered by hand, each man taking those that lay along his homeward route in the early morning. The provision of a substantial supper helped to reduce the strain of the long hours, but I well remember getting into trouble through dropping off to sleep while standing at the machine, thus spoiling many sheets. At other times my eyes must have been open and observation alert, as one little incident will show. The newspaper office was to me as the discovery of a new world. It inspired the writing out of a record of the workers, their duties and qualifications; with certain personal comments. Everybody, from the proprietor to the 'prentices, figured in the list. In changing a coat this compromising paper fell from my pocket and, being picked up, was read out during supper time, to the great amusement of all save the unwary author.

OVERCOMING A DIFFICULTY.

Liberal payment for the night's work and a plentiful allowance of beer usually sufficed t keep up the animal force for the driving of these hand machines. Once upon a time, however, a difficulty arose in a certain office, and thereby hangs a tale. It was a time of hot weather, when ailments were prevalent, for which beer had no curative effect. The men put in an appearance, but it could readily be seen that one of them would never get through the customary work. As there was no one in the office who could possibly take his place, the situation began to look awkward. Suggestions for a way out of the difficulty were hastily sought in various directions, and among those consulted was the governor of the local gaol, who happened to be a friend of the proprietor. "Well," replied this official, "I have got just the man you want under my care, and if you offer him as much beer as he likes to drink, he will no doubt take on the job. Only, if I let him out for the night, you must undertake to keep a watch over him and see that he comes back to me when he has finished in the morning." Every assurance was quickly given; the liberated prisoner duly appeared, and the sense of freedom, coupled with free drinks, sweetened his weary toil through the night, without his knowing how indispensable were his services in saving the publication of the paper.

OLDEN CUSTOMS.

Great importance was attached to the Queen's speech on the opening and closing of Parliament. Directly the speech reached the office it was customary to have slips specially printed, and a copy sent round by hand to each regular subscriber to the weekly paper.

The leading reporter was quite a notability—a man of wide knowledge, and qualified beyond all competitors as a shorthand writer. His one weakness was an inordinate love of gin-and-water. After finishing any report he would settle down in an underground bar, to steadily drink his favourite mixture, until he became speechless and unable to reach home without assistance.

One effect of the No-Popery cry was to intensify the Town and Gown riots that were sure to break out on the slightest provocation. On both sides it was simply an orgy of reckless rowdyism.

A "tossing pieman" perambulated the town with his tin of hot mutton-pies, the disposal of which was generally preceded by the spin of a coin, to decide whether the tasty delicacy should be enjoyed for nothing, or the ordinary price doubled.

Dogs were employed in drawing country carts; the dog tax being twelve shillings a year.

Photography came into being with the Daguerreotype process. "Sun portraits" (as they were called) were taken on every fine day in our garden, each sitter being able to select a pretty natural background.

Tomatoes were cultivated with care, the object being to secure rich colouring for table ornaments; no one thought of eating them.

HOLIDAY IN LONDON.

As Prince Albert, in face of bitter opposition, pushed on his scheme for the Great Exhibition of 1851, the country grew more and more interested. The fact that the Palace of Glass was designed by Paxton, on the plan which he had carried out as gardener to the Duke of Devonshire at Chatsworth, naturally excited my father. He had somewhere met Paxton, and regarded all the followers of Adam's calling as being united in a common brotherhood. There was a further attraction in the novelty of using glass, seeing that the Window Tax, which had been in force for nearly two centuries, still existed, bringing in close on two millions a year. When the illustrated papers made the splendour of the Palace of Crystal known, everybody was agog to see it; my mother amongst the rest. In her company I saw the display in Hyde Park—truly a great exhibition—and something of London; too much to remember many details. One night, however, stands out clearly—the night of Wednesday, July 9th, when Queen Victoria paid a visit to the City, passing through Fleet Street about nine o'clock. Mother would not venture in the crowd, but her boy was there, watching the scene, and eagerly applauding Her Majesty as she drove by. Things were more simply managed in those days, coloured oil lamps being chiefly used for the illuminations. Economy characterised the

Guildhall arrangements for the ball. According to a paper of the time, the royal visitors sat down to supper in the crypt, the walls of which were hung with coarse canvas, roughly painted in imitation of tapestry.

PEEPS BEHIND THE SCENES.

Returning from the brief holiday, another year was spent in the newspaper office. When it was found that I could decipher difficult manuscripts, I was allowed to act as "reading boy," and my service got near to being satisfactory. Printing had certain attractions; scraps of poetry and songs were surreptitiously set up and worked off; willing assistance being rendered in the casting of rollers and the required wetting and turning of paper. During the dramatic season there was always a volunteer ready to carry proofs of playbills to the theatre, no matter how late at night they were ready. This took me behind the scenes, where I experienced the delight of meeting actors and actresses face to face. They would stop me at the stage door and ask to look at the bill; sight of it being the first intimation of the piece or pieces in which they would be required to appear. Of course all were stock plays, for which they were expected to be ready at the shortest notice. Looking back to this time, I recall dim impressions of rehearsals tending to mar the effect which the wonderland of the drama should exercise on the mind of every healthy boy; still it was a happy experience, fraught with fruitful lessons for after-days.

A little confession will show how my youthful mind was affected by this atmosphere of the stage.

Following closely the lines of a story appearing week by week in the *Family Herald*, I laboured secretly, but steadfastly, until what seemed to be a play was ready. The manuscript was dropped one dark night into the letter-box of Mr. Hooper, manager of the Norfolk circuit, then residing in Jesus Lane. That, of course, was the end of the precocious effort.

LIVELY DOINGS AT AN ELECTION.

For real excitement there was nothing to approach an election. Little boys waved their party flags, while bigger ones, following the parental lead, talked a great deal, and sometimes fought. With public nomination at the hustings, open voting, and unblushing bribery, a Parliamentary contest became an event of overwhelming importance. Various causes combined to make the struggle of 1852 very severe. Working on a Conservative paper I was in the thick of it, and had the advantage of access to the hustings erected in the open area of Parker's Piece. The nomination of four candidates, with long speeches full of personalities from each one, extended over many hours, rousing public feeling to fever heat. Next day came the polling from eight till four o'clock. Great efforts were made to secure early voters, and as the numbers became known hour by hour the excitement increased. By two o'clock it was considered that the Conservatives were sure of a majority; soon after I was sent up to wait for the final figures. Down the centre of the hustings from front to back there ran a strong wooden barrier, designed to separate the two political parties, who entered from opposite sides. They were thus kept perfectly distinct from each other, while their respective supporters similarly divided themselves as they stood crowded in front. Shortly before the close of the poll the proprietor of the paper, who was beside me in the reporters' box, waved a sprig of laurel in the face of the defeated party. Directly it was seen there came volley after volley of stones, which fell rattling on the sloping desks as we ducked beneath them and thus escaped injury. Many persons sitting and standing behind were badly hurt before they could gain shelter. The official declaration was no sooner made than the band of the losers moved off into the town, thrusting their flag-poles through the plate-glass fronts of certain leading drapers, known to be on the opposite side in politics. Half-bricks were freely flung at their other windows, till scarcely a pane of glass remained whole. Rejoicing over the victory proved of short duration, as the newly-elected members were unseated on petition. A special inquiry followed, resulting in remarkable disclosures. Bribery was admitted to have taken place in very open ways. Ladies went round with envelopes containing five and ten pound notes; while new sovereigns fresh from the Mint were handed over in bags without so much as being counted. At the first sitting of the Commissioners, the proprietor of the suspected paper was said to have left the town for the Isle of Man on urgent private business. There was no escape; he had to return, and I heard him tell the full story of his share in the sorry work, which consisted in receiving and paying out the money provided by the party expressly to bribe doubtful voters.

Corruption of this kind goes a long way back, for I have a record of 1571, when a returning officer received four pounds to secure an election. On the transaction becoming known the member was removed, the borough amerced, and the offending officers fined and imprisoned. In Cambridge the leaders were granted certificates of indemnity; only a few of the humble tools receiving punishment.

HOME INFLUENCES.

The club of the district assembled in the tradesmen's parlour at the Pickerel Inn, beside the river Cam, where evening after evening politics were discussed on quite imperial lines. The *Times* was my father's standard authority on well nigh all public questions, and with that backing he delighted to argue out whatever topic was uppermost. A pleasurable association with the Pickerel circle is recalled by a silver tankard which remains in my hands. It bears this inscription: "Presented to Mr. Edward Catling by his fellow parishioners, as a testimonial of esteem for efficient and long-continued services as guardian of the poor of the parish of St. Peter, Cambridge." The silver, be it added, was accompanied by a purse of gold.

In matters of serious moment, as affecting belief, my father's broad-minded views were sharply condemned at home. The simple Puritan type of my mother's devout Wesleyanism caused her to express the deepest horror of any approach to freedom of opinion. At the mention of Volney's "Ruins of Empires," she mourned over my father's peril in having even read it. Just opposite our own door was a Primitive Methodist chapel, to which came crowded congregations from the country-side. The judgment on their very demonstrative services, an occasional "love feast," or late night sitting, was always tolerant, if not entirely favourable. With my mother's reverent faith was mingled something akin to superstitious belief in certain mystic readings of the Bible. The thirty-first chapter of the Book of Proverbs, having thirty-one verses, was studied in a spirit of divination, each verse being fitted to the date of one's birth. Some curious results were arrived at by this reading. Burns was the favourite home poet, appealing strongly to one who, with increasing years, felt more and more deeply how sharp was the struggle to get a living out of a small plot of land. "Man was made to mourn" became such a familiar theme with my father, that one morning I committed the whole poem to memory before getting out of bed, without in the least appreciating the meaning of its deep melancholy.

IN A NEW OFFICE.

As my fourteenth birthday approached there was some talk of an apprenticeship. This meant beginning at three shillings a week, with a rise, first of a shilling, and then two shillings, which would bring up the wage for the last year, when I should be over twenty, to fourteen shillings. It seemed little enough; too little, in fact, even for those days. Anyhow, nothing was done. I drifted on week after week and then left.

For a few weeks freedom in the home garden,

with release from night work, proved a pleasant change. As autumn arrived, necessity—stern mother of industry—called for renewed exertion. Various things were discussed in a dreamy sort of way, till one afternoon the master of a small jobbing office arrived. He had heard of my leaving the *Chronicle*, and had been told that I knew enough of printing to be useful. The afternoon when I was called down from a convenient perch amid the branches of a damson tree, laden with ripe fruit, to accept the offered engagement is well remembered. In the new office I gained an insight into many branches of printing. There was neither machine nor any division of labour: whatever came in, card, handbill, broadside, or auction catalogue, was composed and printed by hand.

When work was plentiful consideration was shown in extra payments; slackness caused depression in all directions. The master starting out for orders was apt, if disappointed, to turn to skittles, and seek solace in beer. It was not the excess so much as the loss of time that proved fatal to business. This period gave me unnumbered hours for reading, and I devoured everything that came in my way, novels, histories, mysteries, travels, even "The Lives of the Stoics." There was no such thing as a free library then, so enough money was scraped up for a subscription one, the first volume borrowed being Dickens's newly published "Bleak House."

PRINCE ALBERT AND THE TOWER.

The winter of 1853-4, with the temperature in Cambridge falling below zero, was gloomy in the extreme, the minds of the people being disquieted by many doubts and fears. The anti-German cry found bitter expression in attacks on Prince Albert. I call to mind my father's excitement when a rumour ran through the town that the Prince had been sent to the Tower on account of his correspondence with Germany. Though there was not an atom of foundation for such a report, the satisfaction with which it was received indicated the state of public feeling. Sir Theodore Martin has since told us how deeply the Court was affected. In a letter to Baron Stockmar, dated Windsor Castle, January 24th, 1854, the Prince wrote, "You will scarcely credit that my being committed to the Tower was believed all over the country—nay even that the Queen had been arrested. People surrounded the Tower in thousands to see us brought to it." Though the writer claims that courage and cheerfulness were maintained in face of all attacks, he acknowledges the touch of nature which caused " stomach and digestion to suffer."

HOW I MISSED COLLEGE.

My own affairs grew darker; to depression at home was added the certainty that my master could not hold out much longer. What was to be done? There were few printing offices in the town; I was familiar with them all, and knew how poor were the prospects they afforded of a living wage. Suddenly a wider outlook opened with the offer of a kindly clergyman, curate at the parish church, to secure my introduction to St. Augustine's Missionary College at Canterbury The old monastery, rebuilt by Mr. Beresford Hope, had opened its doors for students, and there was a vacancy for one acquainted with printing, who would be content to accept education as a set-off against his practical labours. Alas! the bright hope of knowledge was dashed to the ground; the demands were greater than my father could possibly meet. Through after life the thought has sometimes arisen, "What might have been my fate with a college training?" No answer is possible; only the deep feeling that I should have made a sorry missionary.

As it was, the opening at Canterbury was passed on to a friend some two years older than myself. He did very well at the printing, but had no inclination for study. Hence he gave up at the end of the trial period agreed on, and made his way to London.

"Why should not I follow?" was the thought that soon arose. A newspaper advertisement opportunely came in the way, and on answering it I received a satisfactory offer. As the "turnover" was wanted to begin work on the following Monday, preparations had to be hurried. My dear mother's anxieties and fears were deep and touching; yet she unknowingly seemed to have anticipated by her thrift the urgent need of that momentous time. The town savings bank held in my name a whole sovereign, the accumulation of many little presents. That was capital enough for a start. My father encouraged me with good counsel and the hope of advancement, bidding me remember that while talent was given to the few all could cultivate tact. Many a time the excellence of this advice has

MY FATHER AT SEVENTY-FIVE.

[To face p. 28.

helped me. For verily tact—the "doing or saying exactly that which is required by or is suited to the circumstances" (as the dictionary puts it)—is one of the high qualities of successful diplomacy in small things as well as great.

SECOND STAGE.

THE CRAFT OF CAXTON.

Early Days in London—My Start on *Lloyd's*—A Time of National Anxiety—Help for a Poor Player—Fleet Street as I Found it—The New Crown Court Office—Salisbury Square Fiction—My Trials and Experiences—War News and Extra Editions—Founding of *Lloyd's News*—Douglas Jerrold as Editor—Shakspere at Sadler's Wells—The Working Men's College—In Front of Newgate—Revolution in Printing—First Hoe Rotary Presses—Whiskers in the Army—Napoleon III. in Hyde Park—Starting of the Sunday League—Boulogne and Foolish Drinking—William Palmer the Poisoner—Lady Bancroft and Ellen Terry—Panic at Mr. Spurgeon's—Death of Douglas Jerrold—The Need of Faith—Notable Benefits—First Bit of Sub-editing—Studying Books and Preachers—Walks and Amusements—I Receive a Police Reward—" Out of My Time " and After—Memorable Year for the Press—Demand for *Lloyd's* at a Penny—Death of the Prince Consort—Development of Stereotyping—The Prince of Wales's Marriage—Teaching Law to a Judge.

WHEN a boy of fifteen-and-a-half sets out from a country home to make his way in London, he does not see, or seek to see, far ahead. Each day opens up its task, and the doing thereof fulfils the claims of duty. A simple diary begins thus:

"*April* 8, 1854.—Rose early. Packed up my earthly possessions, contained in one box; walked to the Eastern Counties Railway Station (sending my box on before), when I started for London, being my first set out in life."

It was the day of the University boat race, and though the contest then created little general interest among Londoners, it drew me from Bishopsgate to Putney. Going and returning along the river's bank and by the rhubarb gardens, then plentiful in Brompton, meant miles on foot before reaching the lodging arranged for me near the printing office in Soho. On arrival late on Saturday evening the little landlady was scared at my appearance. Instead of a tall stripling, decently dressed and wearing a top hat, she expected a fit companion for another lodger—a grimy, dissolute printer from the same office. The good motherly soul would not allow me to come into contact with such a creature. I therefore had to find shelter in the nearest coffee-house.

EARLY DAYS IN LONDON.

The diary records a stroll in Hyde Park before Sunday's dinner; afterwards a walk to Chelsea and back in time for evening service at St. James's Church. Next morning work began, the hours being from eight till half-past seven all through the week. Saturday half-holidays were not even a dream of the future. Nothing eventful occurred, but the change from my sovereign was soon spent. With the first wage I received a week's notice, as all the work in hand would be completed. Here was a staggerer, which brought the stern reality of my position sharply before me. In the diary it is written, "Am rather dull, but don't despair of getting another situation; determined not to go home again under any circumstances." From my friend I learned on the second Sunday that an advertisement for "three turnovers at case" had just appeared in the *Morning Advertiser*. Next morning, Easter Monday, found me an early applicant at the address given in President Street, Goswell Road. The quest was successful, and having arranged to commence piece work on a newspaper the next morning, "with a light heart and gladsome step," I turned towards Greenwich. According to a topical song of the day, the railway then offered "Pig-pens open and free" to third-class passengers. Into a long truck with low sides, no roof or seats whatever, so many as could stand entered by a single opening and packed themselves close together for the journey. The crowding, though attended by a good deal of roughness, was borne patiently enough, and it being a very fine day, the wild fun of the famous fair soon roused my youthful spirits and shut out all anxiety.

MY START ON "LLOYD'S."

With the next day came the beginning of labour on *Lloyd's*. Although the paper was then, as now, printed in Salisbury Square, it was composed on an upper floor in Wheatsheaf Yard, Farringdon Street. The machines left the type in a fearful condition, so that many weary hours had to be devoted to washing it with the strongest pearlash or potash procurable. Dirt mingling with the ink caked the letters together, thus making distribution a heavy task, and seriously handicapping the compositor. I mention this because it kept down wages to a serious extent, despite the fact that there was no Society or other bar to the number of hours spent in the office. Journeymen were content to wait about all day on the chance of getting a night's work. Public-houses were of necessity their chief resort, affording amusement as well as shelter—cards, bagatelle, skittles and other games being permissible. An incident that might have made shipwreck of my whole career marked the first week. When apprentices were bound, or completed their period of service, certain fees were demanded by the men. The fact of two being "out of their time" together led to a double allowance for drink, to the potent influence of which my young stomach was altogether unaccustomed. In a state of insensibility I was carried up to the office, and there left to sleep off the effects of the London gin. My miserable condition stands confessed in the diary, but is accompanied by the entry " am resolved not to get so again." All round there was a plentiful amount of chaff, but excess was too common for any word of serious remonstrance.

A TIME OF NATIONAL ANXIETY.

The period of my arrival was one of national stress, accompanied by gloomy fears and dire anticipations. A comet brandished its crystal tresses in the sky, and Dr. Cumming, seeking to unravel prophecy, was predicting the speedy end of all things. War with Russia had just been declared; naval and military preparations were in progress; martial music filled the air. At the wish of the Bishops a national fast was proclaimed.

It meant making matters worse by the closing of all places of business, though the diary tells me my newspaper work went on as usual. The record of daily labour, relieved by a little sight-seeing, is homely enough. A second trip to Greenwich at Whitsuntide was noted as a warning; the holiday cost too much, and spoilt the work of the week. Wet Sundays proved specially disagreeable. Though it in no way concerned me, the fact may be noted that the Income Tax jumped from 5*d.* to 10*d.* in the pound. What came nearer home was the rise in the price of bread to 10½*d.* and 11*d.* the four-pound loaf; other articles of food going up in proportion. [In the note which accompanied the sketch of the comet of 1854 the *Illustrated London News* said Mr. Hind gave the nucleus a diameter of rather more than 5,000 miles, with a tail of 6,000,000 miles.]

HELP FOR A POOR PLAYER.

Poor though the printers were, there oft came occasions for kindness, and it was never lacking. Before a month passed, I call to mind being one of a goodly gathering at the Standard Theatre, drawn thither for the benefit of Henry Gaskell Denvil, who was known to the overseer. *Clari, the Maid of Milan*, was not an exhilarating entertainment, but tickets were readily bought, as the poor player needed help badly. Twenty years before, when he came out at Covent Garden as the creator of Manfred, he was the dramatic star of the London season. On looking up the records of this time I found high praise lavished on his "refined

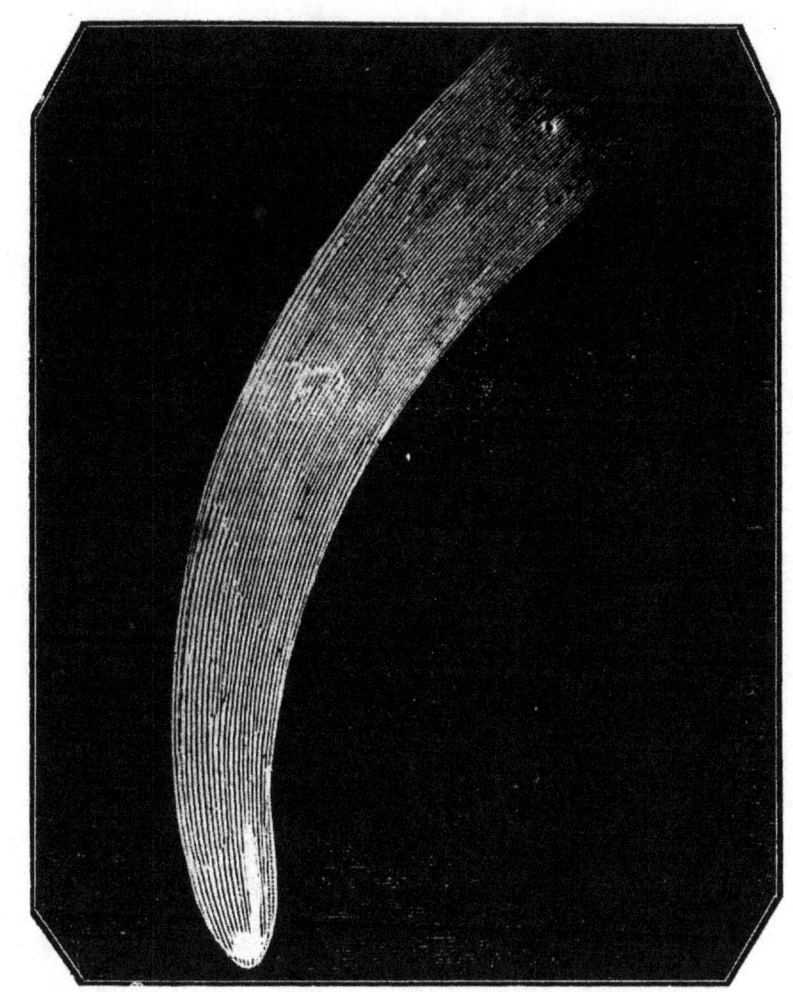

THE COMET OF 1854.

"THE IMPALEMENT" BY CHINESE JUGGLERS AT DRURY LANE.

[To face p. 34.

melancholy, so expressive of Byronic feeling." Alas! only the melancholy endured, and the actor ended his labours as a checktaker at Drury Lane. Still I owe him something, as his sad life story set me reading Byron with an admiration that has never faltered.

Drury Lane, when I first saw it, had for the chief attraction a marvellous feat by some Chinese jugglers. This was known as "The Impalement." One man stood with his back against a board while another darted sharp knives at him. They penetrated the wood close to his ears, his throat, his head, his hands, and between his fingers. The throws were made with an appearance of certainty as to the aim that excited the utmost astonishment.

FLEET STREET AS I FOUND IT.

Fleet Street at this period showed no sign of so soon becoming "the hub of the newspaper world." Though railways were represented by the office of Bradshaw's Guide, the Bolt-in-Tun and Kings and Key still figured as starting points for coaches. Among the retail traders, who were mostly content to live over their shops, there was a "hatter to the Queen" and a looking-glass manufacturer with the "largest mirror in the world." A hairdresser flourished in the sham palace beside the Temple, opposite the two oldest houses, one of which was famous as a cheap pie-shop. Peele's coffee-house maintained a special attraction in files of certain newspapers. *Punch* enlivened the approach to St. Bride's by keeping its windows crowded with humorous pictures; on the north side were the offices of the *Morning Advertiser* and the *Dispatch*. Prominent among a dozen other weeklies appeared the *Sunday Times*, on which my good friend Lord Burnham was just beginning his journalistic career, indulging (as he has since told us) in " visions of a future " destined to be so fully realised in this historic street. A struggling entertainment, conducted somewhat on the plan of the famous Evans's, was carried on at the Johnson Tavern, running alongside Bolt Court, but with the entrance from Fleet Street through Three Kings Court. I there heard Sam Hall, Ross, Penniket, and other comic men. The arrangements were free and easy enough. No side door being available, the performers had to walk through the company the entire length of the hall, thus affording opportunity for words of welcome or chaff that were highly appreciated. Quite naturally this familiarity led to invitations for a drink, which, when accepted, rendered the bliss of the evening complete. Payment was made in a lump sum just before leaving, when the waiter would ask " What have you had ? " and then add up the charges for your chop, Welsh rabbit, beer or spirits as the case might be. Gossip associated the tavern with Dr. Johnson, but it did not exist in his day.

THE NEW CROWN COURT OFFICE.

Of any definite aim, or even hope or anticipation, when *Lloyd's* compositors were moved, I am altogether unconscious. The change, however, opened up possibilities of acquiring a knowledge of many things. In the new Crown Court office it was realised that we worked on the spot where

Richardson carried on his printing during the time that he wrote his famous novels, and was assisted in the reading by Oliver Goldsmith. The windows, overlooking Hanging Sword Alley, recalled the Alsatia of Sir Walter Scott's "Fortunes of Nigel." Douglas Jerrold's neatly written copy came regularly to hand. Everything was clearly marked for the compositor. The following facsimile of a scrap which has been preserved shows the minute care bestowed upon a small matter. All leading articles were advertised each week, and Jerrold wrote out the list in this manner:—

[facsimile of handwritten list]

Another great name grew familar from the fact that on entering the service the three "turnovers" were nicknamed "the Newcomes," after Thackeray's famous story, then in course of monthly publication. The real life of the day, however, had little romance in it.

Crown Court, like nearly all others in the district, was thickly populated; and our immediate neighbours proved a very mixed lot. A burly sweep and his buxom wife, weighing some sixteen stone, were a terrible couple when they broke loose. Industrious, silent and orderly all through the week, these people on Saturday nights, when saturated with beer, sank into a condition of veritable savagery—snarling and quarrelling till insensibility overcame one or the other. The cause of dispute was often as to which of them had drunk most of the sixteen quarts of beer, for which the man vowed he paid. As to language, no description is possible of the vile and abominable epithets hurled indiscriminately at each other and one and all of the near residents. The epidemic of quarrelsome drunkenness seemed to run round the court at certain seasons, when men and women fought with brutal ferocity. One of the saddest scenes recalled was when two comely young girls, who had been close friends, were egged on to a pitched battle, scratching and tearing each other in presence of the whole disorderly gang. It must be recorded, nevertheless, that these folks kept their disputes entirely to themselves. Of the scores of people who passed through the court to and from the printing office on business of one kind and another, I never heard of one being molested or insulted in any way.

SALISBURY SQUARE FICTION.

In the office there remained bills and other evidences of the flood of fiction which was gradually running out. "Ela, the Outcast," and "Ada, the Betrayed," continued in demand, while "Claude Duval" and "Dick Turpin" were perennial favourites. The authors of these and a multitude of other tales no longer poured their manuscripts into Salisbury Square, but the air was full of anecdotes of the methods they had pursued. When, in 1844, all Paris was raving over "The Wandering Jew," each part of the French edition was translated as soon as received, and a hitch in the supply at times compelled the English adaptor to furnish whole chapters of his own invention. A new writer was required to send in a complete story, but the stock authors worked from hand to mouth. Each penny number consisted of eight pages, ten shillings being paid for the copy as soon as completed. The idea of a plot was submitted for something like eight weeks. Number one would be given away with some other work, and if it caught on, the serial might run for twelve months, or even two years. On the other hand, if it failed to attract, a summary ending was quickly provided. Mr. Rymer was the most prolific author, having kept as many as ten different stories running serially at one period. When Mr. Lloyd ceased to issue fiction, Rymer transferred his labours to another publisher, and ultimately accumulated sufficient money to enable him to end his days in comfort.

A droll experience occurred with one lady writer, who unexpectedly sent in what she called the last instalment of her tale. "That will never do," said Mr. Lloyd, when he heard it; "why the story is just going well, and ought to run for months." After discussion, a trusty man was sent to inquire what the sudden stoppage meant. He found that it was due to the lady expecting a speedy addition to her family. As delicately as possible he inquired further, and was told that the important event was anticipated in about a fortnight. To meet the publisher's wish the authoress promised to write all the copy she possibly could during this fortnight, in order to bridge over the period of quiet that must ensue. So the tale went forward, "to be continued," as usual; at the end of the week, instead of the anxiously looked for fresh chapters, came news of baby's arrival. As will be seen on varied occasions, Mr. Lloyd was equal to any emergency; when one literary tap failed, he never hesitated for a moment to get another turned on. There was no one in the place who had read the lady's story, and no time to do it, as the printers were waiting for copy. Just glancing at the closing lines of the previous number, a new writer, regardless of what had gone before, dashed off sufficient for an instalment, which duly came out next morning. Instead of being grateful to those who thus saved the situation, the authoress appeared in a surprisingly short time with an imperious demand to know who had dared to interpolate such stuff into her story. Her anger was softened on being told that the tale was a success, and she could safely go on writing another dozen numbers, with the prospect of more being wanted.

MY TRIALS AND EXPERIENCES.

This first summer in London, with small wages and no sign of any future, was a time of severe stress and trial. A youth who had never before been beyond his mother's guidance naturally fell into some errors and follies; and blundered sadly in spreading the expenditure of his scanty income over the week. One lesson was never forgotten. After working all night I found myself with a sore throat, tired out, and penniless. All efforts to borrow a shilling proved unavailing. As a forlorn hope, my belongings were overhauled, and happily a crooked sixpence, the gift of an old aunt long before, was discovered. This sufficed to provide the much-needed breakfast. Temptations were near at hand. When a few men were called on for night work, the "Father of the Chapel" would undertake to make provision. This would take the form of sandwiches, bread and cheese, a can of ale, and at least a bottle of gin. Instead of paying equal shares, they would "throw" or "jeff" to see who should bear the cost. The throwing was with "em quads," the nicks on one side of which served as the spots on dice for the counting. When, as was often the case, the entire charge fell on a single loser, it became needful to tide him over the payments for a week or two, particularly if he happened to be married. On more than one occasion I well nigh discovered what it meant to "dine with Duke Humphrey," and certainly learned to appreciate a meal of dry bread washed down with a draught of spring water, then obtainable from a pump fixed beside the churchyard of St. Bride, or one beneath Mr. Linn's fish shop in Fleet Street. It is on record that there was a return of cholera in the City during this year, but I cannot recall any personal memory of it whatever. The pumps, however, were soon closed in consequence. At one time there came a tempting offer to make for Australia, but the family ties were too strong to be severed in this way. August, indeed, found me paying a visit to the old home in Cambridge. My position on returning to London demanded immediate consideration, and I resolved on a change at all hazards. In order to raise the money required for an advertisement in the *Times* I had to follow the example of young Master Copperfield and make my way to a pawnbroker's shop. However regrettable the necessity of this may be, it is surely the most independent form of borrowing known. Several replies came quickly, and of two promising openings I agreed to accept one at Kensington. Going there after my work was completed on Saturday evening, I made final arrangements and engaged a new lodging. All that remained to be done was to call back at the newspaper office for my apron and composing stick. Though the hour was late, I found the master printer still on duty. This good man from the west country, Mr. Thomas Cunningham, proved a true and lasting friend. A little talk ended in his offering me terms for which I agreed to abandon my Kensington engagement and enter on a further apprenticeship to him for five years. Thus it was that most unexpectedly I remained a worker on the paper.

WAR NEWS AND EXTRA EDITIONS.

Fighting in the Crimea was just beginning, and in a few weeks I was called on to assist in bringing out extra editions on the afternoon of Sunday, October 1st. Official despatches received during the morning contained the names of the killed and wounded at the battle of the Alma, fought on September 20th. Papers containing these lists, it is needless to say, were eagerly sought after, the demand being far in excess of the number which one machine could supply. It was on this historic occasion that I first saw Mr. Edward Lloyd, who throughout the week drove round the country supervising his advertisements, but always returned for the publishing on Sunday. Long years afterwards he told me that never but once was he late for the early morning issue, and that was on an occasion when a servant had been trusted to call him. A common order in the office was for "more slips for palings and gates," and "six sheet bills for the rocks in Wales." The more remote the place for sticking a bill, the more tempting it was to Mr. Lloyd. He was shaved very frequently, and had his hair cut and trimmed several times a day, in order to chat with barbers concerning their neighbourhoods and the possibilities of pushing the paper. A free copy was sent each week to every toll-gate keeper who could be persuaded to put up a bill by the roadside. Another feature consisted in stamping copper coins with his own advertisements, and paying half the wages of the men with this money, so that it should be well distributed. It was a plan that answered admirably, until the Government took action and passed a Bill making it a punishable offence to deface the coin of the realm.

FOUNDING OF "LLOYD'S NEWS."

My story will be better understood by a brief record of the progress of the paper to the period when I became a worker on it. When started by Mr. Lloyd in September, 1842, it was as an unstamped illustrated penny paper of eight small pages, with two serial stories. News had to be avoided, and so pictures were given of a national event or a murder, without any descriptive letterpress. The police cases were entirely fictitious, but theatrical and other amusements received considerable attention. All passed quietly for a few weeks, and then the Commissioners of Stamps swooped down with an ultimatum, notifying the proprietor of the paper that he must "stop it or stamp it" forthwith. One assumed reason for this was a story told me by Nelson Lee, that he sent up an account of the escape of a lion from a travelling menagerie in Kent, and this was held to be "news." No trace of any such paragraph can be discovered in the early numbers that exist, but there is one respecting Nelson Lee that might have provoked complaint, Here it is:—

"Messrs. Nelson Lee and Johnson have taken the theatre at Canterbury, and there is every reason to believe that the good folks of that city will reward them with the liberality they merit by their exertions to please. On completing their season they go to Deptford, where they open on Boxing night with various novelties, amongst which will be a pantomime written by Nelson Lee, who, we understand, has furnished every theatre in London with fun for the holidays. By the by, we heard lately that these gentlemen had received very harsh treatment at Enfield, from Dr. Crosswell, the parson magistrate, and a stripling named Williams. It seems that having no real ground of complaint against Messrs. Lee and Johnson, these administrators of justice turned informers on their own account, and sentenced the defendants to pay a fine of twenty shillings. The inhabitants, however, subscribed more than the amount, which was handed over by the defendants to the treasurer of the Philanthropic Society. This is a pretty specimen of justice!"

Hazardous as the course appeared, Mr. Lloyd at once had his paper stamped, and produced it for the unprecedented price of twopence. No interval was allowed to occur, the first of the new stamped issue appearing as another No. 1, on November 27th. As fiction had to give place to news, the serials were hurriedly wound up in a couple of extra numbers, appearing simultaneously. Two months later the paper was greatly enlarged and made twopence-halfpenny, illustrations being abandoned. A further change came in September, 1848, the paper expanding to twelve pages for threepence. Difficulties beset every step, trade troubles being aggravated by newsagents combining with the proprietors of higher priced papers in endeavouring to check circulation. All in vain, for *Lloyd's* had come to stay. Still, for seven or eight years, the struggle was very severe. A tax of eighteenpence on every advertisement shut out receipts from that source; the penny stamp on each copy had to be paid for in advance; and in addition there was an oppressive duty on paper. Mr. Lloyd told me that repeatedly he found himself, at the end of the week, in the position of not knowing where the money would come from to bring out the next number. The profits from the sale of a large run of tales, with gardening and other practical handbooks, proved the main source of revenue. Mr. Ball—the original "Censorius" of the *Weekly Dispatch*—was Mr. Lloyd's first editor; he being quickly followed by Mr. Carpenter, known as the author of a scathing "Peerage for the People."

DOUGLAS JERROLD AS EDITOR.

Soon after the Great Exhibition, which gave an impetus to many industries, Mr. Lloyd looked around for an editor who would give a literary character to his journal. Douglas Jerrold was then at the height of his reputation, despite the fact that his own sixpenny weekly paper and also his shilling magazine had failed to command paying circulations. Going straight to Jerrold, Mr. Lloyd asked him to accept the editorship. Jerrold hesitated; offering to write an article for the paper at any time, but saying that, owing to his engagement on *Punch*, he must consult his friends before giving an answer respecting anything permanent. After a day or two he wrote, declining the post. Mr. Lloyd (who usually thought out every detail of a scheme before entering upon it) at once replied to the effect that he had omitted to mention one thing in the course of conversation. That being, what he was prepared to offer. He thereupon named a thousand a year as the sum he was willing to pay Mr. Jerrold for editing his paper. Jerrold's immediate answer was that the letter put a different face on the matter, and he would come to see Mr. Lloyd in the afternoon. At the interview everything was quickly arranged, Jerrold's proposal that the salary paid should be £20 each week being conceded. The agreement with the new editor was acted on at once, without a line of preliminary notice in the paper, the date being April 18th, 1852. Despite the great interest created in the literary world, there was no immediate advance in the circulation, which ranged between 60,000 and 70,000 a week. Marked progress came with the issues relating to the death, lying-in-state, and funeral of the Duke of Wellington, extending as they did over more than two months. In 1853, the abolition of the Government duty of eighteenpence on each advertisement proved helpful, albeit traders were slow to take advantage of the cheaper rates. Steadily growing in every way, the paper moved onward and upward. The impressed penny stamp on each copy enabled the sale to be accurately known. When I entered the office on the 18th of April, 1854—two years exactly from the beginning of Douglas Jerrold's editorship—the official returns showed an average weekly sale of 89,385 copies.

The story of Jerrold's appointment came to me from Mr. Lloyd's own lips. An old workman assured me that the salary was supplemented by a weekly basket of poultry, butter, and eggs—these things being supplied from a small farm owned by Mr. Lloyd. Jerrold resided at Kilburn, and many messengers were engaged in going to and fro for copy and proofs. It was no uncommon thing for a boy to wait the whole day, and out of this arose complaints from parents, who objected to their sons being kept in the garden through all weathers, as sometimes happened. On the other hand, Jerrold showed personal kindness by ordering a meal for those who waited, and often gave them sixpence.

SHAKSPERE AT SADLER'S WELLS.

The revival of *Pericles* at Sadler's Wells is the chief theatrical memory of my first year in London. Performances then began at seven o'clock, the struggle at the doors occurring half an hour earlier. There was no order or supervision whatever; the crowd pushing from either side in the endeavour to overcome the pressure from behind. This meant success for the stronger party, after a severe scrimmage for all, regardless of any rights on the part of those who had been waiting longest. On reaching the pay place it was needful to have the right coin ready, and not to put it down till the disc, which served for admission, could be instantly secured in exchange. If this care was not observed, awkward mistakes were liable to occur with the pittites, as well as those fighting more fiercely for the sixpenny gallery. There were no stalls; the whole floor being given up to a shilling pit. Only alternate rows of seats were provided with backs; between ran a bare form, too narrow for comfort, irrespective of having to balance the body without relief throughout an entire performance. That mattered little; playgoers were earnest folk, and when every form was packed full, late-comers were content to stand.

THE WORKING MEN'S COLLEGE.

It has been said that a compositor's calling furnishes a means of education, but the need for something more was soon forced on me. Happily an opportunity arose through a strange course of events. For doubting "the eternity of the future punishment of the wicked," the Rev. F. D. Maurice had been dismissed from his professorship at King's College. A man of his broad and noble views naturally sought another field of labour, and this led to the founding of a Working Men's College in Red Lion Square. Cordial support was given to the new project in *Lloyd's*, and thus it came about that I was an early student. There, I not

MYSELF AT SEVENTEEN.

To face p. 48.

only received instruction in English that was of immediate benefit, but had my mind opened to a wider range of knowledge. When Ruskin and Robertson, with other great thinkers, rallied to the side of Maurice, many old shibboleths were shattered. Ignorance was no longer to be insisted upon as the chief ally of humility. Thomas Frost, who would be accounted a very moderate reformer now, says in his "Recollections" that when he asked "Why do rich people support scripture reading associations?" the answer was, "In order that the poor may be taught contentment, so that the rich may live in peace."

IN FRONT OF NEWGATE.

An execution soon attracted attention. Writing of the Mannings, Charles Dickens had condemned the hideous crowd brought together in London; I determined, as far as possible, to see everything for myself. Accordingly, very early on a January morning in 1855, when Barthelemy was to be hanged, I formed one of a dense throng in the Old Bailey. To break the pressure, numberless stout barriers were set up, so that once you were wedged in one of the small pens there was little danger. I managed to edge my way gradually to the front of the scaffold, and there waited as the daylight strengthened. All had come prepared for one object, but the depth, variety, and grossness of the language marked widely different views as to the sight in prospect. Barbarous and degrading as the scene might be, there was no mistaking its tragic significance. Every sound and every period of silence became more and more intense as the minutes passed and the gallows loomed out grimly. No mimic drama has ever awakened any approach to the deep feeling that pulsed through the compact mass of human beings. When the bell of St. Sepulchre's Church sounded its solemn knell a few minutes before eight, hoarse murmurs arose, expressing satisfaction that the long night's vigil was nearing its end. Every eye became fixed to watch the fatal doorway. Ingoldsby's lines exactly fit the scene :—

> " God ! 'twas a fearsome thing to see
> That pale wan man's mute agony,—
> The glare of that wild, despairing eye,
> Now bent on the crowd, now turn'd to the sky
> As though 'twere scanning, in doubt and in fear,
> The path of the spirit's unknown career."

Barthelemy's record was a black one, for he had shot a gendarme, killed a man in a so-called duel, and was the means of two others being done to death. Of the facts there could be no question, but legal quibblers averred that the culprit had been wrongly convicted of murder. The wretched man clung to the hope of reprieve till the last, and then went to his doom an avowed unbeliever. His last words to Calcraft, after urging him to be quick about his work, were: " Now I shall know the secret." I can recall the piercing gaze as his eyes beheld the crowd, and were then lifted with wondering intensity to the sky above.

REVOLUTION IN PRINTING.

Printing burst upon the world in the middle of the fifteenth century as one of the most perfect of the arts, and then remained without vital alteration for four hundred years. Of designs for new presses there were no end; but one and all followed the original plan of keeping the type on a flat bed and impressing the paper on it. Even when steam was applied to the printing of the *Times* in 1814, the same system was adopted; only one side of the paper was printed at a time, and the flat formes received a to and fro rectilinear motion in the cylinder machine. While Governments kept back newspapers by heavy imposts, printing inventions languished. In the middle of the nineteenth century progress could no longer be hindered. Mr. Applegath set up for the *Times* a vertical rotary press, which was probably the most marvellous machine ever constructed, though much too complicated and costly for general use. The description reads like a fairy tale. The type revolved on an upright cylinder, but each column rested on a flat bed. For the printing, the impression cylinders were padded for each column, so as to overcome the flatness and secure the effect of a true circle. With a boldness that shows the folly of proclaiming finality for any human invention, the *Times* asserted that the vertical system was the only one to be relied upon. In a leading article of December 29th, 1848, it said:—

"No art of packing could make the type adhere to a cylinder revolving round a horizontal axis, and therefore aggravating centrifugal impulse by the intrinsic weight of the metal."

Yet at this very time Mr. Richard Hoe had invented in New York a rotary press that carried the type round a horizontal cylinder; moreover, it was patented in England as early as May, 1847. Some time elapsed before one of these machines reached Europe, and then it was set up in the office of *La Patrie* in Paris. There it lingered until the abolition of the compulsory stamp duty in England, in the summer of 1855. The effect of this change was immediate and far-reaching. Newspapers appeared throughout the country, the most important among the many London productions being the *Daily Telegraph* and the *Clerkenwell News*, the latter many years after expanding into the *Daily Chronicle*.

Under the old system the methods of working were sluggish in the extreme. Paper had first to be sent to a Government office, and when returned, duly stamped, it went through a double process of wetting and turning. For printing, each sheet was separately stroked by hand into the machine, then taken off, and kept in convenient piles. The same process was repeated in printing the other side; the completed newspapers being then counted, folded, and packed in quires for the agents. With the increase of circulation improved facilities for production were soon in demand.

FIRST HOE ROTARY PRESS.

Mr. Edward Lloyd, himself a practical printer, went over to Paris, where he studied the new Hoe machine, and ordered one to be supplied with all possible despatch. This was set up in London during the summer of 1856, the first copies of *Lloyd's* printed from it being dated July 6th.

DOUGLAS JERROLD, FROM MY OFFICE PHOTOGRAPH.

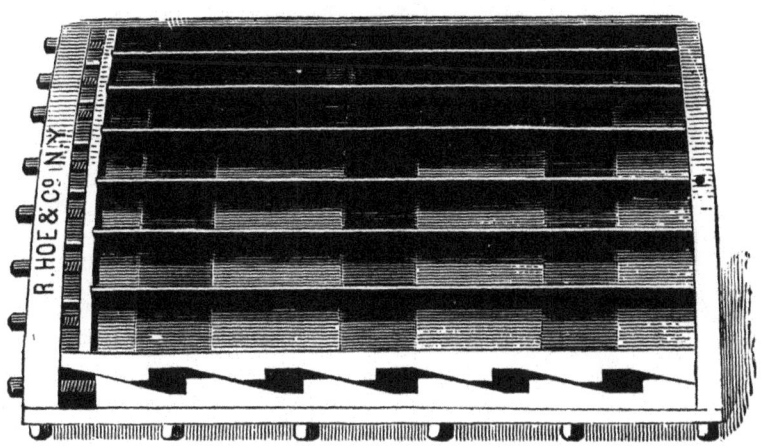

HOE'S "TURTLE" OF THE FIRST ROTARY PRESS,
WHICH REVOLUTIONISED PRINTING.

[To face p. 52.

American workmen were sent over to secure successful running of the machine, and their appearance in quaint coloured blouses created quite a sensation in Fleet Street when they turned out during the dinner hour. The necessity of having a second machine being quickly recognised, Mr. Lloyd brought his keen business faculty to bear on the negotiation. Mr. Hoe had been so eager to introduce the machine into England that he sold the first one at half-price, but Mr. Lloyd's offer to take a second at the same figure was rejected. While making arrangements for going out to New York to discuss the matter, Mr. Lloyd wrote the inventor that he thought it was greatly to his interest a second machine should be supplied. If there should be any failure with the first, the repute of the Hoe press would be seriously damaged; whereas a second machine would ensure success, and thus be certain to lead to a demand from other papers. Mr. Hoe saw the matter in this new light, and a second machine was quickly supplied on the same easy terms. It was only after much correspondence, and considerable research in the Patent Office, that I was enabled to trace the dates of the rotary machines. Being an alien, Mr. Richard Hoe could not obtain a patent in his own name, and it was something of a puzzle to discover it under an entirely different initial. According to the technical description, the first machine consisted of a horizontal central cylinder about 4 feet 6 inches in diameter; around it were six impression cylinders about one-fourth of the circumference of the central cylinder. Each page of the paper was locked up upon a detached segment of the large cylinder called a turtle, which constituted a bed and chase. The column rules ran parallel with the shaft of the cylinder and were straight, the head, advertising, and dash rules being in the form of segments of a circle. The wedge-shaped column rules were held down to the bed or turtle by tongues projecting at intervals and sliding in rebated grooves cut crossways in the face of the bed. The forme was locked up by means of screws and wedges, the type being more secure than on a flat bed. This entirely novel machine, which for the first time swept away the necessity of keeping the type on a flat bed, revolutionised printing; and in the course of a few years led to further developments that are described in a chapter on stereotyping. Every practical man recognised the great merit of the invention, but it was not understood outside the offices. No adequate description can be found in any work of reference; records and dates are alike incorrectly given. In 1868—twelve years after the machines had been set up in London—a high authority like "Chambers' Encyclopædia" said, "As types must necessarily stand on a flat surface in order to be held together and properly printed, it will seem incomprehensible how they should be built up on the exterior of an iron drum. Yet, this is done by Hoe's process. Each column of type stands on a level strip of the turtle." This was directly contrary to the fact, for no part of the surface of the turtle was level. The central idea of the invention consisted in its providing a means for type set by hand in the ordinary way being lifted into grooves arranged to receive columns, and then secured firmly on the curved bed of the chase. The imposition of the pages involved new methods, close attention, and careful handling. At my age anything fresh was welcome, and progress with the first Hoe machine secured me advancement in the composing room. As time went on success there became my aim, owing to the knowledge that the overseer received a more tempting wage than the sub-editor.

WHISKERS IN THE ARMY.

With the passing of the Duke of Wellington many old and narrow views concerning the liberty of the subject faded away, and the frightful errors of the war in the Crimea, due mainly to the deplorable blundering and weakness of our home Government, led gradually to much-needed reform. Small things marked the changes that were in progress, one of the first to be beaten down being the anti-Gallican sentiment which had prevailed for threescore years and more. At one period the managers of London theatres were protesting against French actors being allowed to perform in the metropolis. In describing a royal visit to the City, the *Illustrated London News* announced with satisfaction that "there was hardly a beard or moustache to be seen." When I first appeared in Fleet Street with slight whiskers and the beginning of a moustache, "Frenchy" was quite commonly called after me. It was not till the Queen's birthday in 1854 that the English army, while serving in Russia, was relieved from wearing the "horrible stock in which our brave fellows had been pilloried for generations." Two months later a circular memorandum was issued allowing moustaches to be grown by soldiers in the field. At home the faddism which has so often been a blot on our army system showed itself in regard to hair on a warrior's face. Whiskers were to be permitted; but, said the order:—

"A clear space of two inches must be left between the corner of the mouth and the whiskers. When whiskers are grown, the chin, upper lip, and at least two inches of the upper part of the throat must be clean shaven, so that no hair can be seen above the stock in that place."

NAPOLEON III. IN HYDE PARK.

When Napoleon III., during the Crimean war, brought over his Empress, he was received with due respect, if not enthusiasm, in all quarters. I saw them on their way through Hyde Park, riding in an open carriage, Prince Albert being seated with his back to the horses, and marked the Emperor's serious sphinx-like expression.

STARTING OF THE SUNDAY LEAGUE.

Sunday was a day of special gloom, but signs of revolt against too severe repression were in the air. A striking letter on the subject from Mr. Morrell appeared in *Lloyd's* for May 27th, 1855. This was cordially supported by Douglas Jerrold, and ultimately resulted in the establishment of the National Sunday League. Lord Robert Grosvenor brought in a Bill designed to prevent Sunday trading in the metropolis. The protests against the measure made by increasing crowds in Hyde Park led to some disturbances, and much brutality on the part of the police. I can speak to this from my own observation on July 1st, the day on which a small body of rowdies moved to the house of Lord Robert and smashed his windows. The Bill was withdrawn next day, and a commission appointed to inquire into the conduct of the police.

BOULOGNE AND FOOLISH DRINKING.

About 1856 the offer, by the South Eastern Railway, of a day trip to Boulogne caused a small sensation on both sides of the Channel. Starting from London Bridge at 6 a.m. on the Sunday, we did not return till seven the next morning. A good opportunity was afforded of seeing Continental life, doing the Cathedral, and rambling around the ramparts where Sir Richard Burton made love. Douglas Jerrold happened to be in Boulogne at the time, and he wrote a humorous description of the antics of some tourists who were overcome by swallowing cheap brandy as freely as if it had been their native beer.

Foolish drinking, as I have recorded, was a sign of the times. At the most popular of printers' outings—the wayz-goose—when all manner of luxuries were on the table, men would move quietly to the bar and toast each other in various mixtures. Small wonder, therefore, was it that when the end of the feast approached some required careful nursing. On the return journey the coachman was ordered to pull up as near as possible to a lamp-post, in order that those who alighted might have something to cling to till they steadied themselves, or a friend came to their assistance. Occasionally the driver was too liberally treated, and then the escapes were almost as narrow as they are in these days of rapid motoring. Once on a dark night I remember an omnibus being driven out of its way to the very verge of the Thames, into which the passengers were only saved from plunging by the fact that the lane ended in a gentle slope that enabled the vehicle to be pulled up sharply. Fearon's, on Holborn Hill, was then one of the most noted and best patronised spirit stores in all London —the fame whereof was celebrated in an ode to his wife by Tom Hood, and a leader in the *Times*.

A favourite custom of the period was to visit the docks with a "tasting order." The idea was to enable a possible purchaser to sample particular wines; but in reality it too often meant a rollicking outing with unlimited free drinks. On the only occasion that I accepted a friend's invitation to join him in a tasting expedition we returned through the city on foot; and as the dusk was coming on, found ourselves passing by the site of Goldsmith's old quarters in Green Arbour Court, at the end of which stood Breakneck Steps, leading to Seacoal Lane. It need only be added that we made our way safely down those notorious steps and so on into Farringdon Street.

WILLIAM PALMER THE POISONER.

Among murder trials, that of William Palmer, for poisoning his friend Cook, created an enormous sensation. It was notable for the most unusual circumstance that from first to last there was no thought or suspicion of any woman in the case. Money was at the bottom of the sordid tragedy; and albeit the condemned man declared with his last breath that he suffered wrongfully, no doubt was entertained of his guilt. Stafford was never before so full of visitors of all ranks and degrees as were attracted by his execution. I was called on to assist in bringing out a special edition devoted to the last scene. One high-class sixpenny paper, in the course of a column report, said, "Perhaps no criminal of celebrity was ever executed in so inconvenient a place, so far as the facility for obtaining a view is concerned."

LADY BANCROFT AND ELLEN TERRY.

Two famous actresses, still happily with us, were seen in 1856. Pretty and piquant in the extreme was the Miss Wilton of those early days. As the boy Henri, in *Belphegor*, she played up to the Fanfaronade of J. L. Toole with rare spirit; the scene in which the scraping of a carrot is described and illustrated causing unbounded merriment. In *Perdita* the future Lady Bancroft proved even more charming, Brough's punning lines being given with delightful drollery. Charles Kean was presenting elaborate pageants at the Princess's. The actor's curious nasal twang sometimes brought a laugh in the wrong place. The line spoken by Leontes in *A Winter's Tale*, "What, has smutch'd thy nose?" caused a titter all through the house, which might well have disturbed an older actress than Miss Ellen Terry, then making her first appearance as Mamillius.

PANIC AT MR. SPURGEON'S.

Mr. C. H. Spurgeon was one of the most impressive preachers of his time. Although his style was very pronounced, I never—at Exeter Hall or elsewhere—heard anything approaching the outrageous utterances attributed to him in early days. On a Sunday evening in 1856, when he was conducting service in the great hall in the Surrey Gardens, I was present in the topmost gallery facing the pulpit. A vast congregation had assembled, and crowds were left outside when the doors were finally closed. After the service had proceeded for some time, there was during a prayer the sound of breaking glass, and the people nearest the window rushed from under the lower gallery into the open centre of the hall. Many cries arose, followed by tumultuous confusion, but I heard nothing of "fire." On the instant those seated to right and left and all around me darted to their feet, making for the staircase—some to lose their lives and others to be grievously injured. Of the entire throng at the end of the gallery only my companion and myself remained. I have often reflected on the incidents of that awful night. It was no effort of will, but simple impulse, that kept me firm in my seat. My impression at the moment was that the building was falling, and I distinctly remember thinking how small the chance of escape would be when we were tumbled down in a mass to the floor below. When I did move slowly to the top of the well staircase nearest my corner, it was to look upon such a scene of death and destruction as I devoutly hope never to witness again. All the galleries opened on to one flight of stairs, and the pressure of the mass of people forced out the side rails, those nearest falling into the well beneath. There they lay, the crushed and maimed piled one above the other, till death had claimed many victims. One sadly injured girl whom I sought to assist begged me to search for her sister, describing her dress. When I did so, it was only to find the missing one among the killed, a discovery so dreadful that it had to be concealed.

Looking to records of the calamity, I regret to see that Mr. Spurgeon ascribed it to "the malicious act of wicked men." No evidence whatever of this was forthcoming at the inquest; my view still is that the efforts of some people outside to get into the building led to the scare and the cries heard inside, "The galleries are giving way," "The place is falling." Of course there were some who regarded the tumult as the result of a "fiendish conspiracy" and "an infernal arrangement"; but this arose entirely from overheated imaginations. What happened was simple and tragic enough; a false alarm led to a sudden outburst of fear; then came the instantaneous rush of the panic-stricken crowd into the very danger they wished to avoid. Those who remained calm and still were never in any peril.

DEATH OF DOUGLAS JERROLD.

Douglas Jerrold passed away on June 8th, 1857, being then in his fifty-fifth year. During his brief but serious illness he was visited by Mr. Edward Lloyd, and it was always understood that in the midst of his pain the sick man said he should die happy if he knew that he would be succeeded in the editorial chair by his son, William Blanchard Jerrold. The promise was duly given by the proprietor, and thus it came about that the name of Jerrold remained on the title-page of the paper. Among the manifold tributes called forth by the loss of the distinguished editor, the *Times* said:—

"The reading public, which knows celebrated men in black and white only, has lost a writer, who, for epigrammatic brilliancy, has never been excelled in this language. But far deeper has been the loss of the circle of friends who delighted to spend whole evenings in catching the stream of wit as it flowed from Jerrold's lips, and acquired for themselves a reflected glory by repeating 'Jerrold's last.' The wits of London have lost their acknowledged chief."

The funeral, though announced to be "strictly private," drew together a remarkable assembly of over two thousand persons in Norwood Cemetery. Dickens, Thackeray, Charles Knight, Horace Mayhew, Mark Lemon, Hepworth Dixon, Monckton Milnes, and Mr. Bradbury acted as pall-bearers, and the gathering comprised the most distinguished men in art, literature, science, and the drama.

Hard by Drury Lane Theatre, the Rev. Dr. Cumming was preaching to packed congregations in Crown Court Chapel. I well remember his frank confession that of Douglas Jerrold's works he knew nothing, until he found himself surrounded by lamentations in the Press as to the loss of the great author. With a view to forming a correct judgment for himself, he sent for some of his books and then emphasised the depth and meaning of the following passage from "Clovernook":—

"It is a fine show, a golden sight, to see the crowning of a King. I have beheld the ceremony; with undazzled eyes have well considered all its blaze of splendour. A tender thing to think of is the kiss of peace; beautiful the homage; heart stirring the voice of the champion, when the brave knight dashed his defying gauntlet on the marble stone; very solemn the anointing, and most uplifting the song of jubilate when all is done. But, Sir, to my coarse apprehension, I have seen a nobler sight than this, a grander ceremony, even at the hearthstone of the poor. I will show you a man, worn, spent, the bony outline of a human thing, with toil and want cut as with an iron tool, upon him; a man to whom the common pleasures of this our mortal heritage are unknown as the joys of Paradise. This man toils and starves, and starves and toils, even as the markets vary. Well, he keeps a heart, sound as oak in his bosom. In the sanctity of his soul bestows the kiss of peace upon a grudging world, he compels the homage of respect, and champions himself against the hardness of fortune. In his wretched homestead he is throned in the majesty of the affections. His suffering, patient, loving wife—his pale-faced, ill-clad children—are his queen and subjects. He is a king in heart, subduing and ruling the iron hours; unseen spirits of love and goodness anoint him; and, Sir—said the Hermit in solemn voice—as surely as the kingdom of God is more than a fairy tale, so surely do God's angels sing that poor man's jubilate."

"There," said the preacher, "is a man worthy of all honour. His wit may pass away, but the wisdom of the kindly heart which inspired that picture of the poor man will endure and help to encourage others."

THE NEED OF FAITH.

We are sometimes told at the present day that "Faith is dead"; it is not true. A workman surrounded by a large family, with no resources save the proceeds of his daily labour, and knowing that everything depends upon his maintaining health and strength to work on for the helpless ones, must have faith in the Providence that rules the world. I like to remember Lord Lytton's utterance thereon, "When shall men learn that, if the great religion inculcates so rigidly the necessity of faith, it is not alone that faith leads to the world to be; but that without faith there is no excellence in this—faith is something wiser, happier, diviner than we see on earth."

NOTABLE BENEFITS.

Immediately after the burial of Jerrold came the announcement of a string of entertainments for the benefit of his family. Dickens gave readings, Thackeray lectured, W. H. Russell described personal incidents of the Crimea, Sims Reeves and Albert Smith united at concerts, Phelps appeared with a star cast in *The Housekeeper* at the Haymarket, and I specially call to mind seeing *The Rent Day* and *Black Ey'd Susan* played at the Adelphi. T. P. Cooke, though a veteran, threw abundant vigour into his part of William, Miss K. Oliver was the Susan, Mr. Buckstone Gnatbrain, Paul Bedford Blue Peter, and Miss M. Keeley Dolly. Many a time have I seen *Black Ey'd Susan* since, and amid all changes it never fails to afford scope for brilliant acting. Originally William was the centre of interest, but in a later revival at Drury Lane, Mrs. Kendal reversed this by a rendering of Susan so emotional and pathetic that William seemed quite a secondary part.

FIRST BIT OF SUB-EDITING.

To "follow copy" is the first and chief duty of a compositor, as the least variation is likely to cause trouble. Early in my apprenticeship an opportunity occurred for something more. The last edition of *Lloyd's* then went to press quite early on Saturday, and a trial which had created much excitement was reported as "adjourned till Monday." When leaving the office I caught sight of the word "Verdict" on the bill of an evening paper. Half a dozen shops were visited without finding a copy containing this news. There were no street sellers, it being some time before my old friend, the late Lionel Brough, introduced the first troop of newsboys in order to push the sale of the *Daily Telegraph*. Walking along to Holborn I secured a paper with the verdict and returned to the office. Believing his work finished, the sub-editor, Mr. J. U. Rea, a very able and painstaking journalist, had gone home. As the paper was printed from type, the overseer remained on duty in case of "batters," which were of frequent occurrence. Indeed, if no accidental slip occurred, the boys engaged on the machine had the credit of deliberately causing one, so that they might enjoy what was called a half-hour's "mike." The printer, seeing the importance of the news, stopped the machine, and my first responsible bit of sub-editing was combined with putting the verdict into the forme. The next week I was rewarded with a florin, and, what was of far more importance, received the thanks of Mr. Rea.

A great deal of proof reading then fell to the sub-editor, and when he found that my slip of gardening copy was set up with few errors, the whole article was given me. Mr. George Glenny, though a great authority on all matters of the garden, showed sublime indifference to punctuation. The grammatical lessons I learned overnight at the Working Men's College were applied next day in practical fashion. Jerrold's reviews of new books were eagerly followed, proofs being pulled for home reading. The " Flower, Fruit, and Thorn Pieces " of Jean Paul Richter in this way came to be known.

STUDYING BOOKS AND PREACHERS.

Following the wholesale method of later days, experts have commended a hundred books to students. Douglas Jerrold, far more wisely, advised beginning with two—the Bible and Shakspere. The first came with me from home; while the second—a cherished edition, edited by Samuel Phelps, with notes by E. L. Blanchard—was bought in three-halfpenny numbers, and still occupies a place of honour among my favourite books.

There were no free libraries; so the younger hands joined with me in starting a " Literary Fund " of our own, towards which each paid three-halfpence a week. The papers and books bought for general reading were afterwards divided. In our little club the *Cornhill Magazine*, from its start under Thackeray's editorship, was read and discussed; also Dickens's successive productions. I call to mind many serious books, as well as *Cassell's Magazine* and the *London Journal*, in which appeared Miss Braddon's great story of " Henry Dunbar," then entitled " The Outcasts."

Owing to the wholesale literary piracy which prevailed in the fifties, Tennyson's poems were rendered familiar throughout America, and Longfellow's became household treasures here. Hosts of young people found in the "Psalm of Life" an inspiration and rule of faith. It taught them the useful lesson—to labour on "heart within and God o'erhead."

Orators and great preachers were always an attraction. Cardinal Wiseman I once heard speak from the pulpit for an hour and twenty minutes, without any sense of weariness on the part of the listeners. Of his doctrine nothing is remembered, but the scholarly style and literary finish were most fascinating. He twitted the English Bishops with having only just discovered the purpose for which cathedrals were built—a pointed allusion to the holding of services for the working classes in the nave of Westminster Abbey, and under the dome of St. Paul's in 1858. When a popular canon was the regular Sunday evening lecturer at St. Bride's the church was crowded, lines of listeners standing along the aisles through the whole service.

WALKS AND AMUSEMENTS.

Salisbury Square, where the paper was published, retained something of its olden character. Two maiden ladies living on the west side (where the Church Missionary House now stands) kept up its tradition for respectability by driving out in an ancient carriage with high springs and a flaming yellow body. Fronting their house was a tiny garden enclosed by wooden railings of restful green. To maintain the privacy of the square an aged beadle did daily duty. This officer was the butt of all the printers' boys around. When he was sprinkling the place to lay the dust, it was their delight to snatch the hose from his hands and turn the water on him. Looney, as he was called, is believed to have been the original of Mooney, "the feeble-minded beadle" so fiercely ridiculed by Dickens in "Bleak House." Passing down Primrose Hill we came to the junction with Hanging Sword Alley and Water Lane (now Whitefriars Street). Puddle Dock, running out of the Thames, alongside the Metropolitan Gas Works, then flowed up to Tudor Street.

It was usual to live within walking distance of the office, and ordinary outings were made on foot. I took part in small pedestrian matches at Lea Bridge Road, Barking Road, and Camberwell Grove. A fellow apprentice came from Clerkenwell, and in his company I soon became familiar with the route traversed by the Artful Dodger when he hurried Oliver Twist to the house of Fagin. Farringdon Street ended northward at the dip of the valley between Holborn and Snow Hill. In Saffron Hill the Great, coloured silk handkerchiefs hung on lines outside the second-hand shops, exactly as described by Dickens. Little Saffron Hill led to the ancient Hockey-in-the-Hole, along Pickled Egg Walk, past the workhouse, through Exmouth Street to Sadler's Wells Theatre, beside which the New River was an open stream flowing between grassy slopes. After passing under City Road the watercourse became more picturesque, rendering the walk along its banks to Hornsey delightfully refreshing.

With Mr. Charles Morton as pioneer at the

Canterbury, music halls were rising from the condition when they were contemptuously regarded as "cock-and-hen clubs." Bartholomew Fair had an interest for the office, from the fact that it marked the beginning of "lighting-up time" for winter evenings. I just saw the last of it; likewise the fairs of Camberwell and Greenwich. A few fitful seasons at Vauxhall Gardens attracted me to see Green making his famous balloon ascents. The glories of the place had disappeared, leaving only struggling entertainments amid melancholy surroundings. The City made a beneficial change by abandoning the Water Pageant part of the Lord Mayor's Show, as the crowding at Blackfriars Bridge had reached dangerous proportions.

Albert Smith's *Mont Blanc* at the Egyptian Hall is remembered with delight for its originality and freshness. His song of "Galignani's Messenger" was kept up to date with a readiness that made topical allusions pass for wit. Both qualities were lightly touched in some happy lines welcoming the first Handel Festival. After referring in this light and easy chaunt to the beauty of the music and the gaiety and charm of the Crystal Palace visitors, there came the following :—

> "And the tea-kettle poured forth its musical strains.
> Whose music that was there's no one can tell ;
> It couldn't be Handel's because it came from the spout."

As the hall rang with laughter, we caught the refrain :—

> "Beside our press, you must confess, all other sheets look small,
> But *Galignani's Messenger's* the greatest of them all."

These lines recurred to me in after years, when I visited Mr. Leopold Graham, almost the last editor of *Galignani*, and learned how accessible politicians, as well as actors and actresses, are to Press people in France.

I RECEIVE A POLICE REWARD.

As hard words must occasionally be used respecting the collective action of the police, it may be permissible to include a record of a different kind. A Scotch friend engaged for a series of dances a room where the Bedford Music Hall now stands. One night a party of medical students created a disturbance and were put out. Clamouring at the door for readmission, they came into conflict with two or three policemen, and in my view acted so unfairly that I went to the assistance of one officer. He had a stalwart young fellow in custody, and between us, each holding an arm, we started to march him off to the station. Before many yards had been traversed the prisoner, by dipping suddenly towards the ground, released his arms, and then darted off with a rapidity that made it hopeless for us to follow. Notwithstanding this droll result of assisting the police, a fortnight later I was surprised by receiving the following letter:—

"Police Station, Albany Street, N.W. *April* 19*th*, 1858.

"Sir,—I have to acquaint you that the Commissioner of Police has awarded you the sum of seven shillings and sixpence for assistance rendered to me in the execution of my duty on the 3rd inst. You can have the amount by calling here any evening (Sunday excepted) between 7 and 7.30 o'clock. I am, Sir, yours much obliged, SAMUEL STOKES, Police Sergeant. —Mr. T. Catling."

"OUT OF MY TIME," AND AFTER.

As soon as my five years' apprenticeship was completed I joined the London Society of Compositors, thus obtaining an intimate knowledge of the working of a trade union. Skilled men had previously been put on the same footing as casual labourers, and were often driven to wait about all day on the chance of a night's work. One winter morning I was ordered in at half-past seven, and by nine o'clock the edition was completed, which meant that the earnings for the day were under eighteenpence. With the aid of the Society better conditions were gradually established, and the change worked well all round.

Here it may be permissible to mention that along with attendance at classes in Crosby Hall, the Leadenhall Street Institute, and the old Polytechnic, was a passing appearance on the amateur stage. A little bill of the Eclectic, 18, Denmark Street, Soho, shows me that I attempted Catesby in *Richard the Third*. Subsequent criticism, when I ventured on Banquo in *Macbeth*, convinced me that I was not cut out for an actor.

Sport had no attraction for me personally, but it seemed well to know how things were conducted. Through temporary illness I missed seeing the great prize fight between Sayers and Heenan, but rubbed shoulders with both these champions in adjacent booths on Epsom racecourse. It was Thormanby's year, when Harry Custance, a boy of eighteen, was put up at the last minute and pioneered Mr. Merry's horse to victory. A glorious day brought a happy crowd, and the Scotch ironmaster's success was very popular. Derby Day is, I always think, the greatest outdoor gathering in all England. The many-sided views of life were much the same in 1860, but they could be enjoyed with less police restraint than now. As Mr. Merry led his horse to the weighing-room I was beside him, and remember the bridle being sent for in order to turn the scale. The jockey, one of the lightest weights of his time, owed his great chance to the fact that Sharpe, who had been brought from Russia expressly to ride Thormanby, was found to have drunk too much brandy to be trusted. Despite the enormous stake landed by Mr. Merry, his gift to Custance was only a hundred pounds; he did not wish to turn the boy's head by giving him a larger amount.

MEMORABLE YEAR FOR THE PRESS.

By the sweeping away of the last duty on the Press, 1861 stands out conspicuously in journalistic annals. In May of the previous year the Bill for its repeal had been defeated in the Upper House, when Queen Victoria wrote: "The Lords have thrown the Bill for the abolition of the paper duties out by a very large majority, which is a very good thing. It will save us a large amount of revenue." Great meetings followed the rejection; I was present at one in St. Martin's Hall, when Mr. Bright roused his audience to a high pitch of indignation against the Peers. Taking a step forward he waved his right arm defiantly, and exclaimed: "I don't see what we want with a House of Lords." With one accord we rose and cheered vociferously. The paper duty disappeared, but the Lords remained. At this period the electric telegraph was coming into use, Reuter's name appearing for the first time in *Lloyd's* on September 29th, 1861. In order that the Sunday edition might have later news of the American war, my hours were made to include Saturday night and onward to eleven o'clock next morning. It was a splendid opportunity, as I was left entirely alone to open the telegrams, decide which were important, set them up, read, correct, put the news in the forme, and send it to press. On occasions my single-handed labours would fill a column; ofttimes, however, few messages came through, when I was able to enjoy a good spell of sleep on a camp bed. While the machines rattled on there was no difficulty in slumbering soundly; the silence following a sudden stoppage usually sufficed to wake me. One advantage of a quiet night was that, after a wash and putting on a clean collar, it afforded me an opportunity of attending Dr. Cumming's morning services before walking home.

DEMAND FOR "LLOYD'S" AT A PENNY.

A few proprietors (Mr. Lloyd among the number) anticipated the date of October 1st, fixed for the repeal of the Paper Duty, by bringing the price of their journals down to a penny. The effect on *Lloyd's* was immense, the circulation increasing so rapidly that the methods in use for printing could not meet the demand. To make the most of the two machines, six pages, forming one side of the paper, were printed off early. The other six pages were set up in duplicate, enabling both machines to go on perfecting the paper throughout Saturday night. The direction of a large portion of this duplicating was put into my hands. On one occasion an attack of gout compelled the overseer to stay at home, leaving me the responsibility of making up the whole paper. It was an anxious time. Clara Morris, the famous American actress, in telling the story of her struggling early life, refers to the supreme crisis of a new play depending on her rendering of its principal scene, and says with great depth of meaning: " I caught myself muttering vaguely 'the power and the glory—the power and the glory,' and knew that involuntarily I was reaching out for the old staff on which I had leaned so many times before." In my case the publication of the paper was at stake. Hoe's "turtles" were in use, and every handful of type had to be lifted separately into the formes. As I looked at the galleys ranged in close order on the imposing slabs, and thought of others in course of correction round the frames, each having its special bit of news, the amount of work to be got through seemed impossible in the time. An involuntary prayer flashed through me; I bent to the task with renewed energy, and all went well. Looking back, the crisis seems a slight affair; but the lesson of the time was too deep ever to be entirely effaced.

DEATH OF THE PRINCE CONSORT.

George Augustus Sala, in his " Life and Adventures," records that on December 14th, 1861, he was living within sight of Windsor Castle. Although feeling very anxious on the Saturday night, he went to bed betimes, but rose early next morning and could "just dimly see in the distance the Round Tower and the Royal Standard half-mast high." Sala's example of going to bed (betimes or otherwise) was that night followed by all newspaper representatives. Perhaps it would be more correct to say that the custom of reporters following up home events did not then prevail. Thus it was that, when suddenly called upon to step from my frame, and hurry off to Windsor, I found myself alone in a position of unusual responsibility. The last train carried me down, and eleven o'clock had struck before I walked out from the station into the dark and silent streets. Making straight for the royal castle, the bearded soldier on sentry duty was seen to be in tears. A few rapid questions elicited the fact that the Prince Consort was dead. Being permitted to pass on to the castle itself, it was there learned that His Royal Highness had passed away about twenty minutes previously. Very few particulars were known, and the most strenuous appeals to get them telegraphed through were of no avail. The wire at the castle (said the clerks) was for Court uses only. A message, however, had to go, and so I hunted out the residence of the clerk of the Electric and International Telegraph Company. On ringing him up, he persistently begged not to be called out, stating that before going to bed he had taken nitre in gruel and put his feet in hot water to ward off a bad cold. My mission was imperative, and the clerk recognised the fact. After waiting for him to dress, we proceeded together to the office in High Street, whence I sent intelligence of the Prince's death, with such brief details as had been gleaned of his last hours and of the grief of the Queen. The receipt for that message has been preserved as a souvenir of the occasion. Of course the night had to be passed in Windsor, but a friendly policeman helped me to needful refreshment at one hotel and an ultimate lodging in another.

DEVELOPMENT OF STEREOTYPING.

Momentous inventions, especially of an industrial character, have often been so slow in development as to awaken wonder when improvements came. In a modern work on stereotyping a technical writer says, "The very simplicity of the process now adopted makes us marvel at its long delayed introduction." As invented, in 1729, by Ged, of Edinburgh, a mould was obtained by pouring liquid plaster of paris over a page of type and allowing it to harden. The mould was then removed and placed in a metal box so as to secure a casting of the required thickness. A touch of romance lingers around the early history of the process, since a younger Ged, after being condemned for participation in the Jacobite rising, had his life spared on account of the usefulness of his father's invention. For more than a century the plaster of paris method, though admittedly slow and clumsy, continued in use. Then papier-maché was tried, many experiments being gradually made in Germany and France. Two Swiss—the brothers Dellagana—having acquired a knowledge of the process, brought it to London. To them the credit of applying it in the most practical and simple way is undoubtedly due; but the desired end was only reached after close application, continued experiments, and prolonged labour. As no record can be found, it may be of interest (for printers especially) to trace the course of events. In the *Encyclopædia Britannica*, under the article "Newspapers," it is said:—

"About the year 1856, a Swiss named Dellagana introduced to the *Times* Koenig's idea of casting from papier-maché instead of plaster of paris, and was allowed to experiment in the *Times* office. After a time the invention was so much improved that matrices of pages could be taken and the stereo plates fixed bodily on the printing machine in place of the moveable type."

Mr. George Wright, the registered printer and publisher of the *Times*, kindly informs me that no documentary evidence on the subject exists in that office. His recollection, however, is that "the *Times* was experimenting with Dellagana's process of stereotyping about the year 1858. Shortly after that date stereo. columns were used, imposed in a curved box. About 1861 this arrangement was superseded by the page curved plate."

While receiving a retainer from the *Times*, the Dellaganas set up a foundry of their own, and executed work for other papers. It was in this way that I became associated, as far as preparing the type was concerned, with some of their experiments. The "turtles" of Hoe's machines, designed specially to hold type, required that any substitute, in the shape of stereo., should be type high, that is, nearly an inch; twenty-nine thirty-seconds of the inch, to be exact. A solid column of metal, with the requisite curve, was secured, but the weight proved too great for the revolving cylinders of the machine. Other methods failed on account of the pressure involved. When the stereo. was lightened, by being cast in the form of an arch, solid at the sides, but hollowed down the middle, the printing caused such a depression as to make it appear with a white space down the centre of each column. An entire page baffled the inventors, because there was no way of securing it on the cylinder. Even after the idea of abandoning the "turtle" in favour of a bed to hold the stereo. plate came into consideration, the way seemed difficult. From a mould taken from a page of flat type a plate of the usual thickness of three-sixteenths of an inch was cast; but it could not be bent to the required curve with any certainty. If it did not crack in the bending, it failed through some defect or inequality in the packing up.

Colonel Hoe, apparently, had not grasped the situation, for he was relying on the continuance of printing from type for some time longer. In that same year an application was made on his behalf for an extension of the English patent for the rotary press. It came before the Privy Council on February 1st, Lord Cranworth, Lord Chelmsford, Lord Justice Knight Bruce, and Lord Justice Turner being present. The scene comes vividly to mind, as I was called upon to exhibit to their lordships the technical method of securing the type in the "turtle" that was before them. With Colonel Richard Hoe was Mr. Edward Lloyd, Mr. Edward Levy (now Lord Burnham), and the legal gentlemen engaged. The petition stated that "the machines were very expensive, and consequently for many years the patentee was unable to induce newspaper proprietors to give orders for them; that he obtained no orders in England till after the alteration of the Stamp Duty, in June, 1855; that the first order was in 1856, for *Lloyd's Weekly Newspaper*, and that up till that time the patentee had only received orders for fourteen machines." After hearing evidence as to the novelty of the machine, Lord Cranworth said:—"Looking at this patent, we are all satisfied on the score of its merits, that it is a most useful invention, possessing the great merit and charm of simplicity as far as such a subject can be made simple." An extension of five years was then granted, to date from the termination of the existing letters patent, which were to run for fourteen years from May 4th, 1847. As the demands of newspaper proprietors became more and more urgent, stereotypers found their opportunity, and the now familiar process was developed. Taking a cast from a page of type on the flat, the papier-maché mould or flong was made flexible enough to be bent, and when this was placed in a curved casting-box, plates were readily made to fit any machine. Before this amazingly simple discovery could be adapted to *Lloyd's* it was necessary for Colonel Hoe to provide fresh beds for the stereo. plates, in place of the discarded "turtles." These were designed and made in America. Thus it was that *Lloyd's* had to wait till February 2nd, 1862, before it could be printed from stereotype. The *Times*, with the assistance of the Dellaganas, had been enabled to secure the great advantage of the new method some time previously.

Looking up the subject, with a view to verification, after the above was written, I found to my surprise that an English patent was granted for a French invention in 1850. The specification, although applying mainly to small papers, not only outlined the exact method of securing cylindrical stereotype, but also described how the curved plates could be fixed on a perfecting machine to print both sides of a paper at once. With such minute and exact details on record, it is amazing that the world waited so long for them to be utilised.

Directly the printing from curved stereotype plates came into use the "turtle," which had brought about the revolutionary change, disappeared. As I could not trace a sketch of one, application was made to Messrs. Hoe, and the block which appears in the page with Douglas Jerrold's portrait was sent to me from New York.

Newspapers are supposed to have originated with the Romans. Has it ever been noticed how near they were to the discovery of one method of printing? Water pipes of A.D. 1 are still in existence with raised letters on them, which if inked over could be printed from almost as readily as from a modern stereo. plate.

THE PRINCE OF WALES'S MARRIAGE.

The last occasion of opening London theatres gratuitously occurred on the night of the Prince of Wales's marriage, Tuesday, March 10th, 1863. It was not a case of admitting a crowd indiscriminately. Notice was given some time before that tickets would be issued at the various houses at a certain hour. I appeared at the Haymarket on the morning in question, and had no difficulty in securing two dress circle seats, as they were held out over the heads of the people by the acting-manager. Passing down the Strand, I found the same scrambling process of distribution being followed at the Adelphi, and took advantage of the opportunity to secure two seats for a friend. At night I saw Sothern as Lord Dundreary, his thoroughly original performance being one of the deserved successes of that time. It may be of interest to recall that the Pyne and Harrison Company were appearing at Covent Garden; Drury Lane, under the management of Falconer, was running *Bonnie Dundee* and a pantomime. *Lady Audley's Secret* was the attraction at the St. James's; while at the Adelphi Benjamin Webster appeared in *One Touch of Nature*, Toole and Paul Bedford in *A Valentine* and *George de Barnwell*. At most places of entertainment special compositions were sung or recited, the enthusiasm of crowded audiences everywhere marking their reception.

TEACHING LAW TO A JUDGE.

At this period no landlord or landlady would listen to the application of any journeyman for a decent house. Time after time was I refused as a tenant, even when payment of rent in advance was offered. It therefore became necessary to consider some way of overcoming the difficulty. The first step was to raise funds for the purchase of a lease. A money club was started in the office, of which I became secretary and treasurer. Into this we paid a shilling or more each week, lending out the capital at five per cent. interest. As repayments were made quickly, and there were no losses, the scheme was successful. Through this club I piled up the £50 that enabled me to secure a house in King Square, Goswell Road, which promised the "retirement and tranquillity" sought by Mr. Pickwick. The lease for twenty-one years had just been obtained from St. Bartholomew's Hospital estate by a speculator, who, after getting all the credit he could in the neighbourhood, was driven to sell it for what it would fetch. He had succeeded in keeping the deed free from any clause restricting his power to dispose of it, and after asking £70 premium accepted my £50. In addition to affording me a good home, the venture curiously led up to my teaching a judge in one of the superior courts a point of law. It came about in this way. The inhabitants of the square wished to keep control over the garden enclosure for the use of their families. A committee was appointed, and it fell to my lot to interview the clerk to the Governors of the Hospital. Step by step I discovered that an Act passed to preserve Leicester Square as an open space was applicable to other places. In order to make by-laws operative it was needful that they should be signed by a judge. After having the laws approved by the committee, I proceeded (without any legal assistance) to lay them before a judge. Mr. Justice Denman, who was sitting in Chambers, received me very courteously, but said quite plainly that he had no knowledge of any law which gave him the power to do what was asked of him. I offered to supply him with the Act of

Parliament, and he promised that if I would send it to him he would study the question, and see me again that day week. The by-laws were then duly signed, and in shaking me by the hand the judge smilingly acknowledged that he had learned a useful lesson in law.

THIRD STAGE.

A BOUND INTO JOURNALISM.

From Composing to Sub-editing—Settling a Libel Case—Demand for Dramatic Notices—Theatres in the Sixties—What is Luck?—Fenian Outrage in Clerkenwell—An Innocent Man Hanged—Journalistic Cliques and Customs—Memories of Charles Dickens—From the Church to the Stage—The Franco-German War—Paris after the Siege—Robert Lowe and the Censor—Gatherings at the Old Albion—The Prince of Wales's Illness—Entrance into Club Land—Colonel Bateman at the Lyceum—How Fortune came to the Colonel—Irving under a Manageress—A Few Fellow Pressmen—Lord Lytton's Example of Work—Burning of the Office—Losing a Case of Champagne—An Emperor's Lying-in-State—The Brothers Wainwright—The Proprietor's Secret Discovered—A Straggler from Napoleon's Court—A Cigar with a Murderer—Sleepless Nights Explained—Lord Rosebery's Early Education—Humorists of Former Days—Over and Under the Channel—Man and the Monkey—How Exclusive News was Kept—A Trip to Bonnie Scotland — Lessons in Divorce — Co-workers on the *Chronicle*—Career of Samuel Phelps—George Cruikshank—Jury of Matrons—Euston Square Mystery—Good Work of Sunday Schools—Running and Rowing Incidents—A Long and Noble Life—Sad Lessons from Bohemia—Momentous Doings of a Day—Henry Marston on Stage Tricks—The Daring Duckling on Free Trade.

FROM COMPOSING TO SUB-EDITING.

THE change from composing to sub-editing came quite suddenly and in an unexpected way. Mr.

J. U. Rea, the youngest of those responsible for producing the paper, without any warning broke down. Consumption placed its cruel hand upon him, and the best efforts to continue his duties only served to weaken him still further. One morning at the end of June, 1866, he asked me to "keep the room supplied with copy" while he went to see a doctor. For a few days his condition seemed to improve and he grew quite hopeful; but strength was never regained. On the morning that he was unable to come to the office the question was put to me, "Do you think you could sub-edit the paper?" My immediate answer was "Yes." There was no time for deliberation, and any show of hesitation would have been fatal. Having ventured into matrimony, responsibilities were growing up, and for some time I had been searching around for a better opening.

A newspaper discussion concerning the truth or falsity of the saying "Every man has his opportunity" deeply impressed me; and here appeared my chance. I embraced it at once, without any question as to hours, duties, engagement, salary, or other possibilities; took off my apron, and stepped from the composing frame into the sub-editorial room.

Looking back, memory recalls little beyond the fact that the task of selecting, arranging, and revising—single-handed—the entire contents of the twelve pages of *Lloyd's* involved the closest attention. I worked at copy and proofs till the last thing at night, and was waked early in the morning to pass the completed pages. The first half of the paper went to press on Thursday; so that extreme watchfulness was needed to prevent anything appearing in those early pages that would read awkwardly on Sunday. Of course it led to some mistakes; but happily my fellow-workers were kindly and helpful. Mr. Lloyd's confidence was gained when he saw the paper produced. Mr. Rea sent me encouraging messages, through the fortnight that he lingered in pain. On the day after his funeral, having brought out three numbers, I sent in an application for the vacant post. Mr. Lloyd replied quickly,

"In answer to yours of July 18th, I have great pleasure in meeting your request, by placing you in the position (so far as the sub-editing goes) of our lamented friend, Mr. Rea. As you say, I am sure you feel as much pleasure in those duties as I do in placing them in your hands."

Some practical advice followed as to what the public wanted, and the letter ended,

"Trusting this arrangement will be as pleasant to yourself as I am sure it will be to yours very truly, EDWARD LLOYD."

There was no mention of salary or agreement of any kind; but that mattered nothing. Here was my opportunity, and I went steadily on to the end of the week, when a cheque for four guineas was sent to me. The change involved much; it meant contact with new surroundings, and constantly accumulating calls to meet fresh responsibilities. During twelve years in the office I had made myself master of well-nigh every detail of the requirements of the paper; yet unexpected demands arose.

SETTLING A LIBEL CASE.

In addition to the routine work, there was the inheritance of an action for libel. The incriminating article, which cast the suspicion of murder upon an entirely innocent man, had been copied from the *Morning Post*. Having drafted an explanation and apology, in which the original report was said to have been quoted from "a morning contemporary," I submitted it to Mr. Lloyd's solicitors. They thought the *Post* should have been named, but deemed the case so serious that counsel's opinion was taken on it. The result was to strike out the *Post* and leave my apology as first written. Its appearance in the paper proved so satisfactory to the gentleman complaining that he at once stopped all proceedings against *Lloyd's*. In the course of the inquiry I saw Mr. Allen, then sub-editor of the *Post*, and related my experience. The authorities there, however, let the case go into court, when the paper was mulct in £250 damages, and compelled to insert an ample apology. In the course of the case I received most valuable legal advice, which was of incalculable benefit to me through succeeding years.

Before the month of July was out, the agitation for Reform caused unwonted excitement. On the Monday afternoon, when a great procession, headed by Mr. Edmond Beales, marched to the Marble Arch and found the gates closed against them on the ground of its being a royal park, I was in the neighbourhood to see for myself what happened. The proceedings officially were placid enough; Mr. Beales, on being told that the police had orders to prevent him holding a meeting there, stepped back into his carriage and drove off. The great gathering of people, however, took the matter differently. Seizing hold of the railings for about fifty yards along Park Lane, they began to sway them to and fro. For a little while the police inside tried to beat the crowd off, but soon drew back. Then, with a mighty shout, the people redoubled their efforts, and over went the railings. Violent encounters ensued in various places, and as the people streamed into the park they were cruelly beaten with the truncheons of the police. It was not until the Guards had been called out that anything like order was established. On this, as well as on many other occasions of popular outbursts, innocent folk suffered sadly. In the end the Government adopted a conciliatory tone, Reform was brought within measurable distance, and Mr. Beales became a county court judge.

DEMAND FOR DRAMATIC NOTICES.

Before I had fairly settled down to the duties of sub-editing, another unexpected responsibility arose. It fell upon me through the strange conduct of a contributor. When Mr. Horace Mayhew dropped writing the theatrical notices, he was succeeded by Mr. Edmund L. Blanchard, a son of Douglas Jerrold's intimate friend, Laman Blanchard, whose Life was written by Bulwer Lytton. The custom was to send a boy for the copy every Wednesday afternoon, so that the article could go to press in one of the pages of the side of the paper first printed. Any notices of plays produced on the Wednesday night, or later in the week, stood over till the next issue. Instead of the usual article coming to hand in the third week of February, 1867, this note was received:—

"MY DEAR SIR,—The British public must manage somehow without any amusements this week. There is literally

HYDE PARK RAILINGS THROWN DOWN IN 1866.

[To face p. 88.

nothing to write about in that way. I have hunted over all advertisements with great unsuccess. Faithfully yours, EDMUND L. BLANCHARD."

The first edition no sooner appeared than inquiry was made as to "where was the theatrical article?" Mr. Blanchard's letter had to be produced. The excuse in no way satisfied Mr. Lloyd, who said to the manager, "I should have thought Catling might have found something to put in." On this hint I set to work; "found something"; and the second edition contained a column of amusements. An intimation was meanwhile sent to Mr. Blanchard that his engagement on *Lloyd's* had ended. Of this step nothing was known to me at the time. I simply obeyed the call of duty, with no thought of consequences, near or remote. On Mr. Blanchard's appeal against dismissal being rejected, Mr. Blanchard Jerrold paid a personal visit to the proprietor, but could not move him. "No man," he said, "who had once thrown over his paper should ever be trusted again." The editor then asked to be allowed to suggest two or three writers for Mr. Lloyd's choice of a successor. This was declined, as an advertisement for a theatrical critic had been sent to the *Athenæum*. For the time, without a direct order, I was left to write any notices that occasion demanded. It was by no means an easy task, but it called forth every power that was in me. Years before, after brilliant nights at Sadler's Wells, I had struggled for hours to put my views on paper ere going to bed. These 'prentice efforts stood me in good stead, and by persistent labour and unlimited rewriting and revision I was able to give satisfaction.

THEATRES IN THE SIXTIES.

It was a period of some activity with theatres. Miss Herbert had Mr. Henry Irving in her company at the St. James's. In my first notice, respecting *A Rapid Thaw*, it was said, "Mr. Irving was unfortunate enough to have to play the O'Hoolaghan, a rude Irishman, who is made to caper about the stage on all fours, and perform other pantomimic absurdities."

Caste was produced in April at the Prince of Wales's—this being my earliest acquaintance with a first night which had the real thrill of novelty and excitement in it. I there shouldered some big lights in the journalistic world, and soon learned that years must pass before I could hope to be recognised. With the best grace possible I strove, with a faith that has never faltered, to cultivate patience and work on.

I greatly admired Miss Glyn as Cleopatra at the Princess's; pointed out the weaknesses of *The Great City* at Drury Lane; and found interest in various dramas of the East End, as well as at the Victoria.

The incidents of the period were Miss Kate Terry's farewell to the stage, and the derision created by unwonted scenes at the Adelphi on the first production of Charles Reade's *Dora*, a play founded on Tennyson's poem. The unwonted mirth began with freaks of the Sun. At the most critical moment his solar majesty fell from his throne; and, on being replaced, for some time positively refused to set, although required to do so by the exigencies of the story. Before the house had recovered from its hilarity there came another episode, also due to inefficient mounting. Farmer Allen was heard rejoicing over his bountiful fields of wheat, but when the audience looked across the stage they saw only a scanty supply of very obvious straw. The peals of uproarious laughter were renewed, and of course proved fatal to any serious interest in the unfortunate play.

Mr. Lloyd had a great belief in the anonymous system. When asked to visit the Standard Theatre, newly built after a fire, I was directed to pay for a seat. Instead of answering its purpose, this had exactly the opposite effect. Some friends in the theatre knew me, and made the fact known to John Douglass; whereupon this most genial manager exclaimed, "What! My old friend Lloyd send a man here to pay! That be hanged for a tale." So I was discovered, most cordially welcomed, and the money was returned. The friendship thus begun was only one of many that resulted from Mr. Blanchard's thoughtless action in stopping his article. He had attended several office dinners, where he sang Thackeray's "Little Billee"; but I never saw him after the rupture. Mr. Lloyd laughed heartily on hearing of Douglass's repudiation of his coin.

Time went on without a word being said either in respect to an engagement or increase of salary. Indirectly, it transpired that sixty-six answers had been received to the *Athenæum* advertisement—several writers offering to do the work simply for the privilege of admission to the theatres. No one, however, appeared; so I continued to write. At length a letter from Mr. Lloyd assured my position and all went well.

WHAT IS LUCK?

Years afterwards, when asked to describe the commencement of my theatrical notices for a periodical, the question of Luck arose. It set me thinking, and a few opinions were gathered up. In the metrical version of the Psalms sung in the Church of England, the line "We wish you good luck in the name of the Lord" is familiar enough; but the Bible (both old and new versions) renders the passage "We bless you in the name of the Lord." Various colloquial sayings in respect to good and ill luck are used by Shakspere, including "there's luck in odd numbers." Puck's work for those he favoured was inspired by the fairies; to me life has never been fairyland. It is always cheering, and sometimes beneficial, to indulge in ideals, though the majority of them may prove as unsubstantial as Bottom's dream. The mass of mankind, however, find it a matter-of-fact, work-a-day world, with ever-growing demands and cares that tax the industry and modify even the aspirations of the individual. When the question "What do you think of luck?" was put to Mr. Lloyd he looked puzzled and said, "What do you mean by luck?" Having given him a more or less lucid definition of the common view, that some men, as it were, met with success ready made, he would none of it. "But," he added, "if you keep pushing on something is sure to occur to help you." My own experience runs very much in the same direction. Those who work for the most chances are likeliest to meet with success in one way or another. 'Tis not in the stars, but "in ourselves that we are thus or thus." The truth, in fact, shines out through Dryden's couplet:—

"The lucky have whole days, which still they choose;
Th' unlucky have but hours, and those they lose."

FENIAN OUTRAGE IN CLERKENWELL.

On a December afternoon in 1867, a little before four o'clock—just as I was preparing to start for the office—a terrific explosion rattled my windows and sent me quickly out to ascertain the cause. A walk of a few minutes brought me to the House of Detention, where the scene was one of desolation and frightful disaster. Well-nigh every window in the surrounding streets was broken, and in many cases the sashes were blown out. At the prison there was a breach of some twenty yards in the north wall, while the houses on the opposite side of the narrow thoroughfare, called Corporation Lane, were in ruins. Injured victims were being rescued, but people moved very cautiously, not knowing whether another explosion was to be feared. My duty was clearly at the office, and there I found my observations, hurried though they were, of essential service in enabling me to prepare a coherent narrative from the varied and scattered reports that came in hour after hour. Among the surprises of this excited time, it appeared that two days before the outrage the authorities at Scotland Yard received an anonymous note stating exactly how and when a plot for the rescue of Richard Burke was to be carried out. It was said, "the plan is to blow up the exercise wall by means of gunpowder; the time being 3 and

4 p.m.; and the signal for 'all right,' a white ball thrown up outside when he is at exercise." Despite this warning, the indifference which so often overwhelms officials stopped the police from affording any real protection for the prison. One man suffered death for the outrage, Michael Barrett, being the last criminal executed in public. The Fenian Richard Burke, whose release was desired, was convicted of treason felony in the following April.

AN INNOCENT MAN HANGED.

In the course of my career many notable trials have demanded close inquiry. One specially engaged my attention in 1867, because the conviction remains firm with me that an innocent man was hanged. Equally sure do I feel that in years past I watched the trial of a murderer who was acquitted. As he may still be a wanderer on the earth, any reference to his case must be avoided. The innocent man was a poor wretch named Wiggins. A woman with whom he had lived was found with her throat cut, and as there was blood upon his hands, he was promptly arrested. His assertion from first to last was that the woman attempted suicide, and it was in his efforts to prevent her succeeding that he incurred the bloodstains. Two doctors called for the prosecution did not deny the possibility of suicide, but after a long deliberation the prisoner was found guilty. Being a man of the lower orders, with no friends, he was left to his doom. There was a terrible scene on the scaffold, and he resisted the efforts of Calcraft, having previously declared, "I am entirely innocent of the crime I am to die for, and I suffer the law innocently. I can assure you on my dying oath that I never done it, and I shall die with a clear conscience. I go with a clear heart to my Maker. It was she who cut her own throat, I am innocent—by my dying words I am innocent."

JOURNALISTIC CLIQUES AND CUSTOMS.

Journalists now have a more open field than prevailed half a century ago. Representatives of penny papers were at first looked down upon with something more than disdain. Sala has truly pictured the narrowness of the cliques of the more expensive journals. Objection took the form of giving the cold shoulder to all new-comers, and shutting them out from the informal clubs which then met in upper rooms of various taverns. "One of the most indignant of the protestants," says Sala, "was George Hodder, but dear old George lived to be my intimate friend."

John Hollingshead—when dramatic critic of the *Daily News*—was very much disposed to stand aloof; but he soon abandoned journalism for theatrical management. Before doing so, however, he brought about a great change by printing short notices of new plays the morning after their production. The scheme of the first Gaiety under his management was novel, inasmuch as the theatre was combined with a restaurant. Visitors could dine comfortably, and then walk through arched openings between the two buildings to their reserved seats. This had the effect of keeping the theatre free from all bars, and enabled Hollingshead to assert that, though a sinner, he was no publican. A few evenings before the dramatic opening in December, 1868, a gathering of pressmen sampled both places. Next me at the dinner table was Mr. Mudford, one of the reporting staff of the *Standard*, who was very speedily, by the death of the proprietor, called on to rule and direct that journal.

Very soon after this Gaiety dinner I was brought into contact with Hodder. Blanchard Jerrold sent a batch of leaders well in advance, notifying that Mr. George Hodder would call in to see proofs and add anything that was required in respect to the subjects dealt with. Outside I had met with a few open and ill-concealed rebuffs, but Hodder came into the office in a very friendly spirit. When, however, Mr. Jerrold's articles were looked at, he frankly confessed that he knew nothing whatever of politics. "Now," said he, "if you wanted a sonnet to the moon I could have dashed you one off at once, but what are we going to say about politics?" This gave me another opportunity, because from boyhood I had taken more than a passing interest in the political conflicts and discussions of the time. The speeches of Bright and Gladstone were then subjects of vivid interest. At a meeting at Spurgeon's Tabernacle in 1868, Mr. Bright said it was "beyond comparison the grandest public and political gathering he had ever attended in any building." I formed one of that gathering, and regard the speech delivered on the Irish Church as one of the finest oratorical efforts of my time. In a tea garden opposite Sadler's

Wells, on the site of which Deacon's Music Hall was afterwards built, I had come face to face with one of the last of the D'Orsay dandies—the Radical member for Finsbury, Thomas Slingsby Duncombe —addressing his constituents. As far back as 1844 Mr. John Lash Latey (who afterwards became editor of the *Illustrated London News*) was writing articles on education for *Lloyd's News* that might profitably be reprinted at the present day. "Education," said he, "means the perfecting of a man's nature; the giving him of a sound mind and of a sound body. It consists rather in teaching persons how to think than what to think. The cry should be not 'educate the people,' but 'people, educate yourselves.'" My efforts in this direction enabled me to relieve Mr. Hodder of all anxiety respecting additions to the leaders.

Poor Hodder's fate was a sad one. He formed one of a party of pressmen invited to an outing in the summer of 1870. Coming back through Richmond Park on a coach-and-four, driven by Captain Harworth, the horses became restless and dashed aside under a tree. Eight gentlemen were thrown off the roof as the coach turned over. Mr. John Allen, sub-editor of the *Post* (whom I had met over the libel suit), had one leg broken, the Captain suffered from fractured ribs, and Mr. Hodder from concussion of the brain, which caused his death a few weeks later.

In the previous year, George Hodder formed one of a party of sixteen who went up with me in the car of a captive balloon at Ashburnham Grounds, adjoining Cremorne. A very high wind made the experience the reverse of comfortable.

The huge car had an opening in the centre through which a massive rope passed to a wheel below. As the wheel revolved the coil of rope lengthened, and when the wind drove the balloon to one side a kind of sawing process went on. This awakened something very like alarm that at any moment the rope might be severed, and the party let in for a free flight. The rope had been bound round with many thicknesses of American cloth, and on being drawn down it was seen that the cloth was entirely cut through. How narrow was the escape became apparent a few days later, when the monster balloon broke loose and soared away entirely unattended.

MEMORIES OF CHARLES DICKENS.

In the office Dickens's death in 1870 revived the memory of a long-forgotten suit in Chancery. While the original issue of Pickwick was running its monthly course with shilling parts in 1837, a very young publisher brought out "The Penny Pickwick." It seems to have been more parody than piracy, as a few extracts from the legal arguments used in the case will show. On behalf of Messrs. Chapman and Hall application was made to the Vice-Chancellor's Court for an injunction to restrain Mr. Edward Lloyd from printing, publishing, or selling any more copies of his "Penny Pickwick." It was pointed out that this work was described as "Edited by Bos, with engravings by Phis," and purported to describe the adventures of certain members of the Pickwick Club, among others of Christopher Pickwick,

Percy Tupnall, Arthur Snodgreen, and Matthew Winkletop. Further, that Mr. Pickwick was represented as standing in one place on a chair and in another on a tub; the pipe, the spectacles, the stomach and the short gaiters appeared in both. When the plaintiff's counsel had exhausted his complaints, the Vice-Chancellor (without calling for a defence) said: In his opinion there was nothing whatever to lay hold of except the mode in which the fancifully-made word Pickwick was formed, and which it must be admitted had some resemblance to the name used in the plaintiff's work, but even in this respect there was a considerable difference, one being printed in a curved form and the other a straight line. Before the Court could interfere, it must know the result of any action he would give the plaintiffs leave to bring. Counsel said he did not know if the matter was worth an action. In this uncertain position the case was directed to stand over. Nothing more was heard of it, Mr. Lloyd soon abandoning any attempt to run against Charles Dickens.

When Dickens appeared as a reader he ever proved himself the finest interpreter of his own works. Apart altogether from the interest of seeing the distinguished author, or any feeling of hero worship, Dickens brought an amount of passionate intensity to bear upon tragedy that held his audience enthralled. I can close my eyes and picture him as he went through that terrible story of the murder of Nancy by Bill Sikes, when it was first publicly read in November, 1868. After a private trial many friends urged him not to risk shocking his audiences with anything so awful; a celebrated actress settled the matter differently by saying, "Do it. The public have been looking out for a sensation these last fifty years, and now they have got it." The gathering which filled St. James's Great Hall to its utmost capacity endorsed this view; other assemblies echoed the opinion of London. So deeply and powerfully was the imagination swayed by the Sikes and Nancy reading that one could almost hear the dog whine as he shrank away from his brutal tormentor. All that I have ever read of the power of Dickens as a reader falls short of the reality and the praise that was really due to him. The painful memory is that the tremendous energy displayed on the platform tended to shorten the author's life.

FROM THE CHURCH TO THE STAGE.

The Rev. Mr. Bellew was a great artist both in the pulpit and elsewhere. He came over from India with the title of Archdeacon, but did not succeed in securing recognition from the heads of the Church at home. Bloomsbury Chapel was accordingly opened as an independent place of worship, and the masterly gifts of Bellew drew large congregations. Never have I heard the Ten Commandments read with anything approaching the majesty and feeling of this Archdeacon. He possessed in a remarkable degree the power of interesting the masses in poetry and literature of the highest order. His lecture on Milton was most inspiring, and among other things sent me home to study the stately prose of the *Areopagitica*. After the work of the evening was over Bellew might be called something of a Bohemian, for his hours of relaxation were marked by free and easy indulgences. When the pulpit failed to hold him, he turned to the stage; and for a while his dramatic readings provided an intellectual treat which made them very successful. For a whole week he drew crowded audiences to the Standard Theatre. The arrangement was "sharing terms." At the end of the week, when John Douglass handed Bellew his portion, the latter turned smilingly to the manager and said, "This is better than being a bishop!"

THE FRANCO-GERMAN WAR.

Although there was known to be growing disquiet in France, the war with Germany came like the proverbial bolt from the blue. Lord Granville, entering upon his duties as Foreign Minister on the 11th of July, 1870, was informed by the Under-Secretary that "in all his experience he had never known so great a lull in foreign affairs." Before midnight the discussions which had arisen over filling the throne of Spain assumed a serious aspect, and four days later the gage of battle was thrown down by the French Emperor. It soon became a very anxious time for those directing newspapers, and the necessity of going to press early on the Saturday night landed me in more than one difficulty. French telegrams commonly got through first, and when I had started printing and sending out bills proclaiming a Napoleonic success, it was perplexing to be under the necessity an hour or two later of transferring the victory absolutely to the Germans. Personally the pressure soon began to be felt, as for sixteen years continuously I had not been absent from a single issue of the paper. Any holiday early in the week was restricted by the necessity of being back again in the office on the Thursday. A friendly doctor, after prescribing for me for some time, suggested that a change in the country would do me more good than any medicine. Casting around, I pitched on a quiet village near the foot of Leith Hill, with a playground on the Common which Dickens is believed to have had in his mind for the opening scene of "The Battle of Life." There was a bar parlour at the Red Lion, frequented by the best people in the neighbourhood. Thinking they would be interested in the events of the war, I one evening took down with me the latest evening papers describing a great battle. These were handed to the landlord with a few words of explanation; on going downstairs next morning I found the papers had never been looked at. The incident was a lesson to me in showing how small local interests prevailed over national affairs in the quiet life of a country district.

PARIS AFTER THE SIEGE.

It remained my constant plan to see for myself as much of every phase of life as was likely to be useful for journalistic purposes. As the siege of Paris went on through the terrible winter, I conceived the idea of having a look at the beleaguered city as soon as possible after the conflict ceased. On Monday, March 8th, 1871, the *Journal Officiel* announced that passes were no longer required to enter or leave Paris. The Saturday night following found me travelling with three friends by way of Newhaven and Dieppe towards the French capital. The train ran cautiously on account of bridges having been blown up, and as it neared the river a stop was made in order that the few passengers might alight and walk over a temporary bridge of boats to pick up another train waiting on the opposite side. Paris was safely reached on the Sunday, and there was no difficulty in moving about, as only very slight damage had been done to any of the buildings during the long siege. On that Sunday the Emperor of Germany withdrew with his troops from Versailles and St. Cloud; the next day our little party reached there to stroll amid the ruins and survey the ravages of the bombardment. St. Cloud had suffered most, the palace being nothing but a heap of ruins; the fragments of houses that remained were defiled in a manner which indicated the most malicious intent. Blackened and broken walls were all around, but the tricolour had been hoisted, and little canvas-covered tents were set up for the supply of such refreshments as were within reach. Returning to Paris we dined on unmistakable horseflesh, but on the whole did not fare badly. A photographer was at work, and a specimen of his excellent handiwork is still preserved. Passing out by the Gate of St. Denis we wandered over the scene of many deadly sorties, the only traces of which were little twigs in the loose soil indicating where bodies lay buried. Every house outside the walls had been levelled to the ground, and German soldiers were still on duty guarding the historic gate. The most noticeable thing inside the city was the absence of discipline on the part of the soldiers. On quitting the railway station from Tours, a force of Chanzy's troops went dancing along, rattling their arms and the tins carried for their food, in a way suggestive of being entirely out of hand. On Wednesday, the day after M. Thiers arrived at Versailles, I was on the hill at Montmartre quietly looking at the cannon which had been concentrated there by the violent section. Nowhere were we molested in any way, though at St. Cloud a cry of " A bas les Prusses," levelled at one of the company who had fair hair, acted as a warning to move off quickly. On the Thursday I was travelling home again in time for *Lloyd's* later editions, and thus escaped the Communist rising which began so savagely at Montmartre on the Saturday evening. The success of this Paris trip led (as the reader will discover later) to further endeavours to see something of the world outside Fleet Street.

ROBERT LOWE AND THE CENSOR.

Robert Lowe, one of the most overbearing of Ministers, came to grief over his abortive Match Tax in 1871; and at the end of the year the Censor of Plays was coerced or frightened into fierce activity. Here is a copy of a letter sent out to managers:—

"40, Weymouth Street, W. *December* 18, 1871.—DEAR SIR,—There are three passages in your pantomime which must be omitted in representation, and I send you—although they are endorsed on the licence—early notice of them, so

BRIDGE BROKEN ACROSS THE SEINE, 1871.

RUINS AT ST. CLOUD, FROM A PHOTOGRAPH OF 1871.

[To face p. 104.

that they may either be struck out or modified in time. They are : P. 4, from 'Though Royal persons now are seldom seen' to 'do his best for trade.' This just now is a very unseasonable remark. P. 11, 'For I'm not Gladstone and this isn't Greenwich.' P. 11, 'Tax on matches and Mr. Lowe's name.' Names and political allusions are not permitted. I have struck Lowe and the matches out of every pantomime for '71. Yours truly, W. B. DONNE."

GATHERINGS AT THE OLD ALBION.

Though clubs, apart from taverns, were beginning to be talked about, the Albion remained as a great survival of the old coffee-houses at which the leading theatrical lights appeared. Here on any Saturday night in 1871 might be seen three-fourths of the managers of London. Each division or pew capable of accommodating half-a-dozen was filled with men of note and ambitious aspirants. Toole and Irving were usually near together; Chatterton and Falconer associated in Bohemia as well as in business; and I remember John Hollingshead, Boucicault, H. J. Byron, Andrew Halliday, Robert Reece, C. S. Cheltnam, E. J. Odell, Charles Warner, James Fernandez, and Edward Ledger. David James, Thomas Thorne, and H. J. Montague (the three lessees of the Vaudeville) were regular frequenters, but Buckstone only came from the Haymarket at intervals. Ben Webster favoured a special corner, where he stood by a little bar and sipped his grog with more deliberation than most. Lord Alfred Paget was the centre of a group of influential patrons of the stage. Right merrily and all too swiftly fled the moments as we enjoyed the excellent fare provided, whether a luscious cutlet, tripe and onions in a dainty entrée dish, or a simple Welsh rabbit. Ah me! we had appetites in those days, alike for the food and the good English ale with which it was washed down. Such whisky as was drunk was Irish. To each one was served a small decanter of spirit, a jug of hot water, a tumbler and a large-sized port glass, with ladle, lemon peel, sugar, and a clean napkin. First the tumbler was warmed, then lemon peel and sugar put into it, hot water poured on, and the glass carefully covered with the napkin to keep in the aroma. More water and the whisky were added; the beverage being then ladled into the smaller glass to be drunk as the palate dictated. As the licensing laws became more strict in respect to the time of closing, the difficulties of publicans increased. After midnight at the Albion the exertions of the manager to get rid of his customers became positively pathetic. An inspector of police would pop in and politely remind the company that he really must call upon them to clear out in another five minutes. The following (taken from William Tinsley's "Reminiscences") fairly describes the scene:—

"Half-past twelve, gentlemen. Must ask you to go, gentlemen," would be Charles's request.

"All right, I'm ready when Mr. Toole is," would be Mr. Thorne's reply.

"Mr. Thorne is ready when you are, Mr. Toole. Must ask you to go. Licence in danger, you know."

"Very well, Charles. Ask Mr. James to come at once. He ought to know better."

"He is talking to Lord Alfred, sir, and when you go his lordship will go, no doubt."

"All right, Charles. Get a cab for Mr. Webster."

"Cab's at the door, sir."

"Very well, Charles; I'm ready."

"But do go, Mr. Toole."

"All right, Charles; you do make me so wild."

The five minutes allowed would grow into ten, to be followed by a visit from another police inspector, greatly increasing the anxiety of the manager, but little disturbing the company, who had no fear of arrest. The end of the fun was always worth staying for, and I vividly remember a scene when the Licensing Act of 1872 came into force. The police were more persistent than before in clearing the house, and got the whole company outside quite early. John Hollingshead, who had been compelled to sever the Gaiety from the restaurant by building up every archway, was very wroth. On reaching the pavement he loudly lamented the lost liberties of his countrymen. It was, he declared, nothing short of an outrage to be thus driven forth by "legislation's harsh decree" just when they most wished to enjoy rest and recreation after the labours of the week.

THE PRINCE OF WALES'S ILLNESS.

The first announcement that the Prince of Wales was "indisposed" claimed only passing notice, and was not allowed to interfere with a promised visit to Lord Carrington at Gayhurst. A week or two later it became known that the illness was typhoid fever. The bulletins grew more and more alarming. Sunday, December 10th, 1871, was a most anxious time throughout the country. In the evening a telegram reached London, dated Sandringham,

5.30 p.m.: "The Prince of Wales has passed an unquiet afternoon, with a return of the more urgent symptoms." Crowds gathered in Fleet Street read this with alarm, and those waiting in newspaper offices prepared for the worst. Happily their services were not called into requisition; but a week passed before the Prince was considered out of imminent danger. One of the favourable reports I call to mind was the appearance of a *Standard* placard bearing the words, "The Prince calls for Bass's ale." Five-and-twenty years afterwards, when preparing a sketch of the Prince's life, an effort was made to trace the truth of this. Charles Williams came into the story as having been editor of the *Evening Standard* at the time; but reference to another quarter enabled me to say on the very highest authority that His Royal Highness had no knowledge of ever having made such a request at any time during his illness. The procession to St. Paul's for the thanksgiving service on February 27th following was the most imposing which Fleet Street had seen for twenty years. At Temple Bar the stately ceremonial of opening the gates for the Lord Mayor to present the keys and City sword to the Sovereign was observed with punctilious care. Inside the cathedral a vast congregation included the largest gathering of pressmen I had seen together up to that time. Very touching was the moment when the widowed Queen, leaning on the arm of the Prince, reached the royal pew. Nothing, either in the service or the progress through the multitudes assembled in the streets, was wanting to add to the sincerity and earnestness of the nation's thanksgiving.

TEMPLE BAR DECORATED FOR THE THANKSGIVING, 1872.

[To face p. 108.

A BOUND INTO JOURNALISM. 109

ENTRANCE INTO CLUB LAND.

My first club membership was with the Scribblers, a band of beginners who followed the Savages in a room at Ashley's Hotel, Henrietta Street, Covent Garden. Here the brothers Grossmith, George and Weedon, made their earliest efforts to follow in the footsteps of their father, a talented and noted entertainer, who also filled the post of reporter at Bow Street Police Court. When the Scribblers quitted their first home, certain pictures which had been left by the Savages were missing, and the proprietor appealed to a magistrate at Bow Street. The removal was really part of an elaborate joke. As a protest against certain claims by the proprietor, some members of the club invited him to take a drink at his own bar, and discuss the affair. While this was in progress another set quietly handed the pictures out of the window, and they were carried away. The magistrate appears to have seen through the fun, for he declined to interfere, telling the complainant if he wished to go further that he must "enter an action for trover in a civil court." In the end the pictures were returned as quietly as they were taken away. A further reason for remembering the Scribblers is that a little flippancy on my part led to delay in admission to the Savage Club. The incident took place at the Occidental Hotel, reared on the site of Baron Nicholson's old Coalhole, which had just been opened by Charles Wilmot, an actor introduced to the London stage as "the Paul Bedford of Australia." Henry Hersee, a member of both clubs, was the representative of a City wine merchant by day, and a musical critic at night. At a Scribblers' dinner Hersee indulged in such high falutin flourishes with respect to the importance of Pressmen as to lead me to make what fun I could out of those present. That little after-dinner speech was brought up against me as a bar to admission among the Savages. My election was accordingly postponed, along with that of Mr. Doughty. The latter, who became well known as O.P.Q. Philander Smiff, author of " The Coming K.," and many clever contributions to *Truth* and the *Figaro*, did not come up again. A minute in the club book records that on April 5th, 1873, H. W. Lucy, Tom Hood, Arthur à Beckett, and Thomas Catling were elected. At that time the entrance fee was a guinea, paid when you liked, with a subscription of two guineas to be paid when you could. The guinea I remember paying down; some time later handing the subscription to Charles Millward, whom I met in the Strand. No receipt was thought of, but the word of Millward as secretary or treasurer was sufficient for anybody. My sponsor with the Savages was good, gentle, cultured Tom Archer, who had taken over the editorship of the *Hornet*, previously directed by Charles Townley (the Geoffrey Thorn of later pantomime days). For nearly two years I had (all unknown to the world) been the " Dramatic Owl " of that publication, the proprietor, treasurer of one of the Inns of the Temple, gaining what prestige he could among the players from his paper. Nothing more homely can be imagined than the single room with its sanded floor and plain table at the Gordon Hotel, under the piazza of Covent Garden, where the Savages foregathered. On a gloomy evening in November,

1872, a few members showed every disposition to unbend and enjoy themselves in simple and natural ways. After a meal, Archer, with a view to something practical for the *Hornet*, asked for a rhyme concerning the atmosphere outside. The following jingle, joint production of the Savages I first encountered in their own wigwam, was the result :—

By the Clerk of the Weather.

Dirty days have September,
April, June, and November;
From January up to May
The rain it raineth every day.
All the rest have thirty-one
Without a blessed gleam of sun;
And if any of them had two and thirty,
They'd be just as wet and twice as dirty.

COLONEL BATEMAN AT THE LYCEUM.

No management ever commenced with less promise than that of Colonel Bateman at the Lyceum; yet there were in the company slumbering forces which in process of time brought about triumphant results. It was on a quiet Monday evening in September, 1871, that my dear friend John Northcott (then on the *News of the World*) accompanied me to the theatre. No invitations had been sent us, and when Colonel Bateman was found in front, he said, "I'm sorry, but there isn't a stall or dress circle seat left"; adding, after a slight pause, "I suppose you wouldn't care to come where I'm going, into the pit?" Being promptly told that what was good enough for him would suit us, we passed through and found only a sprinkling of pittites present. *Fanchette*, a new version of a French story by George Sand, had been chosen to introduce Miss Isabel Bateman. The young actress was greeted with friendly applause; the poor little play afforded no hope whatever. Henry Irving, frolicking through the part of a peasant lover, bided his time; while Bateman, firmly believing in his daughter, tried to bolster up *Fanchette* with a version of *Pickwick*. This was prepared by James Albery, down to that time one of the firm of Albery and Back, rope merchants in Blackfriars Road. He was a clever man, but the lionising which followed the triumph of *Two Roses* seemed too much for him. The *Pickwick* is only remembered from the fact of Irving's Jingle being a conspicuously telling performance. Although I openly laughed at Bateman for his faith in *Fanchette*, we remained on the best of terms. Never again was I left without an invitation, and the house, both before and behind the curtain, was always open to me.

Starting as he did with very little capital, six weeks of absolute failure brought the lessee of the Lyceum practically to the end of his resources. The house had been greatly neglected, and there seemed so little hope of avoiding disaster, that Colonel Bateman made preparations for returning to America. The manager's extremity was the actor's opportunity. Henry Irving had been pining for an opening, having fixed his mind on tragedy. It was only when the position became desperate, and the choice lay between closing the theatre or risking a forlorn hope, that *The Bells* was put in rehearsal. The success of the actor and the play

A BOUND INTO JOURNALISM.

are matters of theatrical history. With the turn of the tide Irving's salary was advanced to twenty pounds a week; but he went on playing Jingle as well as Mathias. Much still remained to be done before fortune followed fame. When *Charles the First* had been chosen for the subject of the next play, there were numberless discussions over the scenes and treatment. Bateman cared nothing whether Cromwell or the King became the hero; as he had George Belmore in the company for one part and Irving for the other. Wisely enough from the theatrical standpoint, though history was travestied, Mr. Wills worked out a pathetic piece which deeply moved English audiences and won still greater favour in America. Irving told me that after his first appearance in New York in *The Bells* many friends said, "We admire your acting, but we don't like your play." On the next night *Charles the First* secured high commendation all round. Once the Colonel's faith in Irving had been established it never faltered, and he showed keen judgment in steadily advancing the reputation of his theatre before attempting Shakspere, which other managers of the time declared "spelt ruin." With half-a-dozen plays he carried on for three years, just making both ends meet. Then came the all-eventful revival of *Hamlet*.

HOW FORTUNE CAME TO THE COLONEL.

Players have been mainly of two kinds: those who lost themselves in the characters they portrayed, and others who treated all the parts as pure acting. Macready and Charles Kean were of the stately order, who strove by every illusion to fancy themselves kings and princes; while Edmund Kean, G. V. Brooke, and Irving typified the opposite school. During the triumphant run of *Hamlet*, Irving stood talking to me on various matters until he received his cue to step upon the stage and continue his performance. If he had taken the part too seriously, it would have been well-nigh impossible for him to have continued it for two hundred performances. As it was, Irving told me later that after the strain of *Hamlet* he "was never quite the same man physically," though Mrs. Bateman with motherly care sought to help him in every possible way. On the final fall of the curtain, when a little knot of intimates used to close round him, the manageress would appear with a basin of turtle soup or some other delicacy and eagerly press it on him. If one of the party would draw Irving on one side and say "Do take this," her look of grateful acknowledgment was something to be remembered. On the night of the hundredth performance—February 16th, 1875—the event was celebrated by a gathering in the saloon. Many much more lavish and expensive assemblies came later, but this early festivity with a small company was by far the most interesting and enjoyable. Irving answered the compliments showered upon him with a modest deference, telling of the times when he had acted all manner of parts for thirty shillings a week and less. Even then he said he had always striven to act with as much sincerity and earnestness as was in him. The truth of this indifference to salary was proved by the fact that while he went on filling the Lyceum he received only thirty pounds a week. Then it was that manager Bateman found his profits rapidly accumulating. At his death, which came with terrible suddenness, he left ten thousand pounds—the result (as Irving assured me) of twenty weeks' run of *Hamlet*. Only two days before he passed away, I was talking to the Colonel of the future. Some of his patrons, he said, were pressing him to change the bill more frequently. He was ready and willing to do so, but not at his own risk; he did not mean to lose the money he had found it so difficult to make by any experiments. Wealthy folk, he pointed out, thought nothing of putting down a thousand pounds for yachting or any other pastime; and why should they not do the same for the theatre? If they did he would bring out any number of plays for their amusement, but not otherwise.

IRVING UNDER A MANAGERESS.

With unswerving loyalty, Henry Irving continued to play on under Mrs. Bateman. The run of *Hamlet* reached two hundred performances, and subsequently *Macbeth* was produced. Public opinion differed widely over this play. Miss Bateman received hearty praise for her fine rendering of Lady Macbeth, but Irving's acting was severely criticised. The indignation of the manageress knew no bounds. "I can't understand you pressmen," she said to me, "it looks as if you must find fault with some one. If Mr. Irving is commended, my daughter is sure to be wrong; and if my daughter is praised, then Mr. Irving gets blamed." When *Fun* came out with a stinging article on "A Fashionable Tragedian," the managerial protest took the form of a summons against the printer of the paper. This was abandoned in favour of two others; as George R. Sims at once stepped forward to acknowledge that he was the writer, and Henry Sampson accepted responsibility as editor. After Irving and Toole had given evidence, Mr. George Lewis pressed the case as a very bad one, and Sir Robert Carden ordered both defendants to be committed for trial. This was exactly what they expected, but the case suddenly took an unexpected turn. In answer to the usual question as to whether they had anything to say, first Sims and then Sampson replied that, after hearing the opinion which had been taken of the article, they tendered apologies to Mr. Irving. A brief pause, and a little whispering resulted in Mr. Lewis rising to say, " Mr. Irving having performed his duty to society, and having done what he thinks was necessary for the protection of the interests of his profession, accepts these apologies." With that the case ended, and I carried the good news to Mrs. Sampson that the fear of her husband's imprisonment was over.

Years passed before any rupture occurred; then it was due to the parental fondness which characterised both the Colonel and his wife. In June, 1873, coming out of Drury Lane, where Madame Ristori had played Medea, I met Bateman. "Well, what do you think of it?" he said. The answer was that the terrific grandeur of the performance had greatly impressed me; whereupon he exclaimed, " I like my daughter's rendering better." The parting of the ways between Mrs. Bateman

A BOUND INTO JOURNALISM. 117

and Irving came when he intimated a wish that Miss Ellen Terry should be engaged in place of Miss Isabel Bateman for the projected revival of *Hamlet* in 1878.

A FEW FELLOW PRESSMEN.

The idea current in some circles that Americans introduced live journalism into England in no way agrees with my experience. Machines which made it possible to wait for late news certainly came from New York, but there was no lack of men in London ready to grasp every advantage possible. Let me glance at a few of my early fellow-workers. Walter Wood, who controlled the news department of the *Standard* for over thirty years, graduated on *Lloyd's*. Between us (the confession may now be made) we anticipated the expansion of telegrams, which has since been made almost a fine art. I remember a message of a dozen words developing into a couple of columns in the paper. That was in relation to some royal function in Ireland. Wood obtained an official programme in advance; the telegram said all went well, and gave the weather, so the task was easy. Wood's first *Standard* engagement was as reporter, and he scored over more experienced men by a bit of smart practice. Driving somewhere out of Dublin, he noted the exact position of the telegraph office, and on the way back with several other pressmen was careful to secure a seat on the jaunting car that enabled him to be the first to alight. Darting into the office, he had ready a long dummy message, which the clerk was directed to send at the end of a brief report of the day's proceedings. In this way the line was blocked against all comers long enough for the *Standard* to appear well in advance of other papers. George Byron Curtis (who succeeded Mudford as editor of the *Standard*) came to me from a local paper in Hackney. We had a busy Saturday together in 1869, on the opening of Blackfriars Bridge and Holborn Viaduct. A bunch of reporters stood in the roadway of the bridge, and marched in quick order immediately behind the Queen's carriage to the Viaduct. In a short time Curtis joined the staff of the *Echo*, but continued to write a report of Thursday and Friday's Parliament for *Lloyd's*. When Baron Grant bought the *Echo*, it was turned from an evening into a morning paper — the first issued at a halfpenny — Curtis being made editor and Horace Voules manager. Having to give up the Parliamentary work, Curtis introduced a young Irishman, fresh from the University, with excellent qualifications, who was desirous of studying the work of the House of Commons, and would write what was wanted. The recommendation being sufficient, the ticket which secured admission to the reporters' gallery was handed over, and Mr. T. P. O'Connor thus entered Parliament as the representative of *Lloyd's News*. Two brothers named Geary did useful work in reporting inquests and accidents. One died prematurely; the other made his mark in an unexpected way. The proprietor of the *Times of India* having sent over for two journalists to act as editor and manager, Sydney Blanchard (a brother of Edmund, previously on *Lloyd's News*) was selected for the first post, and Geary for the second.

After a time there came news of Blanchard quarrelling with his chiefs, and Geary being placed in the editorial chair. The dispute was carried into a court of law, when Blanchard met the complaint that he failed to fulfil his duties, especially on mail days, by pleading that "they had no right to expect a racehorse to do carthorse's work." Geary held the post till he was able to exchange it for the more advantageous one of proprietor of another prosperous Indian journal.

LORD LYTTON'S EXAMPLE OF WORK.

How is it that the genius of Bulwer Lytton is so little recognised at the present day? On his passing away in 1873 the *Times* said: "With the exception of Scott, who like Shakspere wrote for all men and all times, it would be hard to find a novelist who contributed more largely to popular enjoyment." Twenty years before, Thackeray had penned this notable tribute: "One of Dickens's immense superiorities over me is the great fecundity of his imagination. Perhaps Bulwer is better than both of us in this quality; his last book, written at fifty, is fresher and richer than any he has done." Another critic pointed to him as a splendid example of work, "famous the world over as orator, poet, dramatist and romancist." In everything attempted he was successful, the only failure being his marriage. On my bookshelves there rest two volumes of "The Poetical Works of Sir Edward Bulwer Lytton, Bart." In the preface he refers to his epic of "King Arthur" as "the child of my most cherished hopes, to which I deliberately confide the task to uphold and the chance to continue its father's name." There can be no hope of any future for Bulwer's poems, but a revival of interest in his now neglected novels would not surprise me. Theatrically his fame will rest on *Richelieu*, which merits the distinction of being the cleverest acting play written in English during the nineteenth century. Beginning at sixteen, Bulwer continued writing till his seventieth year, when, like Dickens, he left a story unfinished. A compositor who had worked in Bentley's printing office told me a yarn of Bulwer one day coming to see some proofs. He found space left for a word which no one could decipher. On the offer being made to produce the copy, the author repudiated the suggestion, remarking that if they had not been able to read it, he certainly couldn't. During the visit he surprised the printers by producing a bottle of scent from his pocket, pouring some into the palm of his hand, and distributing it over his daintily curled hair.

BURNING OF THE OFFICE.

The Monday after Christmas, 1873, has never been forgotten by reason of two sharp experiences. Being free from duty at the office, I had attended a meeting called for the winding up of the first company in which I had ventured to take shares. Dogberry prided himself on being "a fellow who hath had losses"; the disappearance of my hundred pounds left no feeling of satisfaction. Walking homewards in the dusk of evening, my somewhat gloomy reflections were swept away on seeing, near St. John's Gate, an evening paper bill announcing

A BOUND INTO JOURNALISM. 121

"Destruction of *Lloyd's Newspaper* Office by Fire." A very few minutes found me in Salisbury Square surveying the ruins. From the City a journey was made to Bow, where a reserve of type and cases had been stored. These sufficed to bring out the paper as usual, though the strain on the workers was severe. Nothing was ever discovered as to the actual cause of the fire, but as it broke out in the machine room it was assumed to have originated in some oily rags thrown too closely together on the previous day. Two or three odd circumstances were associated with the calamity. My desk perished entirely, but among a few scraps of charred paper recovered from the ashes was this letter from a famous author:—

"*Woolman* v. *Reade*.—SIR,—It would seem by your report of this case that I stated in my evidence that Mrs. Freeman was my mistress. What I intended to convey was that she was mistress of the house where the goods in question were delivered, and not my servant, as the plaintiff maintained. I am, Sir, your obedient servant, CHARLES READE, 2, Albert Terrace."

In another desk the master printer had left between eight and nine pounds in gold and silver, while mine contained a bag of nearly a hundred farthings. Although for insurance purposes the whole of the ashes were sifted, not one single coin was reported to have been found.

LOSING A CASE OF CHAMPAGNE.

Shortly before Christmas, Mr. Thurgood had started business as an auctioneer in Chancery Lane; and he told his fellow-members of the Fleet Club that some champagne would be sold cheap. Along with several others I bought a case, which, for convenience, was delivered at the office. Neither Sundays nor holidays were allowed to interfere with the production of a newspaper, and accordingly we were busy on Christmas morning. So were the staff of the *Dispatch* on the opposite side of the street. One of the number was John Thomson, a thorough Bohemian, who had been associated with Mr. Swinburne. About noon John came over with a friend on the off-chance of finding something to drink. He was greatly disappointed at hearing there was no whisky, but revived on being shown the champagne. The case was opened, and the contents voted to be good. Thomson, though pressed, would not trespass on me for more than one bottle. When we met in the following week, after expressing sympathy over the fire, his first question was, "What became of the wine?" On hearing that it all perished, his regrets over the waste were both deep and forcible, and he never forgave himself for declining the invitation to open a second bottle on that Christmas morning.

The "Dear John" of the letter on the opposite page was Thomson. He had undertaken to make inquiry for me as to Victor Hugo's comparison of Shakspere to the sea, and had added a little criticism on his own account, which brought forth Swinburne's defence.

AN EMPEROR'S LYING-IN-STATE.

Napoleon the Third lived so quiet a life at Chislehurst that few followed the reports of his illness

Holmwood
Nov. 25th

Dear John,

1. The similitude of Shakespeare to the sea forms the overture of Victor Hugo's book — "William Shakespeare" pp. 15, 16 (ed. 1864).

2. The license of using a singular verb ↄ after two substantives (as in the verses you quote) has always been admitted, I think, in modern English verse. Of course it *is* a license to say "the flower-dust & the flower-smell *clings*"; but even if unpardonable, the offender will find himself chastised in good company. Mille amitiés.
Yours ever
A C Swinburne

very closely. Hence the news of his death a week after an operation for stone came upon public and Press people alike as something of a surprise. It was mid-morning of Thursday when he passed away, and on the Friday Mr. Lloyd sent to inquire if a supplement could not be brought out to deal fully with the dead Emperor's career. Machines for printing the entire paper from a so-called endless roll had not then been completed, and thus it was found impossible to risk any kind of supplement. All that could be done was to boil down the story of Louis Napoleon and the Third Empire to the compass of a page of small, closely-printed type. I contrived to do this single-handed in a way to satisfy the readers. Nothing more was heard of any need for a supplement for a number of years. Tuesday being fixed for the lying-in-state of the dead Emperor, I was enabled to escape from the office and go down to Chislehurst. Evening had closed in before the fifteen thousand persons had passed through the chamber, but a friendly inspector took me in when all was quiet. The solemnity and awe of the scene were thus intensified. The hall door of Camden Place being closed, the visitor entered at one side and moved along what seemed a vast passage, roofed, walled, and floored from end to end with black cloth. About the centre the black hangings parted and formed two great curtains, looped up to disclose the mortuary chamber. The coffin, set some distance back, was so sloped that the whole of the interior was visible. The dead Emperor, with eyes softly closed, showed no trace of pain or suffering; and the moustache and imperial being untouched gave the same mystic expression to the face that was familiar in life. He was in the uniform that he wore at Sedan—a blue tunic and red trousers, the latter being covered by a dark military cloak. A little crucifix rested on the breast, and gold rings glittered on the pale fingers. The red ribbon of the Legion of Honour crossed the body, and on the left breast was a row of medals and crosses. At the head rose a brass crucifix, and behind that a large Latin cross stretched its silver arms over the black hangings.

THE BROTHERS WAINWRIGHT.

The startling circumstance under which Henry Wainwright was arrested made the Whitechapel tragedy rank as a thrilling sensation of 1875. A young woman named Alice Day was with him in the cab when the mutilated remains were moved from Shoreditch over London Bridge. On the two prisoners being brought up at Southwark Police Court, a crowd pressed so closely upon the dock (which was simply surrounded by an open iron railing) that Wainwright's hat was several times knocked down. My seat enabled me to lean against this rail and therefore to watch the accused very closely. After a lengthy opening speech by Mr. Poland, he said the Crown withdrew any charge against Alice Day, and she was at once ordered to be discharged. Her seat in the dock was on the left of Wainwright, so she had to pass him in order to move out. She shrank as far as she possibly could from even brushing his coat, a look of mingled fear and disdain on her face. Wainwright, on the other hand, regarded her with a leer which no effort to smile could make pleasant. In the course of the examination the father of the victim suddenly spoke of her bearing a mark on one of her legs, where she was either burned or scalded when young. Counsel instantly jumped at this as a link in the chain of identity that was wanted. Mr. Benson, the presiding magistrate, afforded evidence that wisdom is not always to be found on the judgment seat, for he resented this questioning, and remarked that considering the state of the remains the point could be of no value. It subsequently, however, proved a very important point. The case started early in September and was carried on to the end of the year. At the trial, which occupied nine days, Henry Wainwright was found guilty of murder, and his brother Thomas of being an accessory after the fact. Thomas, who was said to have begun his working life as an apprentice to an ironmonger in Fleet Street, was sent to seven years' penal servitude, Henry being hanged just before Christmas. A ticket for the execution was sent to the paper, but I could never bring myself to witness the carrying out of the last sentence of the law after it ceased to be in public.

THE PROPRIETOR'S SECRET DISCOVERED.

A little surprise was sprung upon Mr. Edward Lloyd one day in the autumn of 1876. He had carried through all his negotiations for purchasing the *Clerkenwell News* with absolute secrecy, but on its completion the manager was called in to see that the needful documents were properly signed and executed. These being finished, he was asked to keep silence, as Mr. Lloyd did not wish knowledge of the affair to get out till he was ready to move with the new property. Now it so happened that at the previous Christmas, through writing some dramatic notices for the *Hour*, I had become acquainted with Mr. Robert Boyle, the sub-editor. When want of funds caused the *Hour* to be suddenly stopped, all the workers on it were thrown out. Pickburn, who had sold the *Clerkenwell News*, being a good Bohemian, invited friends to rejoice with him over the receipt of a cheque for thirty thousand pounds; and as Boyle lived in the neighbourhood, he heard of the purchase forthwith. To hurry down to me, with an inquiry as to whether there was any chance of an opening for him, was the work of half an hour. Of course I was entirely in the dark, but said I would soon see if the report was correct. He assured me there was no doubt whatever about it; so I stepped into the manager's room, and in a quiet, matter-of-fact way asked, "What is Mr. Lloyd going to do with the *Clerkenwell News*?" Hance nearly tumbled off his chair with astonishment; and, instead of replying, said, "What do you know about it?" On being told, he hurried to Mr. Lloyd, and recalling the fact of his being asked to keep the purchase secret, added, "Catling has just been in to me to inquire what you intend doing with the paper." As it was part of my business to gather news, Mr. Lloyd smilingly admitted it was no use trying to keep me in the dark. So I was taken into his confidence with regard to changes contemplated. No journalistic opening was likely for some time;

but as the weeks went on I was able to keep hope alive with Boyle, and ultimately he became the first editor of the *Daily Chronicle*.

A STRAGGLER FROM NAPOLEON'S COURT.

Baron de X—— was a fine old fellow, with some stateliness of manner, when he first figured in Fleet Street, despite the fact that his clothes were beginning to show signs of needing renewal. How or in what way we met I cannot recall. Gradually his story was made known. Bearing a title derived from some petty German State, he entered the service of Napoleon, and in the circle of the French Court met and married a young and charming American lady. After the flight of the Empress from Paris, the Baron and Baroness, with two or three children and the lady's mother, sought refuge in London. For a time the disposal of their jewellery provided for daily wants, and when these were gone the Baron cast about to find some means of earning an income. No economical and comfortable tea rooms then existed, but a company had been formed with a large capital to bring about their introduction. The directors met in Soho Square, and there I went to support the application of the Baron for the management of a coffee tavern to be opened at the corner of Bouverie Street, Fleet Street. It was an act that I am afraid was prompted more by kindness than discretion. Anyhow, the Baron was duly appointed; Blanchard Jerrold presided over a small gathering of pressmen, at which hopeful speeches were made. There was neither chicken nor champagne; nor even cigars. It was a simple, straightforward, honest effort to improve on the old coffee-shops, without sacrificing temperance principles; but the business mind was lacking, and therefore the scheme soon went awry. The shutters were finally closed in Fleet Street, and it was not long before the company, with all its good intentions, had to be wound up.

A CIGAR WITH A MURDERER.

Years ago the police were not always shy of pressmen. On the afternoon of Friday, December 15th, 1876, London was startled by news of a shocking murder in Pimlico. A young man of two-and-twenty named Frederick Treadaway was paying his addresses to the niece of a Mr. and Mrs. Collins. After taking lunch with the old couple, he was left alone with Mr. Collins, and immediately shot him down across the table. Fearing that he had only wounded instead of killed his victim, Treadaway dashed out of the room, and meeting Mrs. Collins, assaulted her so brutally that she was left unconscious while he made his escape. The police were soon hot on the scent, and next morning I sent out a reporter to watch and follow up the police. The busy hours of Saturday passed away without any news of the search; the paper went to press as usual just before midnight; and I was preparing to go home when the reporter made his way slowly and not quite steadily upstairs. "They've got him," he said, in a thick, confidential whisper, so as not to be heard by any one else. Drawing him into my room, I tried to extract further information, but "They've got him" was all he could say, and indeed all that he knew. The man had been out for sixteen hours, possibly with little to eat, and though he brought no details, the fact of Treadaway's capture was unquestionably important. As quickly as possible I made for Bridewell Police Station, but there they knew nothing of any arrest, and could only refer me to Rochester Row. A hansom soon carried me there, where quiet reigned. Only one officer was busy at his books in the small station. After a few words of explanation as to who I was and what I wanted, he confirmed the news that Treadaway had been captured somewhere up the river, and would be brought there during the night. With this official confirmation of the arrest I was able to drive back to the office and insert a brief report. Before leaving I asked to be allowed to revisit the station an hour or two later. "You won't get anything more," said the kindly officer, but I urged that there might be something, and obtained permission to return. When I did so it was to find the police station even more quiet than before. An hour of silent waiting seemed a long one, even though I was seated in front of a good fire. At half-past two o'clock on the Sunday morning a vehicle drew up outside, and the next minute two police officers ushered in a man securely handcuffed. There was a whispered inquiry at the desk, evidently with respect to my presence, but the answer proved satisfactory. Once inside, the handcuffs were removed from the prisoner, and he was treated with marked gentleness. Asked if he was cold, he replied firmly, "No, sir," and declined any refreshment, saying he had had supper. One of the officers then said, "Now we have brought you here our duty is ended. Once you go inside we can do nothing more for you; but (he added) I know you like this," and offered him a cigar. I took one, the detectives followed suit, and all four sat down in front of the fire smoking. The weather and other indifferent subjects were touched upon, but no word was said respecting crime or murder or anything disagreeable. At the end of half an hour a significant glance drew me outside. Then I was shown the things found upon the prisoner when he was arrested in the cottage of a friend at Isleworth, where he had gone to borrow a sovereign. Once the facts were obtained I jumped into my cab and drove back to the office. At seven o'clock an extra edition of the paper appeared with a full column of the capture—omitting of course all mention of personalities and the humanity which afforded even a murderer a last smoke. Before leaving, the inspector on duty asked me to send up some copies of the paper, and he was well supplied. When reporters of the various dailies appeared in the course of the Sunday at Rochester Row station, asking for particulars, each one was handed a copy of *Lloyd's*, with the intimation that all the information the police could possibly give was included there. It was a source of great satisfaction to me to find that in a comparatively short time every one of the officers concerned in the case had obtained promotion in the Force. Treadaway, it may be added, was tried, convicted, and sentenced to death for the cruel murder; but the sentence was reduced to penal servitude on the ground of his being an epileptic. The case scarcely came within the scope of a comic paper, but Henry Sampson gave me the first public pat on the head by printing the following in *Fun* :—

"The Fight for Life. It is an ill-wind that blows nobody good, and *Lloyd's* made its first tremendous triumph as a special Sunday paper over the Pimlico murder. While other journals said nothing whatever about the assassin being taken *Lloyd's* took the wind out of the *sales* of the dailies by a column of special details of the Saturday night's capture. We mention this fact, as it gives us an opportunity of being first for once with the information, special and exclusive, that Mr. Catling, the man at the wheel in Salisbury Square, arranged it all, and had the unhappy young man concealed on the premises until the other Sunday papers had gone to press, then sent for the police, and set the machinery of the law and of *Lloyd's* in motion at once. We are not jealous, but in the interests of those of our weekly contemporaries that had to go without the 'latest tip,' we should like to ask, Now, *is* this journalism?"

SLEEPLESS NIGHTS EXPLAINED.

Presswork, like poverty, makes a man occasionally fall into strange company. In connection with my first ill-advised speculation I met a middle-aged man who was full of enterprise, but confessed to a strange inability to sleep. No matter at what early hour in the morning he woke he could never go off again, and was perforce obliged to get up and turn out. After a meeting in support of a scheme for bringing out a new process for preserving meat from abroad, this man asked me into his office in High Holborn, where I learned that he was the secretary and manager of the Sun Permanent Building Society. He was specially anxious that I should look at his method of bookkeeping; all I remember is that he had an unusually large number of ponderous ledgers. Not being interested in the society, nothing more was thought of the matter until a year or so later I read a report that William Robert Warner was charged with embezzling £12,000. Here was an explanation of the sleepless nights. He pleaded guilty at the Old Bailey and was sentenced to seven years' penal servitude.

LORD ROSEBERY'S EARLY EDUCATION.

It is of interest to recall the views on education expressed by Lord Rosebery in early life. Speaking at a presentation of prizes at the Cowper Street School in 1874, his lordship said in the very classical public school to which he was sent they taught him where the villa of Cicero was, but did not teach him the whereabouts of San Francisco, or the difference between Protection and Free Trade. By way of illustration, he related the experience of a colonial sheep farmer, who had in his employ, as shepherds, a man who had been at Oxford University, another from Cambridge, one from Trinity College, Dublin, an army lieutenant who had been educated at Rugby, a Winchester man, and two Germans. This result of classical education he held to show the greater advantage of commercial training. So far as the ignorance of America was concerned, Mr. Cobden had emphasised it ten years previously. In a speech at Rochdale he referred to a London newspaper article, which made a river 580 miles long turn up hill into another river. These two rivers were then made to fall into a third, though not a drop of water reached there from either.

HUMORISTS OF FORMER DAYS.

Douglas Jerrold's flashing wit was so distinctly personal that when he passed away no successor appeared. Instead we had a small army of humorists, following diligently in the path of the arch-punster, Tom Hood. Word-twisting prevailed in all directions, leading to many mirthful stage productions. Gilbert à Beckett and Talfourd, the Brothers Brough, Burnand and Byron, Gilbert and Reece, ransacked mythology and history for themes capable of burlesque treatment. The more outrageous the pun the louder was the laughter or the more general the chorus of "Oh's" that burst forth. When Talfourd made an ancient goddess command a young one "To your room, miss; you'll find room in it to ruminate a bit," he struck the chord of fun. Then, becoming more daring, the maiden let fall her veil as she fled away. This being produced to the anxious parent as evidence of flight, was met with the despairing cry, "Think you to cheer me with her drop her veil? (drop of ale!)" These burlesques called forth some of the best acting of the time, but were never perfect till they had been played for a few weeks.

Artemus Ward was carried off by death too quickly for his droll American lectures to have created any very deep impression.

Three or four years later came Mark Twain, who made the realism of travel the basis of humorous reflections. Wonderfully neat and happy was his account of the many cents he had contributed for missions while attending Sunday school. In respect to native dress he described the women as gorgeous in earrings and bangles, while the men wore a smile! On recalling the fact of my hearing this to the memory of Mark Twain some thirty years later, his eyes twinkled as he said, "Yes, yes; that's quite right." Judged as a newspaper writer, Mark must have been the most brilliant of his time, for the non-travelled reader revels in his fun; while those who have been over the same scenes—Rome, Venice, Athens, Palestine, Baalbec, Damascus, Egypt—appreciate still more highly his just, eloquent, and discriminating word pictures. Let any one who doubts turn to the last page of "The New Pilgrim's Progress" and his eyes will be opened.

Tom Hood the younger, who while a clerk in the Government service wrote several poems which I put into type, appeared in clubland and Fleet Street during the early seventies. My first meeting with him was in a wine shop where the Express Dairy now stands; above the first floor being a huge board inscribed "Anderson, Engraver." When Hood undertook the editorship of *Fun* (owned by a looking-glass manufacturer on the other side of the street) Henry Sampson acted as sub-editor; and Anderson, beginning on the *Referee*, later became a very successful descriptive writer for the *Daily Telegraph*. Hood was an imposing figure, resembling Sir William Treloar. I remember Tom Archer, who was friendly with both, one day saying to me "Aren't they a fine pair, and aren't they alike?" Having inherited his father's delicate constitution, genial Tom Hood soon passed away; and George R. Sims appeared on the scene, writing vigorously for *Fun* when Sampson was editor. It is impossible to think of Henry Sampson without a feeling of deep regret. A more encouraging friend and adviser never crossed my path. Shrewd, diligent, and a strenuous worker himself, he inspired confidence in others; and was able, when occasion required, to give just the light touch of a spur which compelled action. His indignation was superb, but it did not damp his kindness of heart. On one occasion, we were beating about with the view of getting sufficient support to start a Press Club. Lovell, manager of the newly-formed Press Association, was traced to an upper room at the Cheshire Cheese, where a rubber of whist was in progress. One of the players was Sydney French, who had that afternoon borrowed ten pounds of Sampson to save his furniture from being seized for rent. There was no scene; going downstairs, however, I heard the lender's emphatic opinion of the transaction. Yet a month or two after, when French fell ill, Sampson was one of the first to visit him and afford help. He said no word of this, but I accidentally met him coming out of French's house. The *Referee*, in which three proprietors were concerned, soon became a success. The early death of Francis improved Sampson's holding, and he stood alone shortly after the passing away of Mr. Ashton Dilke. Fortune, however, I am persuaded, brought more disappointment than pleasure. New friends did not make amends for the old ones that were shuffled off. The early days, when he was fighting for recognition, and slowly climbing

A BOUND INTO JOURNALISM. 137

the ladder, were undoubtedly the happiest in the comparatively brief life of Henry Sampson.

OVER AND UNDER THE CHANNEL.

Captain Webb's success in swimming the Channel was a triumph hardly likely to be repeated by those who attempt it with the additional strain attendant on modern press enterprise. I met and chatted with Webb, and entertain the highest opinion of his simplicity and courage. Admitting that it was a very hard task, especially towards the last, when nothing but determination made him hold on, Webb simply said, "I did my swimming in a fair honest English manner." It may be worth while to recall the facts. Diving from steps at the head of Dover Admiralty Pier, just before one o'clock on the afternoon of Tuesday, August 24th, 1875, Webb reached Calais in twenty-three and three-quarter hours. As the crow flies the distance would be twenty-one miles, but drifting with the ebb and flow of the tide was estimated to make the course thirty-five miles. After necessary rest, Webb appeared none the worse for his great exploit. He already held the medal of the Royal Humane Society for jumping overboard in a gale to save a fellow sailor, and many other honours were conferred upon him. Nothing but sorrow can be felt for his pitiful end in the terrible rapids of Niagara.

Inquiry into the Channel Tunnel project involved my paying a visit to the works as they stood in the spring of 1883. As a pioneer, Sir Edward Watkin was one of the most energetic of the time, but he played too much for his own hand. Descending the shaft, the party were conveyed on trollies a goodly distance under the sea, nearly a mile if memory serves me right. From an engineering point of view no reason was apparent why the work could not be completed. On returning to the surface there was a luxurious luncheon, with speeches descriptive of the whole scheme and the hopes of the promoters. In print I strongly opposed the tunnel, and hold, with Tennyson, it to be the imperative duty of Englishmen to keep our shores " compassed by the inviolate sea."

MAN AND THE MONKEY.

The descent of man from protoplasm, through a long line of monkeys, has often been a subject of discussion. One day in 1878, at the Westminster Aquarium, I was enabled to study the matter in good company. A gorilla newly arrived from Africa was proclaimed to be the "Missing Link." Representatives of the Press were offered the first chance of shaking hands with the new brother; I arrived there simultaneously with Mr. Frank Buckland, the well-known naturalist, one of H.M.'s Inspectors of Salmon Fisheries. As an attendant opened the door of the room, in one corner of which Master Pongo was crouching, under no restraint, Buckland said "Come along," and I was bound to follow. My companion said that if an animal was gently seized by the mouth it would not bite. I soon had an opportunity of proving the truth of this. Having laid hold of my leg, Pongo was proceeding to what seemed very like biting, when a

CAPTAIN WEBB LANDING AT CALAIS AFTER SWIMMING THE CHANNEL.

TRAM-LINE RUNNING INTO THE CHANNEL TUNNEL.

[To face p. 138

playful rubbing of its chin had a soothing influence, and we became quite friendly. Buckland, talking softly, shook one paw, then stroked the other; gradually inducing the huge beast to extend its limbs and stand upright. Further efforts were directed to making it exhibit any possible intelligence that might be there. This was all in vain, though the interview was very interesting. As we left, Buckland quietly quoted the words, "And God saw everything that He had made, and behold it was very good"; adding with significant earnestness, "And it remains good to this day."

HOW EXCLUSIVE NEWS WAS KEPT.

The most remarkable of many instances of securing an exclusive item of news occurred in 1878. Shortly after one o'clock on the afternoon of the last day of August a serious collision took place at Sittingbourne Junction, on the London, Chatham, and Dover Railway. While shunting operations were in progress, a passenger train ran into some carriages, with the deplorable result that five people were killed and forty others more or less badly injured. Lloyd's paper mill being close at hand, a brief telegraphic report was sent up, and appeared in a portion of the edition issued at four o'clock in the afternoon. Fuller particulars were subsequently sent up by train, and I despatched an assistant sub-editor to the scene of the collision. This was done in order to avoid any of the general reporters getting knowledge of what had happened. Next morning *Lloyd's* appeared with nearly two columns of details, including lists of the killed and injured. As the passengers who were in the train came on to London, they were greatly surprised that no mention was made of the accident in any of the Saturday evening papers; still more were they astonished to find the Sunday papers equally silent. *Lloyd's* was the only one to give an account of the disaster.

A TRIP TO BONNIE SCOTLAND.

Travelling by boat from the Thames I reached Leith on a Sunday evening, and found myself under the necessity of carrying my own bag till shelter was secured in an hotel some distance away. Outside, the Sabbatarian law was strictly observed; indoors it was possible to obtain refreshment and drink very much as usual. After climbing Arthur's Seat, and admiring the picturesque beauty of Edinburgh—not overlooking the worse than Whitechapel squalor of the poorer parts—my steps were directed to Loch Katrine. Day after day I waited at Inversnaid in the hope of ascending Ben Lomond; falling mist rendered this impossible. So, crossing the loch, a coach carried me through the Pass of Glencroe to beautiful Inverary, and thence onward to Dalmally. It was the summer of 1878, when Mr. John Bright was seeking restoration to health by a prolonged holiday. One morning the famous statesman entered the hotel, greeting the proprietor very cordially, and inquiring with keen interest as to the political feeling of the district. Scotch ways did not appeal to a humble journalist. Luncheon, I remember (whether you partook of a biscuit or made a substantial meal), was at the fixed charge of three and sixpence. A clergyman, who came in with some ladies and two boys, groaned very audibly when presented with a bill at this rate. The rail then ended at Dalmally, making a carriage drive needful to see the wild Pass of Brander. Going and returning I greatly enjoyed the "land of brown heath and shaggy wood"; crossed the Bridge of Allan, climbed Ben Ledi, and surveyed the battlefield of Bannockburn from Stirling Castle. The railway journey from the latter place to Glasgow taught me something. Fierce war was being waged between two companies, and quite innocently I travelled on one line with a ticket issued by the other. Protests against paying a second time were all in vain; a passenger had to choose between parting with his money or being detained. A final burst of indignation was calmly met by the Superintendent, who asked, "How long have you been in the country, Mr. Catling?" "Only a fortnight," I answered. "What do you think of the scenery?" came next. "Oh, the scenery is attractive enough, but I don't see that is any reason for your making me pay twice." However, payment had to be made, and it is fair to add the amount was subsequently returned by the other company on the circumstances being explained.

One morning, when I was getting up in quite a pretentious hotel, Burns suddenly came to mind, for there on the bedclothes was just such an

"Ugly, creepin', blastit wonner,
  Detested, shunn'd, by saunt and sinner,"

as the poet saw on a lady's bonnet at church.

LESSONS IN DIVORCE.

The artistic temperament in many cases appears too self-centred to bend in accord with the give-and-take principles which alone can make married life successful and happy. This reflection is called forth by a letter of 1877, in which the famous tragic actress, Miss Glyn, wrote, "I cannot afford to advertise. Will you notice these readings? Upon them I depend to keep my home over my head. Eleven years of legal and domestic wars have left me worse than penniless." The lady's case was indeed a sad one. At an early age she was left a widow, and in the winter of 1853 met Mr. Dallas, a literary man of some repute, at Glasgow. One evening, at his lodgings, the pair married themselves after the Scotch fashion, in the presence of her maid and the landlady. Mr. Dallas read over the English marriage service, and placed a ring on her finger; she repeated the part put down for saying by the lady, and the law was satisfied. On returning to London some time afterwards a more formal marriage ceremony was gone through at St. George's, Hanover Square. The union was not a success; when pecuniary troubles were added to those of a domestic character, the lot of the pair became very unhappy. While living in Hanover Square, in 1868, the lady lost many of her dresses and other property by fire. A few years later she regained her freedom through the Divorce Court; but, as her letter shows, it by no means meant a return of prosperity.

Another divorce case of the seventies, in which the Rev. Newman Hall figured as petitioner, was

A BOUND INTO JOURNALISM. 143

the greatest scandal of the time. *Lloyd's* was drawn into the matter through a paragraph announcing the case as forthcoming. The report came from a young reporter, who was pursued by Mr. Hall, with what I felt to be far more indignation than the matter warranted. It was positively denied that there had ever been any cause for dissatisfaction with the conduct of Mrs. Hall. When years later the case came into court, the utter falsity of the reverend gentleman's assurance was proved beyond question. After commencing action he let it drop for five years because (as he admitted in the witness box) he thought it would interfere with the collection of subscriptions for his new church. Both parties made a miserable show in court, and perjury was rife. Mr. Willis spoke for eight mortal hours in the endeavour to show the innocence of Mrs. Hall: it was all in vain. The jury at once proclaimed her guilt, and a decree was granted. On the other side the *Standard* said, " A middle-aged man with a young wife, who allows her to sit up at night and smoke with her riding-master, may be fairly said not only to deserve, but to have created his own disgrace and dishonour." The reverend gentleman six months later married again.

CO-WORKERS ON THE "CHRONICLE."

When Mr. Lloyd entrusted the reviewing department of the *Daily Chronicle* to me, I was brought into familiar association with many good fellows. Building up what was virtually a new daily on imperial lines meant earnest work for all concerned. At first publishers were so shy that I had to go round and ask for new books; some even then declined to send any but cheap publications. That mattered not; if a column had to be filled, a pamphlet or a leaflet of the day sufficed. One I specially remember dealt with "The Hours and Holidays of Bank Clerks" in such a way as to lead the publisher to send copies of the paper round to every bank in London. The early closing on Saturdays had not then been introduced. Kegan Paul gave me a kindly welcome, but Messrs. Bentley required a good deal of persuasion before they could be made to understand that the *Chronicle* had come to stay as a daily paper. Henwood Thomas, while still engaged in the Customs, contributed sound political leaders; Phipps Jackson, an official in Somerset House, wrote vivid art criticisms; Skinner was the skilled financial expert, and A. E. Fletcher dealt with social leaders and notes. The wide and extensive reporting staff had Mr. Sharp as chief sub-editor. Mr. Lloyd paid £30,000 down for the *Clerkenwell News*, and then proceeded to spend further large sums on improving the property. All the profits—about £5,000 a year—which the previous proprietor had been gaining from the local sheet of course disappeared. This fact was only admitted by the income-tax people after a sharp fight. Mr. Lloyd told me at the outset that he had made up his mind to push the paper for five years, and then see what were its prospects. Some time before that period had expired it was paying interest on capital, and no question of turning back ever arose. Mr. J. R. Fisher (now editor of the *Northern Whig*) was foreign editor; Mr. F. W. Pattison analysed blue books and statistical papers, Mr. J. Lysaght

Finigan writing on general topics. We were proud of Finigan, and had high hopes of his future. He studied for the Bar, and when he got through, the staff presented him with wig and gown at a complimentary dinner. At one time he took a short holiday, and returned M.P. for Ennis. The latter feat was due to the fact of Finigan being Parliamentary secretary to Mr. Parnell. He disappeared more suddenly than he had risen, and was understood to have sacrificed political ambition for the pleasures of domestic life.

CAREER OF SAMUEL PHELPS.

What the stage owes to the fifty years' strenuous labour of Samuel Phelps has never been adequately recorded. Like Irving, he took to acting from deliberate choice, having been brought up in quite a different sphere. His father dying when he was very young, he was apprenticed to a printer at Plymouth. Just after his sixteenth year he made a move to London, with only a few shillings in his pocket. In the office where he gained employment he was what is technically known as a "twicer"— that is, a man who can turn his hand from composing to working at press. The method is still common enough in the country, but does not obtain in London. During a period of struggling hardship Phelps met Douglas Jerrold, a year older than himself. Both were full of ambitious ideas, the fulfilment of which was being sought in the direction of the stage. Having become recognised as a promising amateur, Phelps at the age of twenty-two married, and soon after accepted a professional engagement. Beginning with the York circuit, he played throughout the country for ten years before being seen in London. Sadler's Wells management—the most famous in Shaksperean annals—was not begun until he had turned forty. Familiar as I was with his appearance on the stage, I only once saw him in private, and that was in the dress circle of the Princess's. A curious snuffle attracted my attention, and on looking beside me in the semi-darkness there sat Phelps. This sniffing of the nose was one of the actor's persistent mannerisms, of which he made most effective use in various comic characters, notably Dr. Cantwell and Christopher Sly. For versatility and supreme excellence in such widely different parts as Lear and Sir Pertinax Macsycophant, Richelieu and Sir John Ogleby, Phelps stands without a rival. He continued to act too long, owing to the fact that the salaries of the time had not enabled him to make adequate provision for his retirement.

GEORGE CRUIKSHANK.

George Cruikshank was a great character to the end of his long life. Artistically he worked through many changes, but the exuberant humour of the man never left him. When he was well over eighty we had a long chat over the ways of Fleet Street. He went back to a period when laborious days were followed by the fierce delights of all-night revels. Bed was left out of the question; after a bath and a breakfast he returned to his drawing. Very few of the fellows could stand it, he said; but it did not hurt him. The rigid teetotalism of his later years led me one day to ask if he did not miss the luxury of an occasional glass. With a merry smile, brimming over with recollections of the past, George instantly replied, "Oh, no; I've had my whack."

JURY OF MATRONS AT NEWGATE.

Two weird tragedies engaged my attention in 1879. On March 5th, a box discovered floating in the Thames near Barnes was found to contain the body of a woman, minus the head and arms. For a while the police strove to keep the matter secret, bidding any probable witnesses "say nothing about the case to the Press." That is the way to put a journalist on his mettle, and it was not long before the accounts I gathered led to the mystery being solved. A young boy, after reading the paper, told his mother that he was sure the box which had been found was one which he had carried for Kate when she pushed it over the parapet of the bridge into the Thames. "Kate," it transpired, was a domestic servant who killed her mistress, a Miss Thompson, boiled her body in the copper, and then bolted to Ireland. As the case was slowly unravelled, the advantages of publicity became more and more apparent. The notorious Peace, it may be remembered, boasted that in spite of the rewards set upon his head he could defy all the detectives; and it certainly was not till after the Press published the news of his arrest for burglary that information was given which enabled the police to identify the notable capture they had made. At the Old Bailey, after Kate Webster had been sentenced to death, there was a remarkable scene. In reply to the question, "Have you anything to say why the sentence of execution should be stayed?" the prisoner answered "Yes." A communication was then made privately to the Judge. In the course of a few minutes great commotion reigned throughout the court. The under-sheriffs came buzzing around, approaching every female present; the jury which had tried the case was dismissed; and the meaning of the excitement was seen in the box being refilled with a jury of matrons. Meanwhile Kate appeared to have fainted in the dock. A warder and two female attendants were busy bathing her forehead and attempting to revive her with a jug of water and a bottle of smelling salts. The matron of the female side of Newgate gave evidence, but as this was not deemed conclusive, Mr. Bond, the well-known surgeon, was directed to make an examination, the convict being taken to the jury room. After a quarter of an hour the case was resumed in court, and the doctor gave evidence. Mr. Justice Denman said that during his experience of thirty-two years he had never been engaged in a case of this kind before. The end of it was that the jury of matrons decided that the plea for stay of execution was not true, and the prisoner's doom was sealed.

EUSTON SQUARE MYSTERY.

The second case, known as the Euston Square Murder, is still a mystery. The remains of a poor old lodger named Matilda Hacker were found by dustmen when clearing out a cellar which had been used for coals. Suspicion fell upon the servant, a woman named Hannah Dobbs, who was arrested and brought to trial. Mr. Gorst for the prosecution insisted that the evidence proved the connection of the prisoner with the murder, and told the jury they must not shrink from the performance of their duty in the presence of the facts which he had drawn attention to. Mr. Mead for the defence contended that as there was only a suspicion against the poor woman on her trial, but more than a suspicion against other persons, the jury should give her the benefit of the doubt. Half an hour's deliberation ended in their returning a verdict of "Not guilty." Two months after the trial I first met Bennet Burleigh, who offered to bring Hannah Dobbs to the office. The idea rather startled the proprietor, but as the case was much in the public mind, the meeting was arranged to hear the whole of the dreadful story. The coroner's jury had returned a verdict of "wilful murder against some person or persons unknown." It is no part of the duty of a newspaper to make accusations, but judges even in these later days have held that the Press has a right to endeavour to unravel mysteries. It was very thin ice that had to be gone over in the daring assertions and accusations of this woman, and I remember sitting up all night to write and re-write, revise and correct my column. The necessity for this was shown a little later when I met Mr. Purkess (proprietor of the *Police News*). When I told him there had been no complaint whatever with respect to my dealing with the story of Hannah Dobbs, he said, "Well, my telling it cost me £2,500." A curious incident arose some eight or nine years after the trial. At a little dinner party in the home of Augustus Harris, Sir John Gorst, Sir S. Bancroft, and Mr. J. C. Parkinson were present. During the evening the conversation drifted into criminal experiences, and I mentioned Hannah Dobbs. "Oh, did you know her?" said Sir John Gorst. "I prosecuted her at the Old Bailey, and while the jury had gone to consider their verdict, the members of the Bar made me very anxious and uncomfortable by telling me that my closing speech would secure a conviction. As I did not feel altogether certain in my own mind it was a great relief when they came back with a verdict of acquittal."

GOOD WORK OF SUNDAY SCHOOLS.

Foremost among the benevolent influences of the nineteenth century I should place the teaching of Sunday schools. Education may be said to have begun with them, and their results reach far beyond all calculations. As these lines are penned, the voices of the children gathered to celebrate the centenary in 1880 seem still ringing in my ears. Despite the rain that fell in heavy showers, the grounds of Lambeth Palace have witnessed no prettier gathering. Fully 18,000 children, with many teachers, had been drawn there, along with the Prince and Princess of Wales and their sons and daughters. The Duke of Cambridge hurried back from a review at Aldershot, the Lord Mayor and Lady Mayoress represented the City, and Mrs. Gladstone appeared on the platform, bowing so low as to recall the curtsey of a child before

A BOUND INTO JOURNALISM. 151

shaking hands with the Prince and Princess. Among the many hymns that were sung nothing approached the processional "Onward, Christian soldiers, marching as to war." As the young folk moved quickly along, raising their voices and waving their banners, the effect was thrilling in the extreme. Writing on the subject in next morning's paper, I recalled the pessimistic view of Horace Walpole in the year that the Sunday school movement started. In a letter to a clergyman, he said, "as to this country, it is sunk perhaps never to rise again. It is my opinion that Europe itself is worn out." We laugh at these gloomy forebodings to-day; they should teach the lesson, never to lose heart. Let us rather inspire the young with high and noble thoughts; bid them press on to a happy future for themselves and their country.

RUNNING AND ROWING INCIDENTS.

Weston's long-distance walks at the Agricultural Hall were closely watched, and I learned a lesson at Lillie Bridge. During a running match a young Jew was well ahead up to within half-a-dozen feet of the winning-post, when he suddenly eased off and allowed another runner to pass him on the post. After the Jew had been duly declared second, I heard a friend ask him indignantly, "Why on earth did you lose the race like that?" "Didn't you see the first prize was a medal and the second a quid," was the response; "I wanted the coin."

One cold April morning in the early eighties I boarded the Press boat with the idea of really following the Oxford and Cambridge race. Our steamer got off badly and kept far behind. One reporter mounted the bow, and with the aid of powerful field-glasses was able to catch a distant view of the competing crews. What he could distinguish was shouted to the rest. Very few of us saw anything of the race. My only compensation for the disappointment and uncomfortable experience was found in the fact that some unknown friend—rumour said a member of the royal family—sent a case of excellent champagne on board.

A LONG AND NOBLE LIFE.

When the daily papers announced that the Baroness Burdett-Coutts was about to marry Mr. Ashmead Bartlett they blundered. There was no excuse for the error, because the gentleman had a wife living at the time. From a private source I received the correct intelligence that it was the brother, William Lehmann Bartlett, who was the prospective bridegroom. Seeing that the lady was in her sixty-seventh year and had enjoyed the title of Baroness for ten years, Mr. Lloyd was incredulous, and said, " I wouldn't notice the report in *Lloyd's*." The policy of silence meant the loss of a special item of news that would have been of great interest. My grief was scarcely soothed by receiving something as near to an apology as was ever offered by a proprietor to an editor.

Opportunity was afforded me on more than one occasion to note how earnest and unostentatious was the Baroness in her private charity. Something in the letter of an unknown beggar attracted attention, and her private secretary, on looking closely into it, found that an article enclosed was cut from *Lloyd's*. So I was written to, and the reference being satisfactory, help was afforded. Of the public benefactions of the Baroness there are enduring memorials in all quarters of London.

The career of the lady constitutes a most remarkable romance of the peerage, especially in the matrimonial way. When her grandfather, Coutts the banker, married a domestic in the service of his brother, he could scarcely have anticipated seeing three of his daughters become titled ladies. As to fortune for them, that must have seemed lost when the banker, at the age of eighty, married, for the second time, Harriet Mellon, a popular actress. On the death of Coutts in 1822, he left all his wealth to his widow, who five years later, being then fifty-six, married the Duke of St. Albans, not quite half her age. Angela Georgina, daughter of Sir Francis Burdett, the famous baronet and Liberal M.P., came of age in 1835, and two years later, to the surprise of everybody, became, under the will of the Duchess, the unexpected heiress of her grandfather's fortune. London society speedily busied itself in suggesting likely husbands for the young lady, who, with the money, assumed the name of Burdett-Coutts. One day rumour asserted that she was to become the Duchess of Wellington; a little later Prince Louis Napoleon was chosen; and in Lester Wallack's "Memories of Fifty Years" a more startling tale is told that Charles Kean aspired to winning the hand of the great heiress. Entering the theatre in Dublin one night, he said abruptly to Miss Ellen Tree, "Ellen, if you wish to marry me, to-morrow or never." He was in a white heat of passion, and the story was that he had just received a flat rejection from Miss Burdett-Coutts. This can scarcely be credited, but it is certain that Charles Kean married Ellen Tree in 1842, while Miss Burdett-Coutts remained single until 1881. For five-and-twenty years after her marriage the good Baroness continued and extended the range of her benevolent works, dying on the last day of 1906.

In my last interview with Sir Henry Irving, while the Baroness still lived, he told me that he paid her a visit on her ninetieth birthday, when she recalled some of her earlier experiences. One notable occasion was that somewhere about 1840 she went to a ball at Willis's Rooms with the Duke of Wellington, and asked him to tell her, as Louis Napoleon entered, if the Prince in any way resembled his great uncle. Wellington's reply was that he could scarcely say, because it was only on a single occasion that he saw a little man in a grey cloak riding at a distance, and was told that was Bonaparte. The Baroness further remembered when out driving with her father he stopped the carriage at Richmond, and she saw him take out a gallon jar cased in wicker. Her curiosity being aroused, she inquired what it was, and her father said, " Well, my dear, Edmund Kean is lying seriously ill, and as I'm told the poor man drinks nothing but gin, I have resolved that he shall have some of the best that can be got for him." Inheriting as she did her vast wealth from the actress who became a Duchess, it was natural that the Baroness Burdett-Coutts should have sympathetic leanings towards the stage; but we know from Mr. Bram Stoker's book that the persistent rumours as to Sir Henry Irving's indebtedness were altogether without foundation.

SAD LESSON FROM BOHEMIA.

The kindliest depths of Bohemia were stirred in the spring of 1882 by the news that E. C. Barnes died at the age of forty-four, after two days' illness with bronchitis. He was one of the brightest among the leading Savages, and personally appealed to me through coming from my native town of Cambridge. Barnes painted popular pictures: "The Light Blue" and "The Dark Blue" were typical of the University boat race. "Family Cares" appealed to a wider circle. He gave lessons to one of the royal princesses, was known to Charles Dickens, a bosom friend of Tom Robertson, and soothed the last moments of Artemus Ward. Companions called him one of the kindliest of men, but there was little kindness for himself. I never saw a sadder sight than when his artistic home, founded on loans, was lotted out for sale under the auctioneer's hammer. It is of little use to moralise; but living beyond one's means in this way is not worth the candle, and when there is a family, it becomes worse than a blunder.

MOMENTOUS DOINGS OF A DAY.

The 6th of May, 1882, stands out on account of two historic events—one a scene of rejoicing and the other a tragic horror. It was a day of bright sunshine as Queen Victoria drove from Chingford to High Beach to declare Epping Forest open for the use of the people for all time. Copying one of the mottoes, " Was never such a May day and never such a Queen," I described the scene. We were quietly snatching a hasty lunch in a marquee beside the dais arranged for the ceremonial proceedings. Suddenly, a few minutes before the expected time, a blare of trumpets announced the Queen's approach. Ministers and Pressmen alike were on the alert; Lord Granville, one of the most homely of Secretaries of State, not only filled his mouth with part of a sandwich he was eating, but carried the rest on to the platform. The happy chronicle of the royal rejoicings in Epping Forest, which closed with one of Messrs. Brock's matchless firework displays, had scarcely been completed when there came " Terrible News from Ireland." The assassination under such savage circumstances of Lord Frederick Cavendish and his under-secretary, Mr. Burke, was clearly and correctly reported. This fact is emphasised on account of its having been so often stated that the London public heard nothing of the diabolical occurrence until Monday morning. Not only was the news given, but in some comments I said, " The crime shatters at a blow Mr. Gladstone's hope of pursuing a gentle policy."

No one dreamed of Fleet Street being in any way associated with the murders, but Mr. Rayleigh in his story of the Cogers says :—

" During the Fenian agitation, Mr. Kershaw, the Grand, denounced the Irish rebels with great vehemence. On that occasion, Tynan (No. 1) and a friend had dropped in, and Mr. Kershaw's strictures harrowed a sympathiser beyond his endurance. No blood was spilt, however, thanks to the protection of the members. It will ever be matter for execration to all Cogers who are Irishmen, and to all Irishmen, that the knives intended for the foul assassination of Lord Frederick Cavendish were deposited in a bag at the bar while the owner was within at the debate. This was discovered in later years; but perhaps it is not so generally known how Tynan was requited, or how the original MS. of Chapter VII. of the American edition of Tynan's book came, to his great discomfiture, to be lodged among the grim curiosities of a past Coger."

HENRY MARSTON ON STAGE TRICKS.

Henry Marston, one of Phelps's great supporters, was a fine actor. Despite a guttural voice, he shone in a wide range of parts, from Iago to Antony, Baradas to Dr. Pangloss. Visiting him a year or so before he passed away, I found him praying for the end. With a cheerful talk, however, he was drawn to speak of acting, and specially of the methods of Edmund Kean. "There was no fuss then," said Marston, " about art, with or without the big A of later days. All was simple and businesslike. In rehearsing, Kean would remark, ' At this point you take the front of the stage,' and when they came to another, ' Here you give way to me.'" With a bright twinkle Marston said, " We called these things tricks of the stage then, and knew no other name for them." Mention of Macready took Marston back to the night when he first played with him. Macbeth had gone smoothly enough on to the final combat, which had no sooner commenced than Macduff was amazed to find himself assailed by the vilest and most opprobrious epithets. " Come on you —— ——" hissed the tyrant of Scotland to his scared opponent, who after a moment's bewilderment hurled back the challenge, and answered curse for curse throughout the encounter. This language was utterly foreign to Marston's nature, and when after the fall of the curtain he was asked to go to Macready's room, he felt a little curious as to what was coming. "Thank you, Mr. Marston," said the star, "it was a very good fight; I haven't enjoyed it so much for a long time!" A similar story has been told of other actors, but Marston's was his own never forgotten experience.

THE "DARING DUCKLING" ON FREE TRADE.

While "The Ship" at Greenwich continued to be the scene of the Ministerial Whitebait dinner, it also attracted other political bodies. A notable gathering occurred in the summer of 1883. Embarking at Westminster Bridge, the party went down by steamer, thus acquiring an appetite for an excellent repast. It is worth recalling, by reason of the chairman's speech. Mr. Joseph Chamberlain was then in the prime of life. After his strenuous career in trade, and as the municipal leader of Birmingham, he had had seven years in the House of Commons. As chairman at this Cobden Club banquet, he said:—

"'They had not to consider whether the world had been wise enough to adopt Mr. Cobden's views, but whether anything had occurred to weaken his arguments or throw doubt upon the conclusions at which he had arrived. The arguments against this system, by which the few were enabled to enrich themselves at the expense of the many, remained absolutely unshaken, and he did not doubt that in the long run truth and reason would prevail."

A BOUND INTO JOURNALISM.

Mr. T. B. Potter, M.P., in proposing "The health of the chairman," said that he endorsed the able speech which had been delivered by Mr. Chamberlain, and he should be quite content in the future to follow the lead of the "daring duckling," as Mr. Chamberlain had been described.

FOURTH STAGE.

THE EDITORIAL CHAIR.

My Duties and Responsibilities—Writing for the *Morning Post*—A City Tragedy made Helpful—Mr. Gladstone and General Gordon—The First Home Rule Bill—Appeal to the Country—A Branch of Religious Work—At an Irish Eviction—Queen Victoria's Jubilee—The Struggle for Trafalgar Square—Where the Armstrong Case led me—A Reporter's Adventure—Result of a State Prosecution—The "Ripper" Atrocities—How the Clues were Missed—Origin of the Safety Parachute—Projects of Lord Winchilsea—How Small Traders were Saved—Americans Welcomed in London—Why I am a Liberal—Reporting under Difficulties—Barnum as a Teetotaler.

MY DUTIES AND RESPONSIBILITIES.

A NEWSPAPER somewhat resembles a State in the manner of its working. No matter what changes may occur, the run of daily duties must go on unceasingly. Mr. Blanchard Jerrold passed away at half-past four on the morning of Monday, March 10th, 1884, and before noon a letter from Mr. Edward Lloyd reached me, setting forth his plans for the future. As no one realised that Mr. Jerrold was seriously ill, news of his death came with a suddenness that deepened the regret for the loss of a most amiable gentleman and kindly colleague. When I studied Mr. Lloyd's new proposal—that henceforth he would secure leading articles of a high character from various writers; and that my

THE EDITORIAL CHAIR.

responsibility for reading them and supervising the entire contents of the paper should continue as before—it led me to look forward and backward.

In the very early days of my sub-editing, Mr. Lloyd strongly disapproved of one article, and wanted to know how it got into the paper. Being told it was Mr. Blanchard Jerrold's, he said " That has nothing to do with it; I look to you to see that everything is kept right." From that time onward, though the editor's name appeared on the front page of the paper, his copy had to be closely supervised by the sub-editor. On occasions it was necessary to suppress a leader, and insert one of an exactly opposite opinion. That happened after the bombardment of Alexandria, when Mr. Jerrold advocated withdrawal from Egypt; his article got no further than a proof, the paper supporting the higher view of England's responsibility in regard to the Egyptians. During the eighteen years that we worked together, the editor only once visited the office (on a Derby day when I was at Epsom), so that we never had a business meeting. Once Mr. Lloyd's wishes were made clear, my responsibility was recognised, and things went much more smoothly than might have been expected.

Some curious experiences followed, because my liability included the filling of any gaps that might occur. At intervals, Mr. Jerrold spent much time in France, and more than once the post failed to bring his batch of leaders on the morning of going to press. It was imperative to maintain the usual appearance of the paper, which meant hastily dashing off two or three columns of leader matter for the early edition. In this way I furnished contributions on a great variety of subjects. When Mr. George Glenny passed away, a fortnight elapsed before his successor was found in Mr. William Earley; the gardening articles printed meanwhile being mine. On a later occasion the sudden illness of Dr. Andrew Wilson let me in for the more daring compilation of a medical article. The only subject never ventured upon was a sermon. Reviews and theatrical notices were everyday duties. Possessing the entire confidence of Mr. Lloyd, I was entrusted with certain special commissions. Sir Edward Watkin's Bill for a railway under Hyde Park to Westminster aroused Mr. Lloyd's opposition from the fact that the arch of the proposed tunnel was shown in the plan to come within eighteen inches of the ground floor of his house in Delahay Street; no compensation whatever being payable.

"We can't stand that, can we?" said Mr. Lloyd to me.

On my agreeing, as a matter of course, the assault was begun. Day after day in the *Chronicle*, and week by week in *Lloyd's*, all manner of reasons were advanced for opposing the projected line. How far this influenced the decision I will not venture to surmise. It is satisfactory to know that the railway was never made, as blow-holes in the park must have been an unsightly nuisance.

WRITING FOR THE "MORNING POST."

Experience ranged somewhat beyond the office. Acting as deputy for Charles Dunphie, the accomplished dramatic critic of the *Morning Post*, I was writing a number of notices for that paper. Whenever he wished for a rest or a little holiday a note sent to my house fixed the engagement. The peculiar arrangement will show how different were the customs of the past from those of the present. I was left with a free hand in the writing, and my copy went straight up to the overseer of the composing room, technically known as "the printer," with the direction that it was to go in. If a theatre ran late I took the copy up myself, so that no hitch should occur through a single minute being lost. In this way I came to know Mr. Dickson, and learnt from him that Mr. Borthwick (afterwards Lord Glenesk) had made him responsible for the paper going to press at a fixed time. When the order was first made clear, the printer, with some surprise, asked what he should do supposing the late leader was not ready. "You will go to press at the proper time, leader or no leader," was the proprietor's immediate response; and this command was regularly obeyed.

On one occasion, when called upon to notice a play at the Court Theatre, the request was made that I would introduce a few complimentary references to the surrounding neighbourhood. The whispered reason for this wish to direct favourable attention to matters outside the playhouse was that Sir A. Borthwick was thinking of going up for Parliament; and it was believed that he had his eye on this particular constituency. The supposition proved to be correct; at the next election the proprietor of the *Morning Post* was returned for South Kensington by a majority of more than two thousand.

Any idea of accepting Mr. Lloyd's proposed new plan of carrying on *Lloyd's* was out of the question. If it had been tried the inevitable friction must have brought about an early breakdown. As it was I pointed out the difficulties, and put forth the counter proposition that (subject to Mr. Lloyd's approval) the selection of writers should be left in my hands, as well as the choice of topics with which they were to deal. After a friendly conference this was agreed to. Mr. T. H. S. Escott, then the scholarly and popular editor of the *Fortnightly*, undertook the political column; social articles coming from George Barnett Smith, Howard Evans, the Rev. Mr. Haweis, and other writers. I approached Mr. John Bright, and received a kindly and characteristic letter in reply.

A CITY TRAGEDY MADE HELPFUL.

Directly the death of Mr. Jerrold became known, Fleet Street was alive with rumours. Those who personally knew the late editor looked upon the post as a " soft job," and among the many applicants was the famous war correspondent, Mr. Archibald Forbes. From what happened later, I am inclined to think that Mr. Lloyd wished to keep me in check, because the word " editor " was never once mentioned by either of us. The foolish Yankee talk of " too old at forty " had not then been heard of; I had passed forty-five, but there was no lack of energy or determination to back up practical knowledge. While I worked on, Mr. Lloyd watched and waited. Before a month was out the matter settled itself through a City tragedy, which

132 Piccadilly
Mar 18. 84.

Dear Sir

My engagements are so many that I cannot undertake to write what you suggest. I am often asked to write for some of our Periodicals, & have always to refuse to do so.

From America such requests come to me — & they are declined. I find writing irksome, & I avoid it when I can possibly do so.

I hope you may find your new office pleasant, & that your success may be all you can wish for.

I am very truly yours,
John Bright.

Mr. Thos. Catling
12 Salisbury Square, Fleet St.

remains a mystery to this day. In a lawyer's office in Arthur Street a young clerk was found murdered on the Saturday afternoon. Not a word came out in the evening papers, and I only heard of the affair late at night. The police absolutely refused any information whatever, and would not even affirm or deny the story I put to them at headquarters. By persistent efforts for some three or four hours after midnight, I succeeded in getting enough particulars to fill over half a column in the morning's paper, this being one more exclusive feature. When Mr. Lloyd heard what had been done, all his doubts disappeared; meeting me as I entered the office a day or two after, he said, "I think I owe you something. How many weeks is it?" I replied that I really could not say off-hand. "Well," said he, "send me a note just giving the dates." This was done, and on the Friday my usual cheque was enlarged to a satisfactory sum covering the new arrangement. From the first the method of combining control with responsibility for the paper worked well; and it remains a source of deep satisfaction with me that I enjoyed the confidence of Mr. Edward Lloyd to the end of his days.

MR. GLADSTONE AND GENERAL GORDON.

"At the age of 65 and after 42 years of a laborious public life, I think myself entitled to retire. This course is dictated to me by my personal views as to the best methods of spending the closing years of my life." So wrote Mr. Gladstone at the beginning of 1875. Five years later the famous statesman entered on a new crusade with a vigour and intensity that astonished the country and commanded the support of the Midlothian electors. Morning, noon, or night Mr. Gladstone was ready to make a flying speech or to deliver an oration covering the entire home and foreign policy of the kingdom. Subsequently, I happened to meet an organist from Edinburgh, who told me that in the throes of that electoral fight Mr. Gladstone soothed and steadied himself with music. Having arranged a time for the organ practice, he was provided with a key, by means of which he could enter the church quite privately. Silently and alone he would sit in one of the pews with his forehead resting on his hands, while the organist played over a number of familiar and impressive hymn tunes. The listener neither looked up nor spoke until the hour compelled him to move; then, with a "thank you," he passed out, to throw himself again into the bustling political contest. In the following year Mr. Gladstone once more became Premier, and speedily had to deal with events fraught with momentous issues. Trouble with Ireland was followed by deeper concern with respect to events in Egypt, culminating in the sacrifice of Gordon. Future historians will, no doubt, deal adequately with the life of the heroic soldier; nothing can tarnish the majestic earnestness of his closing days and final hour in the Soudan. On the other hand the Cabinet of the day showed absolute indifference as to Gordon's fate. When the question was pressed home to Mr. Gladstone in the House of Commons one afternoon in April, 1884, he asserted that "There was no military or other danger threatening Khartoum."

It was not only the words but the scornful tone in which they were uttered that created such a painful impression in my mind. Again and again in *Lloyd's* I joined with other papers in forcing the question of Gordon's rescue to the front. Nothing was attempted until the time for action had passed, leaving the mournful words "too late" to be written as the record of the nation's sacrifice of one of its noblest sons. The verdict of the Press of that time has since been confirmed in the most emphatic manner by Lord Cromer, who says: "The Nile expedition was sanctioned too late, and the reason that it was sanctioned too late was that Mr. Gladstone would not accept simple evidence of a plain fact, which was patent to much less powerful intellects than his own." Mr. Gladstone's error of judgment in delaying too long the despatch of the Nile expedition left a stain on the reputation of England which it will be beyond the power of either the impartial historian or the partial apologist to efface.

THE FIRST HOME RULE BILL.

Home Rule for Ireland involved me in deep personal anxiety. *Lloyd's*, with the strongest Liberal principles, "broad-based upon the people's will," had always supported and upheld Gladstone. He was regarded not only as the greatest intellectual force of his time, but as a veritable high-priest of true radical principles. To suggest at a critical political period that the paper should turn round and boldly oppose Mr. Gladstone seemed a perilous proceeding; the more consideration was given to the proposals the greater seemed the obstacles. Patriotism and the sincerest wish for the good of both countries, however, prevailed. It was with immense satisfaction that in various conversations with Mr. Edward Lloyd I found the proprietor in sympathy with my objections. None the less was the fact recognised that if things went wrong and the paper suffered (within a couple of years of my editorship) I must expect to pay the penalty. Sir Henry Lucy, in the story of his brief editorship of the *Daily News*, throws an interesting light upon the period. He decided to let the paper follow Gladstone, but the readers would not have it. In a very short time the decline in circulation told its tale ; and proprietorial discontent led to the speedy retirement of the editor.

With a view to fulness of knowledge, I was in the Press Gallery of the House of Commons during every one of Mr. Gladstone's five speeches, and also seized the advantage of discussing the subject with various members in the lobby.

The introduction of the Bill, when Mr. Gladstone spoke for nearly three and a half hours, was an occasion of marvellous interest. Lord Morley, after describing the intense excitement which prevailed, says, "No such scene has ever been witnessed in the House of Commons." A week later came the Land Purchase Scheme, the objectionable features of which were so obvious as to meet with instant condemnation. For two months the agitation continued both in and out of the House, until, on the early morning of June 8th, the ill-advised Home Rule measure was rejected by 343 to 313 votes. All that matchless eloquence and passionate earnestness could achieve was evident on the Ministerial side, and almost to the last the aged Premier seemed to cherish hope of success. The defeat, therefore, by a majority of thirty came as a heavy blow. His biographer says, " As I passed into his private room with Mr. Gladstone that night, he seemed to bend for the first time under the crushing weight of the burden that he had taken up." A few minutes later I watched him in the first hour of the calm summer morning come down with Mrs. Gladstone into Palace Yard, where he stood waiting for his carriage. A cape had been thrown over his shoulders, and was pressed tightly across his chest, but his bearing was as calm as if he had been a listener rather than the leader in the tremendous political conflict of that memorable night.

APPEAL TO THE COUNTRY.

When Parliament had been dissolved for an appeal to the country, it was with no half-hearted resolve that *Lloyd's* championed the side of the majority of the Commons, including Mr. John Bright, Lord Hartington, Mr. Goschen, Mr. Chamberlain, and so many other leading Liberals. Week by week, while the Bills had been before the public, the facts and arguments were presented as clearly as possible for the instruction of the people. Among the eminent writers specially approached was Mr. Froude, with whom I had an appointment on Monday, May 2nd. That was the morning on which Mr. Gladstone's manifesto to his Midlothian constituents first appeared in the *Edinburgh Daily Review*. It was immediately telegraphed to London, and on my way to Brompton I secured a copy in the second edition of a morning paper. On entering Mr. Froude's library with the paper in my hand, I mentioned what it contained. "You are not in a hurry, I hope," he said, as I handed him the sheet; thereupon he sat down and read through the address of some 2,500 words. We then discussed the situation and the whole question. Mr. Froude was firm in the conviction that Home Rule as first proposed by Mr. Gladstone was really John Morley's scheme. Lord Morley, we know, disclaims this responsibility, but it is certain that in a speech at Chelmsford he had strongly advocated the exclusion of Irish members from the House of Commons. In a colloquial way this was the first great charm and attraction of the proposal—it would get rid of the troublesome Irish element, and thus afford means for pushing forward legislation much more rapidly. Mr. Froude's objections were based on the soundest historic reasons, as was set forth in a letter which appeared in *Lloyd's*. He wound up by saying: "Our fault has been too fond a belief in the regenerating virtues of our own particular Constitution. A firm and just administration, with a distinct assurance that separation would never under any circumstances be tolerated, would produce the same effect in Ireland as it has produced in every country which has been resolutely and wisely controlled. Is it prudent to venture an alternative which, if it fails, will leave us to choose between a separation that might ruin the British Empire, and a bloody and disgraceful reconquest?" In the general election which followed Mr. Gladstone was left in a hopeless minority.

A BRANCH OF RELIGIOUS WORK.

In respect to one phase of the great statesman's character Mr. Froude spoke with all seriousness and deep concern. Evidence, he declared, had been brought before him of such a nature in regard to Mr. Gladstone's private visits to certain notorious houses at the West End, that if he dealt with it on historic lines there was no possibility of avoiding its acceptance. Coming at the moment of the extraordinary change of front in regard to Ireland, it was mentioned only as a perplexing feature in the life of a notable man. No opinion beyond this was even remotely expressed. The story faded from my mind, and would never have been recalled but for my finding in Mr. Morley's "Life" the following passage referring to and explaining those visits:—"On his first entry upon the field of responsibility in life, Mr. Gladstone had formed a serious and solemn engagement with a friend—I suppose it was Hope Scott—that each would devote himself to active service in some branch of religious work. He could not, without treason to his gifts, go forth like Selwyn or Patterson to Melanesia to convert the savages. He sought a missionary field at home, and he found it among the unfortunate ministers to 'the great sin of great cities.' In these humane efforts at reclamation he persevered all through his life, fearless of the misconstruction, fearless of the levity or baseness of men's tongues, regardless almost of the possible mischief to the public policies that depended on him."

AT AN IRISH EVICTION.

My interest in Ireland having been thoroughly roused, I made a holiday excursion there in the autumn of 1887. The idea was to travel from Dublin to Cork, and so round by the royal route to Bantry, Glengariff, and Killarney. On reaching Cork, however, a whisper was heard of an eviction. No evening paper was published, but on visiting the office of one journal late at night I learned particulars. It meant my being up and off by a six o'clock train next morning for Knock Long Station. There I discovered that the scene of trouble in Limerick was nine miles away, but by great good fortune a single jaunting car was available. Signs of suppressed excitement and alarm were noticeable along the route: as I approached Herbertstown eager eyes peered at me out of many windows by the wayside. Finding the road dug up at intervals, with the view of obstructing vehicles, my boy driver said he dare not go any further. The last mile therefore had to be covered on foot. Endeavouring to look as unconcerned as possible, I quietly approached a group of men, stating that I was a tourist from London, and should be very glad if they could tell me where I might obtain breakfast. For the rest of the day my path was strewn with kindnesses, and I learned something as to the way in which facts on the spot differed from the news printed in Fleet Street. Great point was made by a London daily paper of an old lady being ruthlessly removed from her home by the police and carried along the roadside, with the result that she died from the shock. The truth was that the bailiffs and police not only begged the old lady to remain, but absolutely refused to lend a hand in her removal. Not to be debarred a dramatic sensation, the relatives carried her out by the roadside, and she was soon sheltered in another home, where she lived for many a day. This opening scene being over, a move was made towards a farm belonging to The O'Grady. For a time I marched with the populace, men and women of all ages shrieking and gesticulating violently. As the police passed along the road where a field sloped upward some four or five feet, showers of stones began to descend, making matters look awkward. Captain Plunkett, who was in command, became very angry, threatening a charge, so I resolved to quit the crowd and trust to the protection of the authorities. On taking the place pointed out by Captain Plunkett between soldiers and police, I found myself alongside an alderman of the City of London and his wife. The lady, who in subsequent conversation evinced a deep interest in Irish affairs, had courageously braved the discomforts of the time, with the view of acquiring a personal knowledge of the state of the people. A short march along the muddy road over a few stone barricades of insignificant dimensions brought us to the cottage of Mary Ann Hogan. The first movement was made by the military, who formed an extended circle round the building. With the police I entered the circle, when the windows of the house were seen to be closed up with hawthorn and other prickly bushes. A dog was lying on the step of the front door. As the official paper calling on Mary Ann Hogan to answer the claim was read, the animal threatened to bite the policeman who approached it. The constables, therefore, drove off the dog with a few stones. The door being fastened, an order was given to break in. As the men moved to their duty, spectators were warned " Don't go too near, they sometimes throw a long way." The meaning of this was soon apparent; boiling water poured down from an upper window. The "crowbar brigade" consisted of four men working in couples. They attacked one side of the house, The O'Grady, who appeared profoundly dejected, and Captain Plunkett looking on. One or two policemen stood quietly smoking in the rear, and there was little sign of excitement until the crowbars had nearly broken through the loose stone wall, some two feet thick, though cries were heard from the crowd in the distance. As the opening was effected the men anxiously drew back for an instant, but finding no sign of hostility made a speedy entrance. All being reported peaceful, an order was given to open the door and guard the place until the names of those within had been taken. This accomplished, the bailiff's men were called upon to turn out, not the tenant, but the tenant's belongings. While the humble home was being dismantled, and every stick placed in the yard, I had a talk with the landlord, The O'Grady, whose family had been in possession for three or four hundred years. The widow, it was known, could readily pay the rent, but as the farm stood in the place where the Plan of Campaign was originated, the command had gone forth she was not to do so. When things had quieted down, Dublin reporters insisted on my seeing the widow.

At first she regarded me with suspicion: on being assured that I was only a journalist and had no association with the Government or the police, she talked freely enough. The eviction was very much a show of authority rather than a punishment, because the tenant was left free to re-enter the premises on arranging terms any time within six months. At a meeting immediately following the eviction, Father Ryan, Mr. William O'Brien, and other speakers declaimed loudly against English domination. The more closely I went into the question of Home Rule, the more certain it appeared that it was ardently desired as a means to an end, that being separation.

QUEEN VICTORIA'S JUBILEE.

Impressive as were the national festivities associated with Queen Victoria's jubilee, they were overshadowed in interest by the family character of the rejoicings. At the close of the stately thanksgiving service in Westminster Abbey, it was a touching sight to look down upon the aged Sovereign as she bent to kiss the array of children and grandchildren gathered round her. The assembled throng of notabilities, in a blaze of scarlet uniforms with glittering decorations, formed a glowing setting for this sweet human picture of gentle motherhood. One manly figure, conspicuous among them all, was the German husband of the Princess Royal. Before entering the Abbey I halted at the entrance to watch and note the arrival of the brilliant cavalcade. Prince Frederick was in the white uniform of a Cuirassier of the Guard, with the

Imperial crest on his helmet. He sat with the firm easy seat of a cavalry soldier, holding the baton of a German Field-Marshal: an ideal prince among princes. Though my notes described him as looking "pale and grey," there was then no thought of impending doom. Stricken down by a fell disease, he rallied to be hailed as Emperor and patiently passed away in less than a twelvemonth from his imposing appearance at Westminster.

THE STRUGGLE FOR TRAFALGAR SQUARE.

"We tingle with shame when we think of Englishmen being bludgeoned by the police." These words of Douglas Jerrold, written in 1855, came to mind when I saw a deliberate and ruthless attack made upon a procession moving in an orderly manner along the Strand on a Sunday afternoon in November, 1887. The wickedness of the affair was only equalled by its folly, as the result quickly showed. On the previous evening Sir Charles Warren, Chief Commissioner of Police, suddenly sent out a decree that "no organised procession shall be allowed to approach Trafalgar Square." As it was known that political processions were being arranged, I went personally to Scotland Yard on the Saturday night to ask for further details, with the view of warning the people in Sunday's paper. My question as to where the procession would be stopped seemed utterly to bewilder the inspector on duty; he could only surmise that the matter would be settled according to circumstances by the officials in charge of the police. Next day I made my way towards Trafalgar

Square and there met David Anderson, who said, "If you want to see the fighting don't stop here, but go to the Strand down by Wellington Street." On proceeding there it was evident that a military trap had been laid for the processionists. They were allowed to march quietly up to the level of Waterloo Bridge. Then, at the order to charge, the line of police dashed on the unarmed crowd and rained down blows with their batons on every one within their reach. Behind a second line of police I watched the sickening sight.

The after proceedings afforded some strange contrasts. Among those arrested at the Square were Mr. Bennet Burleigh, Mr. Cunninghame Graham, M.P., and Mr. John Burns. It was asserted that my friend Burleigh threatened to knock down the first policeman who touched him, but the presiding magistrate at Bow Street disposed of the charge by making an abject apology to the correspondent. Burns and Graham were sent for trial, Mr. Haldane being bail for the latter.

At the trial Mr. Asquith, Q.C., M.P., defended the Scotch member; Burns, described as "socialist," represented himself. Among the witnesses called was Mr. Lorraine, engineer, Gray's Inn Road, who gave Burns an excellent character in regard to his capacity as an engineer and his industry and steadiness as a workman.

"And when the jury acquit us," asked Burns, "you will allow me to resume work, won't you?"

Mr. Lorraine: "Certainly."

The jury found defendants guilty of taking part in an unlawful assembly, and they were sentenced to six weeks' imprisonment without hard labour.

Writing long years afterwards in reference to the Czar's "Bloody Sunday," Mr. Stead likened the proceedings to those around Trafalgar Square. At home, he said, "Two men were killed, hundreds were injured, and hundreds more were dragged off to prison. Nothing but the forbearance of our workmen saved London from a massacre as bloody as that which took place in St. Petersburg. Our excellent police when their blood was up bludgeoned right and left with the utmost brutality, even using their batons on the prisoners in their cells."

All this reckless violence was professedly in defence of law and order. Before a year had passed the Chief Commissioner of Police, having upset those in authority over him, the magistrates, his own officers, and the main body of his men, resigned amid the rejoicings of the public. The Government gave way, and Trafalgar Square became a recognised place for public meetings.

WHERE THE ARMSTRONG CASE LED ME.

"You're the man who sent me to gaol," was the exclamation with which Mr. W. T. Stead greeted me when we met at a journalistic dinner in 1906. He thus recalled the result of a State prosecution of twenty-one years previously, concerning my share in which full confession may now be made. A poor mother's appeal to a London magistrate for aid in seeking her lost child quite naturally found a place in *Lloyd's*; and as the mystery deepened special correspondents were set to work with the view of unravelling it. In the same week that the disappearance of Eliza Armstrong was reported,

Mr. Stead began publishing in the *Pall Mall Gazette* an account of his secret commission. The main event was the alleged purchase from her own mother of a girl of thirteen, called Lily. Every incident of wrongdoing was traced with apparent fidelity; and then the writer said, "That was but one case among many; it only differs from the rest because I have been able to verify the facts." *Lloyd's* search for little Eliza was commenced without the slightest idea that it had anything to do with Mr. Stead. Gradually, however, the sweep's daughter was traced; the facts of the domestic drama of humble life showing that the purchase of "Lily" was as unreal as it had been made painfully sensational. When the Salvation Army were found to be mixed up in the affair, Mr. Bramwell Booth endeavoured to silence *Lloyd's* through the intervention of a friend; at the same time he admitted having " Eliza in safe keeping." One Saturday he called at the office and waited over half an hour to see me, this making it plain that the case was deemed important. Then he wrote saying, "I cannot help regretting that you have allowed the matter to assume the direction it has taken in your columns." Having a doubt as to what he wished to convey to the public, I sent a special messenger to Mr. Booth's house the same evening. While he was kept waiting for the answer several Salvationists gathered round him, and plumping down on their knees held a prayer meeting for "the young man from *Lloyd's*." Mr. Booth's second letter took a startling turn, for he wrote, "To show my *bona fides* in the matter I am quite prepared to hand the child to you on Monday or Tuesday if you will take the responsibility."

A REPORTER'S ADVENTURE.

Lloyd's story of the mother's search for her lost child attracted the notice of Parliament, the Home Secretary announcing that he had felt it his duty to lay the printed evidence before the Attorney-General. For the following Sunday's issue Mr. Hales, the reporter, crowned his labours by tracing a French woman who figured in the case. Some of the incidents are dramatic enough to be recalled. The reporter says:—

"I discovered that a manservant and several women servants were kept in the house, and that no carriage or cab was allowed to drive up to or take up at the door. Having determined to take Mrs. Armstrong there, it was arranged that the father should be near at hand in case of need. The door was opened to the mother, and I immediately followed. An English servant said I could not see Madame without an introduction, but on my saying I would introduce myself, she ran down some stairs, and we followed into what appeared to be a consulting room. The servant ran out of another door through the yard into what looked like a glass house, which seemed to have a bed in the centre with curtains round. The servant was heard exclaiming, 'There's a man in the house, there's a man in the house, and he is down in the room.' A Frenchman appeared in a state of great excitement, and was followed by a second female. While they were talking and gesticulating violently, a large Newfoundland dog was panting, barking and tugging at his chain just outside the consulting room window, which was wide open. I told the Frenchman I only wanted quietly to ask Madame a few questions, and when they had been answered we should both go away. The parties went out, and eventually Madame came. After many questions and denials, Madame admitted that she had examined the little girl. On further questions being asked, more excitement ensued, and one of the servants raised the cry of 'police.' Mrs. Armstrong, fearing that I was going to be attacked, or that the dog might get loose, rushed out of the room up the stairs and along the passage, calling to her husband, 'Charlie, Charlie.' Opening the door she let in her husband. Being a tall, powerful man and a sweep in his working clothes, his demon-like appearance had an electrical effect. The female servants ran back, the Frenchman seemed paralysed, and the old lady threw up her hands, while her eyes remained fixed on the black figure before her. Mr. Armstrong was the first to break silence by coolly saying, 'Well, you are a fine colour, all of you. Why, you are all as white as turnips.' As no harm had been done we all quickly and quietly left the house."

RESULT OF A STATE PROSECUTION.

The day after the publication of the reporter's discovery there came a letter from the Treasury, written by Sir A. K. Stephenson, and marked "Confidential." He asked for any information possessed by the paper, and on my taking Mr. Hales to the Treasury, we learned that the police and detective force had failed to trace either the name or address of the French woman. When the facts were made known a State prosecution was at once entered upon, the case exciting intense interest both at the police court and the Old Bailey.

In the course of the inquiries I had met Mr. Stead in Mr. Bramwell Booth's office. During one of the intervals at Bow Street (where I had a seat on the bench) he asked me if it was not a mistake for me to be there, as witnesses were ordered out of court. "I'm not a witness," was the reply, "I've said all I have to say in print." With dry humour Mr. Stead added, "So have I, but they won't be satisfied with that."

Mr. Bramwell Booth, Mr. Stead, Mr. Jacques (a *Pall Mall* reporter), Madame Mourey, and Rebecca Jarrett were brought to trial. Only the first named escaped conviction. Jarrett and Mourey were sentenced to six months' imprisonment, Stead to three months, and Jacques to one month.

Mr. Poland, counsel for the Crown, warmly complimented me on the part *Lloyd's* had taken in the recovery of the girl, and a subscription on her behalf brought in a goodly sum. Eliza was well looked after till her marriage. A few years ago I heard with regret from Mr. Stead that she was left a widow with five children very insufficiently provided for.

THE "RIPPER" ATROCITIES.

Of the blacker mysteries of London, none quite equal the Ripper atrocities of 1888. Very early in the morning of Sunday, September 30, an hour after I had turned into bed, a messenger drove up in a cab with news of the murder of two women. The first had been found dead about one o'clock in a back yard in Berners Street, Commercial Road; the second at twenty-five minutes to two by the entrance to Mitre Square. A subsequent comparison of times showed that the man who conveyed the first news to the office must have been on the spot within five minutes of the discovery, and then walked very rapidly to Salisbury Square. As the result, I was back in the office within an hour, and, hastily gathering up the particulars which were already in the paper, made for Bishopsgate Police Station. There the constable on duty whispered that if I would wait a minute I should see someone who could speak with authority as to what had happened. Directly after, the chief superintendent of the City force, Major Henry Smith, appeared. In response to my inquiry, he said he feared both murders must be put down as the act of the unknown "Ripper." Proceeding next to Mitre Square, I learned from kindly-disposed policemen a number of details of both crimes. The bodies had been taken to the City mortuary, and I followed them as quickly as possible. There it was my good fortune to find a friend whom I had known in school circles, Mr. Gordon Brown, one of the medical officers of the police. He gave me facts—more than could be published—as to the condition of the bodies. Thus, when I returned to the office I was able to spin out a column and a half of accurate particulars very quickly. As fast as the copy was written it was composed and put into the paper. All through Sunday special editions were printed as rapidly as the machines could turn them out. These were sent to the newsagents in all directions, to be substituted for papers printed before the murders were known.

Prior to this date newsagents did not enjoy the privilege of taking papers "on sale or return"; if an agent took twenty copies and failed to sell more than eighteen he had to bear the loss of the two. From the date of the Mitre Square tragedy a more liberal system came into use.

HOW THE CLUES WERE MISSED.

If ever the police blundered they did so in a most melancholy way over these two crimes. While the City constables were guarding and watching every place within a wide range, Metropolitan officers appeared on the scene. At the inquest it came out that the Mitre Square murderer cut off a piece of the victim's rough apron in order to wipe his weapon upon it. This piece of apron was picked up an hour or two later in a passage leading to the staircase of a common lodging-house in Goulston Street. When daylight came some writing in chalk appeared on the wall of the lodging-house. The house was neither searched nor its inmates examined. Sir Charles Warren drove down in the early morning and personally ordered the writing to be "washed off."

ORIGIN OF THE SAFETY PARACHUTE.

Thirty years have passed away since "a professor" came from America to show that he had discovered what may be called the safety parachute. I met the bold balloonist at the Alexandra Palace on a July afternoon in 1888, and had a pleasant chat with him. When he commenced his experiments, he told me that he followed the old plan of trying a parachute shaped like an umbrella with a closed top. This never answered, so one day he cut a small hole in the centre, leaving space for air to rush through. Experiments quickly proved that herein was the secret of safety. In America he made just half a score safe descents from a lofty elevation;

then started for London expressly to make a little money. Baldwin from his manner evidently regarded each ascent as risking his life. Prior to the ascent he drew his wife into a little private dressing room, and from the earnestness of the people I feel sure that they took a prayerful farewell of each other. The parachute first used was made of the finest silk attached to cords; being of considerable size, it weighed forty pounds. In order to alight as near as possible to the Palace, Baldwin released himself when little more than a thousand feet high, and came down in forty-eight seconds in a field adjoining the racecourse. The crowd was far more demonstrative than pleasant; when the hero of the occasion had pushed through to the Palace, he discovered that a valuable presentation watch and chain had disappeared.

PROJECTS OF LORD WINCHILSEA

In October, 1888, I formed one of a party which sat down to luncheon in the decaying Great Hall of Kirby, where Queen Elizabeth was entertained by Sir Christopher Hatton. The occasion was inspired by an effort to reintroduce the use of Weldon stone. It had an interest for Fleet Street, because the stones of which St. Dunstan's Church is built came from Kirby. The Earl of Winchilsea, at whose invitation the party was gathered together, said if Kirby Hall was ever to have a roof on it again, it would be derived from the funds of the Weldon stone. Though Colonel North (then reputed to be a millionaire) was of the party, nothing came of it beyond the enjoyment of a pleasant outing. Years afterwards Lord Winchilsea paid me a return visit in Crown Court, when he was interested in a project for bringing farm produce from the country direct to the London consumer. The assistance I was able to promise had to be guarded, because one phase of the project was not free from the suspicion of a protectionist tendency. Incidentally, the Earl said he had been putting forward a proposal of a sliding scale for the Income Tax. When he mentioned this to any friends and gave the various amounts that were to be made liable for increased payments, every listener, he said, paused in order to make a mental calculation as to how far he would be affected before approving or disapproving the scheme.

HOW SMALL TRADERS WERE SAVED.

Is it not an error to suppose that the manifold burdens of everyday life may be removed by the restrictions of Acts of Parliament? In the spring of 1888 a Bill was brought forward to enforce the closing of all shops at eight o'clock on five days and ten o'clock on the sixth day of the week. It left public-houses free, and made the sale and purchase of a loaf of bread a criminal act. Letters condemning the proposals came to me in shoals, and Lord Charles Beresford took the chair at a meeting of small traders and costermongers who crowded Exeter Hall. The main points in the letters sent me were used up by the chairman, and his arguments were enforced by five other members of Parliament, Mr. Maple, Mr. G. Howell, Mr. L. H. Isaacs, Mr. R. Cooke, and Mr. Pickersgill.

Freedom of discussion being welcomed, an amendment in favour of the Bill was moved; it only obtained the support of 100 out of the 4,000 present. Lady Charles Beresford accompanied her husband, and two other ladies were on the platform. As they proceeded to leave by the small stairway at the back, an ugly rush was caused by three or four men. Mr. Blundell Maple, squaring his shoulders, thrust them aside, making way for the ladies to pass. As he looked round with a smile of satisfaction, it was somewhat damped by Mr. Isaacs exclaiming, "I've lost my watch," holding up the end of his chain to prove the fact. In the following week the House of Commons rejected the Bill by 278 to 95 votes.

AMERICANS WELCOMED IN LONDON.

A party of Americans brought to London in the summer of 1889 by the Scripp League proved very interesting. It was known as a working men's expedition; but the half hundred (all of the artisan class) included four women. We dined together at the Tavistock Hotel, Covent Garden, and wound up a long sitting by visiting the printing office of the *Daily Chronicle*. Mr. H. M. Ogden was in the chair, and Mr. R. Lincoln joined in the welcome to his country folk. Mr. L. M. Barry, an Irish American, referring to the small number of women amongst so many men, said the American woman had learned to trust the American man; adding, perhaps what was more to the point, that she was also very well able to take care of herself. In my separate conversations with all the women and a number of the men I found them out-and-out free-traders. They not only recognised the advantages which English people enjoyed, but said American working people would be very glad to share in them. Another interesting personality was Mr. Biggar, M.P. The Press represented him as an ill-tempered ogre in the House of Commons; he shone in social life by reason of his buoyant humour and good spirits. Chatting away with the utmost freedom, he threw new light on all the subjects touched upon. His gallantry recalled the story of a few years previously when he was sued by an Irish lady for breach of promise. It was sworn that he went down on his knees, lifted the lady's foot and kissed it, saying, "Now you see how much I love you when I stoop and do this." On his attentions attracting notice, he seemed to grow more cautious, as he advised the lady to consult her confessor as to the propriety of being kissed before marriage. The confessor thought there was no harm in it, and as the lady plainly told Biggar she liked being kissed, he took advantage of the invitation. There was an obstacle to the marriage in the form of two children by another lady. This ultimately led to a rupture and an action for breach of promise. A verdict for £400 was given in the lady's favour, and the Irish M.P. had to submit to unlimited chaff in the House of Commons.

WHY I AM A LIBERAL.

In the university town from which I came those "in authority over us" were accustomed to demand awe and respect, in addition to obedience, from simple folk. "Dons" were monuments of learning; the rich were ruling authorities; and employers resembled the centurion of old who directed the coming and going of men. A spirit of revolt arose in me out of one incident. It found expression when I was asked to contribute to a work entitled "Why I am a Liberal." Therein I wrote:—

"While the good government of a State can only be secured by the rule of the wisest, history fails to show that any one class possesses a monopoly of wisdom. Hence, instead of fostering the privileges of the few, Liberalism seeks to utilise all the forces of the sovereign people, with a view to the diffusion of happiness among the many. As a result of this action, the English men and women of to-day enjoy more personal freedom than the inhabitants of any other country. In the provincial newspaper office, where I learned my first political lessons, a printer who had dared to vote for a Liberal was fiercely challenged by his Tory employer. When the man ventured to say that he had voted according to his conscience, he was met with the rejoinder, 'D—n your conscience!' and summarily dismissed. The incident is significant, because it represents a principle—the despotic claim of one class to override the feelings and opinions of others. Against such straitened views it is the province of Liberalism to wage constant battle. Free Trade, a free Press, the free expression of opinion, and all our social and religious liberties, have been won by beating down the narrow Conservatism which so long barred the way. Wider avenues are now opening, and it is because of my earnest belief that legislation may do much to brighten the lot of the humblest workers that I desire the triumph of the Liberal cause which means progress, the growth of freedom, and the advancement of the general good."

This contribution called forth a few words of special comment in a *Times* leader devoted to the book.

REPORTING UNDER DIFFICULTIES.

However much the Press may be lauded as an institution, its representatives have often had to work under peculiar disadvantages. Years back a Cambridge paper was anxious to secure a list of the visitors at a reception given to the Prince of Wales. The reporter found himself the only newspaper man present, but all his appeals for information were met with a direct refusal. Not to be baffled, he made terms with a local policeman off duty, and secured the loan of his clothes. When evening arrived, the disguised pressman duly appeared at the entrance to the mansion and busied himself in opening the doors of carriages. This expedient worked well till one of the Court officials recognised his face. "Very smart, no doubt, but not gentlemanly," was the tart comment with which the unfortunate reporter was dismissed. Still, he had secured a goodly number of representative names to figure in his report.

In later times difficulties occurred with the City of London. When Lord Mayor's day fell on a Saturday, important speeches had to be secured by hook or by crook for the Sunday paper. On occasions I have acted as my own messenger, sometimes gaining admission to Guildhall and at others having to wait outside. One year an arrangement was made with the representative of a daily paper to send out notes to me at the entrance. The Lord Mayor's footman brought the first batch of copy, but firmly declined to go back for a second, even if the tip was doubled, saying, " I dare not, sir, and if you had heard the language that was used to me as I pushed by them, you wouldn't ask me." It being absolutely necessary to obtain the copy somehow, the matter was pressed further. At last the footman said, "I will take you into the hall if you like." The offer was instantly accepted, and I found myself launched by a side door into the crowded hall, very near to the Wellington monument. Folks looked at me with my top hat and overcoat, but before the committee could decide whether I was a detective or a burglar, the popular councillor, Sir John Bennett, roused himself from a half slumber and, putting out his hand, said, " How are you, and what are you doing here?" The way was thus smoothed; I signalled to the reporter, secured my copy, noted the surroundings, and sped back to the office as fast as a hansom could carry me.

The Royal Academy's official dinner on the Saturday night preceding the opening of the Exhibition was long a difficulty, as no reporters were admitted save those of the *Times*. A friendly Royal Academician (now passed away) once promised to bring me a programme with some notes of the speeches. We met by appointment. Alas! the artist had forgotten the programme; all he could give me was the assurance that it was a rattling good dinner, and there were some capital speeches. He had apparently enjoyed himself so fully that no single sentence of any speech was remembered, nor even the subjects touched upon. Having failed in this direction, another method had to be tried, and it worked so well that it was followed for many years. By adroit arrangement a reporter obtained admission in the guise of a waiter so soon as the speeches began. With a napkin over his arm concealing a notebook, he managed to hover around, now at one table and then at another. In this way he secured sufficient notes without attracting observation, and then quietly left to write out his copy. All this was for the public good, and though presents had, of course, to be made, I hope they will not be regarded in the light of corruption.

BARNUM AS A TEETOTALER.

Barnum's first visit to Olympia in November, 1889, happened to be made at a time when I was there. Having walked round the building and listened to his chaff with Kiralfy at cutting off his profits by taking so much room for the stage, we sat down together at luncheon. When a decanter of sherry reached me I hesitated for a moment, knowing that the great showman was reputed to be a total abstainer, and then said, "I suppose it is of no use offering you this?" "Oh! yes," was the reply, "you may give me a little. I'm a teetotaler, but not a bigoted one." It is only fair to add that, though he sipped his glass in courteous recognition of the toasts, his drinking did not amount to more than a spoonful.

FIFTH STAGE.

THE OLD ORDER CHANGED.

Mr. Gladstone becomes a Contributor—Stanley Declines a Blank Cheque—A Quarrelsome Author—First Run of Short Stories—" Lucky in Murders "—Winning a Libel Case—Compositors and Overtime—Lord Northcliffe's Beginning—Sala and his Salad—Lord Rowton describes his Houses—Cardinal Manning's Lying-in-State—The Prince and the Republican—*Lloyd's* Jubilee Number—Right Royal Time in America—Wilson Barrett's Experiences—Meeting with President Cleveland—Whisky for Medicinal Use—Among the Mormons—Return through Canada—The Falls of Niagara—Henry Pettitt and His Work—A Bishop and His Income—Death of Mr. Jonas Levy — Oscar Wilde's Ruined Life — Queen Victoria Favours the Editor—I am Ordered to the Mediterranean—Labours of Sir Augustus Harris—Increasing the Million Circulation—Blondin's Triumphs and Losses—Pennies for the Royal Hospital Fund—Result of Getting into Print—A Thames Tragedy Leads to Comedy—Are Delusions an Excuse for Murder?—Concerning Authors.

THE OLD ORDER CHANGED.

AFTER continuing *Lloyd's* for forty-seven years as a twelve-page paper, entirely devoted to news, the founder recognised that the time had arrived for further developments. Before any enlargement could be carried out entirely new machinery was needed. The prolonged delay in securing the requisite plant greatly worried Mr. Edward Lloyd, and a serious illness was the result. Notwithstanding this he continued to push forward arrangements for improving his paper. A novel by the late Grant Allen was purchased. Its title, "The Scallywag," fascinated him, and he had letters five or six feet deep specially cut for a huge poster, intending the one word "Scallywag" to blaze over the country. On my representing to Mr. Lloyd that if the enlargement was to be marked only, or mainly, by the introduction of a serial story by an author not of the front rank it might create a wrong impression, he promised to think over the matter. A little later he said, "Well, you shall have your way, and we will put this tale aside for by-and-by."

It then became my immediate duty to make another proposal, and an article by Mr. Gladstone was mentioned. During my thirty-six years in the office I had garnered up many ideas, and this was the first to be acted upon. The ex-Premier had passed his eightieth birthday, and his weighty contributions to the *Nineteenth Century* gave little encouragement to the hope of his being induced to write for a penny Sunday paper. However, the matter was left in my hands, and a personal application was decided on. It was not without some trepidation that I called at 10, St. James's Square, on the morning after the marriage of his third son to a daughter of Mr. Rendel. A brief note stated my object, and offered explanations. Mr. Gladstone met me with marked courtesy and politeness, but said he must decline any proposal for writing. He had been repeatedly asked to do so for American papers, and always refused. The answer was so decided that it left no room for appeal, and my mission looked like a failure. Disappointment, however, only quickened the resolution to watch and wait for another opportunity. It was no part of my training under Mr. Edward Lloyd to accept any first "No" as final.

MR. GLADSTONE BECOMES A CONTRIBUTOR.

Very shortly after Mr. Gladstone's personal refusal an American paper appeared with a long postcard from him which seemed to afford an opening for renewing the attempt. As the letter then sent sets forth my editorial aims at the time it may be given:—

"*March* 21, 1890.—Sir,—Your address to the members of the Mutual Building Association of New York, in which you pointed out the advantages of thrift and self-help in man-making, induces me again to appeal to you to write a paper or letter for the two million readers of this journal. *Lloyd's* has secured its weekly sale of six hundred thousand copies by constant efforts to give the latest news; but a change in the direction now opens up an opportunity for extended usefulness. It is a family newspaper that goes into tens of thousands of British homes, and is very largely read throughout the whole of Great Britain. May not good be done by putting before this vast body of working people a loftier ideal of life? If writers of weight and authority will aid me by providing a series of papers dealing with the moral and material, the physical and the intellectual progress of the masses, I venture to hope that the lessons thus scattered abroad will exercise a beneficial influence. What I would beg from you is a paper—about 2,500 words in length—on any subject relating to social advancement of the people that you may please to select. As *Lloyd's* has been increasingly prosperous for more than forty years, I need scarcely assure you this is not an effort to push a struggling journal. The proprietors, however, have no right to trespass on you; and, therefore, permit me to say that if you furnish such a paper, a cheque for a hundred pounds shall be at once sent you. Pray regard my appeal as one for generous assistance in commencing what I trust to make an instructive and useful feature, and aid me if you can. I am, your obedient servant, THOS. CATLING."

By return came a postcard:—

"SIR,—I have this morning received your letter and will carefully consider, as soon as I am able, the suggestion you are good enough to make. Your faithful and obt., W. E. GLADSTONE."

This was promptly acknowledged, and the matter rested until April 3rd, when another postcard arrived:—

"DEAR SIR,—I write to inform you that I have completed a paper which I hope corresponds with your description, and that I am prepared to send it if you are ready to receive it. Your faithful and obt., W. E. GLADSTONE."

This reached me by the last post at night, and with a letter of thanks my own cheque for the hundred pounds was at once despatched to Mr. Gladstone, who replied next morning:—

"10, St. James's Square. *April* 4, 1890.—DEAR SIR,—Many thanks for the cheque so promptly sent. Herewith document, the MS., which I hope may be found suitable for the purpose. You kindly promise a proof, and this will find me here on Tuesday morning. My address till then will be St. George's Hill, Weybridge. I remain, dear sir, your faithful and obedient, W. E. GLADSTONE."

The copy, occupying ten folios of foolscap, all in Mr. Gladstone's handwriting, almost went astray, as the writer throughout his correspondence addressed me as "Mr. Dabling." There was no heading to the article, so it was christened "The Rights and Responsibilities of Labour." This was adopted when Mr. Gladstone saw the proof. A notable feature of Mr. Gladstone's paper was expressed in the following passage:—

"The spectacle presented by this country at the present time is a remarkable one. The ultimate power resides in the hands of those who constitute our democracy. And yet, our institutions are not democratic. Their basis is popular; but upon that basis is built a hierarchy of classes and of establishments savouring in part of feudal times and principles; and this, not in despite of the democratic majority, but on the whole with their assent. I do not know whether history, or whether the present face of the world presents a similar case of the old resting on the new, of non-popular institutions sustained by popular free will."

Mr. Gladstone's article, after careful revision by the author, duly appeared on May 4th, the day fixed for a great working-class demonstration in Hyde Park; and attracted considerable attention. In addition to its own importance as an exclusive feature, it had the advantage of attracting other writers.

STANLEY DECLINES A BLANK CHEQUE.

A few weeks before the enlargement Mr. Edward Lloyd passed away, leaving the paper in the hands of four of his sons. Mr. Frank Lloyd (the managing director) expressed a great wish to secure an article by Mr. H. M. Stanley, who was then returning from his prolonged expedition in Africa. Time pressed, and the occasion was one in which only the

MR. GLADSTONE'S CONTRIBUTION.

[To face p. 198.

THE OLD ORDER CHANGED. 199

boldest bid offered the slightest hope of success. Accordingly I sent an invitation to Mr. Stanley, offering him a blank cheque if he would write the paper required. My letter reached him during his visit to the King of the Belgians, and brought forth —not the wished-for article—but this reply:—

"Palais de Bruxelles. *23rd April*, 1890.—DEAR SIR,—I have to acknowledge, with many thanks, the receipt of your letter of the 21st inst. With regard to the matter of your communication I am much obliged to you for your kind offer, but extremely regret that I am so deeply involved in engagements, that it would be quite impossible for me, however much I might desire to do so, to accede to your request. Again thanking you for your kind note and very liberal offer, I am, dear sir, yours very truly, HENRY M. STANLEY."

Another contribution of this year to which I look back with the keenest satisfaction came from Mr. Henniker Heaton, M.P. This doughty champion of an extended penny post unfolded his proposals with striking force and power, basing his arguments on facts and figures, while appealing to the people for the support which has enabled him to bring about so many important and beneficial reforms in the postal service of the country and the Empire.

A QUARRELSOME AUTHOR.

With the consideration of fiction a difficulty cropped up. Mr. William Black had been given a commission to write a serial, saying that he fully appreciated the necessity of making his work suitable for a very wide and popular circle of readers. My mind was not free from doubts, and sitting beside him one evening at a public dinner, I endeavoured to draw him into discussing the plot.

The attempt failed, and he stuck to his assertion that a story depended upon the manner in which it was told. When, after a while, he sent in two-thirds of the copy the worst fears were realised. Typewriting had not then come into general use, and it was a task to read through Mr. Black's small crabbed manuscript. The contract provided for the payment of a thousand pounds for the first serial publication of the story, which was to be commenced before the end of the year. To my dismay I found that the work was not only unsuitable, but utterly impossible for the purpose in view. In giving my opinion to Mr. Frank Lloyd I asked him if he would look at the copy. After reading it through, he remarked: "We had better throw the story into the waste-paper basket than attempt to print it in *Lloyd's*." Then the trouble began. Editors are sometimes censured for hasty and inconsiderate dealings with writers. My constant desire was to avoid trouble, and a fairly wide experience demands recognition of the kindly courtesy that was ever shown me. Poor Black was the only author who became quarrelsome. On my intimating, as gently as possible, that the story was not suitable for *Lloyd's* he bounced into a passion. An attempt to soothe him by paying over two-thirds of the purchase money before the tale was completed only made him more obstinate and disagreeable. Authors are now reasonable folk, though swelled heads are not quite unknown; when a novelist is attacked he suffers badly. Black in his temper wrote nonsense; bidding me "remember that the story was written for *Lloyd's Newspaper*, and for *Lloyd's Newspaper* alone"; asserting that he had put his "best work" into it; and talked of enforcing publication. Having determined not to print it, I made many efforts to dispose of the unfortunate purchase, and would have sold the rights for half the money, or less. No one wanted this story by Black, and it looked as if the serial publication would be allowed to lapse. As a last resource one of the proprietors suggested printing it in the *Daily Chronicle*, which also belonged to them. To give it every possible chance the story was announced as the chief feature of a literary supplement, forming a new departure in morning journalism. " Donald Ross of Heimra " was duly commenced on the first of January, 1891, and met with the fate it deserved. The literary supplement, however, proved an attraction that has flourished to the present time.

FIRST RUN OF SHORT STORIES.

While perplexities over a serial were causing a troublesome waste of time, the question of fiction for the weekly paper was solved in a bright and pleasant style by a run of short stories. My old friend B. L. Farjeon led the way, and among those who followed him were Walter Besant, G. Manville Fenn, Clark Russell, Stanley Weyman, James Payn, " Q.," Henry Herman, Mrs. Lynn Linton, Mrs. Oliphant, and Ouida. It was Rudyard Kipling's first year in London, and though he was being talked about his writings moved slowly. Proof of this is afforded by the fact that I had the pick of a batch of stories from his pen at five guineas each, and selected several. One was held over for the Christmas number, and appeared in conjunction with tales by Bret Harte and the Queen of Roumania. A little later Kipling's story, "The Light that Failed," was offered for a hundred pounds, and I agreed to accept it. The Americans who held the copyright, however, failed to agree as to date of publication, and ultimately the British serial rights were abandoned.

"LUCKY IN MURDERS."

Mr. John Delane, the famous editor of the *Times*, while taking a somewhat prolonged holiday, wrote to his representative in the office, "How lucky you are in murders." This disposes of the superstition that the first newspaper in the kingdom held its position entirely by reason of the handling of home and foreign politics. A murder mystery has always been of great service to every newspaper. Reports were formerly given at enormous length, and with much wider freedom than is now permitted. Towards the end of October, 1900, a typical case occurred in London, the early particulars coming to *Lloyd's* in rather a curious manner. Directly after the body of a murdered woman had been found lying in Crossfield Road, Hampstead, a young artist appeared on the scene. With the view of turning his knowledge to practical account, he made his way to the office of the *Daily Graphic*. Failing to get his offer of news accepted there, he resolved to try in another direction, and reached Salisbury Square about midnight. My eldest son, who was in charge, secured enough details to print in the Saturday morning edition, at the same time arranging with the artist that he should bring down a sketch of the scene next day. This gave us a start that, followed up, helped to increase largely the demand for the paper. When Mrs. Pearcy was arrested I well remember my reflection: "If Miss Braddon can make an imaginary murderess the object of such thrilling interest, ought not something more to be possible with a female assassin in real life." The case, from the first discovery of the slaughtered mother and babe to the execution of the unhappy woman two days before Christmas, extended over eight weeks, and once more proved the truth of Delane's judgment as to a newspaper being "lucky in murders."

WINNING A LIBEL CASE.

Early in 1891 my journalistic experiences were enlarged by having to undergo a severe cross-examination at the hands of Mr. Jelf, Q.C. (late one of His Majesty's Judges). The action was one for libel brought against me personally in the Queen's Bench. When the offending paragraph appeared Mr. Edward Lloyd was the proprietor of the paper, but he died before the case came into court and the proceedings were at an end. A fresh action started against Edward Lloyd Limited failed, because no company can be made responsible for anything done previous to its formation. With a determination worthy of a better cause, the solicitor then made a third start against the editor. The long delay, extending over fifteen months, was vexatious in the extreme; and the proprietors were willing to get rid of the trouble by the payment of a certain sum which it was known would be accepted as damages. My back was up, however, and the editorial wish for the case to be fought out prevailed. It turned on questions coming under the Act for the Prevention of Cruelty to Animals, and ended in the jury giving an immediate verdict in my favour. Besides enjoying the discomfiture of the solicitor for the prosecution, I had the satisfaction of finding the paper congratulated on thus enforcing the duty of kindness to animals.

COMPOSITORS AND OVERTIME.

My practical knowledge of the composing room quite naturally led to an invitation to take part in a conference between employers and workers on a demand for an increase of wages. There were seven representatives on either side, and every detail was carefully considered, the result being a settlement that, with comparatively slight variations, has continued to this time. Mr. William Clowes, always thoughtful and patient, made a model chairman. When one of the delegates of the men contemptuously offered to forgo the right to a fortnight's notice, thus following the unhappy example of the builders, it was Mr. Clowes who brought about a wiser and more kindly conclusion. Overtime was a rather thorny point, and here I am bound to censure the workers. In their unions and trade meetings they cry out for the suppression of overtime, but in practice the best men are eager for opportunities to secure some extra payment. I am unable to see anything wrong in a man doing the best he can for himself.

THE OLD ORDER CHANGED. 205

While the subject was being warmly discussed, Mr. Clowes raised a laugh by saying that if it was pressed home to him he would have to confess that his firm was "reared on overtime." A parallel was instantly suggested in the great publishers, W. and R. Chambers, of whom it was said that they personally kept their booksellers' shop open during the day and did their printing at night; when they found time for sleep being a mystery.

LORD NORTHCLIFFE'S BEGINNING.

Fifty years ago, when Samuel Smiles' "Self Help" was a text-book for those who wished to get on in the world, the examples held up for imitation were those who had won success by their "strong individuality" and "indomitable spirit of industry." These remain enduring qualities with Englishmen. A newspaper cutting of 1892 furnishes a vivid illustration of what may be accomplished by untiring energy. It reads thus:—

"Rather less than four years ago it occurred to a young journalist and Bar student, Mr. Alfred C. Harmsworth, that while the public appetite for reading was greatly on the increase, the taste for litigation was distinctly on the wane. Taking considerable interest in the spread of pure literature, he proposed to several well-known publishers the starting of a penny periodical which, along with the ordinary attractions, should have the co-operation of the most distinguished novelists of the day. Mr. Harmsworth was told that such a journal could never pay expenses. Eventually, however, he managed to make a bold plunge on his own account, and in June, 1888, launched the first number of *Answers*. Within four years Mr. Harmsworth's establishment was the largest in the world for the production of periodical literature, and there was a branch office in Australia."

The above story of Lord Northcliffe's beginning is given in his own words. No sharper uphill fight was ever waged by a young man of twenty-three; and who can for a moment doubt that his victory was won, like those of earlier date, by "strong individuality," "indomitable courage," and unflagging industry.

SALA AND HIS SALAD.

Early in this same year I sat beside George Augustus Sala at the dinner of Correctors of the Press. He was an excellent chairman, and laid himself out to do justice to a body of worthy men whose labours are by no means adequately recognised. During the evening he talked over many experiences, though (if truth is told) G.A.S. was never sympathetic with his brother journalists. *Sala's Journal*—a poor little weekly periodical at which people laughed—was then coming out; and belief in his name inspired the hope that it would one day be a flourishing property. His own words to me were that it would be a provision for his widow when, according to the French proverb, "he was eating his salad by the roots." The dream was soon over, for the paper died of inanition years before Sala passed away.

LORD ROWTON DESCRIBES HIS HOUSES.

For every newspaper man of his time the career of Lord Beaconsfield had all the fascination of romance. His statesmanship abounded with surprises, which only came to an end with his death, in the spring of 1891. With the spirit of Carlyle's hero-worship strong in me, I sought to secure a souvenir at the sale of his effects. The writing cabinets fetched prices far beyond me, and I had to be content with a modest purchase of a very personal character. Three months afterwards I was asked one afternoon to step down into Mr. Lloyd's room, and there found Lord Rowton, the famous private secretary of the great Conservative leader. The mission of the caller was to talk over the project of improving the "doss-houses" of London. Having had some experience and devoted much time to the study of the housing question, I was able to enter into Lord Rowton's views pretty thoroughly. The result of our talk was the appearance in *Lloyd's* the following week of a column and a half explanatory of the scheme. Three weeks before, altogether unknown to the public or the Press, his lordship, accompanied by a little niece, had laid the memorial stone of the Vauxhall building. The cost was estimated at £20,000, and Lord Rowton's own money being devoted to it, he was deeply interested as to the financial probabilities. He spoke of himself as a "poor man," that is "a poor man for the House of Lords." Just a year afterwards Rowton House had been erected, and it was possible to say of the building "what has been done is a wonderful step in advance of anything that has ever been attempted in any country of the world. It is, if it may be said, the outcome after many years of the Young England principles with which Lord

Beaconsfield's name will ever be identified. The sensationalism of that school has at length justified itself in a tangible and useful form, and it now only remains to await with the deepest interest the results."

Fitting and furnishing occupied the rest of the year, so that it was not until the last day of 1892 that the first Rowton House was available for use. At a previous private view I found Lord Carrington and Lord Suffield being conducted over the house by Lord Rowton, thus obtaining the advantage of hearing their questions and comments. It was never my custom to join in the abuse of the private owner. Even jerry-builders had their uses, for they reared roofs over the heads of struggling workers at the cheapest possible rents. In the common doss-houses many a stranded wayfarer is trusted for a night's lodging, and I pressed Lord Rowton very hard as to what would be the custom in his new home. He evaded the question for a time, but at length said, "The charge will be sixpence a night, and I am afraid, Mr. Catling, if there is no sixpence there will not be any bed."

CARDINAL MANNING'S LYING-IN-STATE.

However touching as a mark of respect and veneration may be the Protestant custom of confining "lying-in-state" to moving solemnly around a closed coffin, it in no way appeals to the imagination as does the Roman Catholic exhibition of the embalmed figure. One specially remembered instance was that of Cardinal Manning, whom I had last seen in life actively engaged with

Lord Mayor Whitehead in settling the great dock strike, while I waited at the other end of the Lord Mayor's parlour at the Mansion House to know the result. For the Cardinal's lying-in-state in January, 1893, the principal room of the Archbishop's house at Westminster was hung with black cloth thickly dotted with silver stars. All daylight was excluded, the only illumination being afforded by candles. On a raised bier, covered by a scarlet mattress, with velvet and gold adornments, lay the body, the sunken cheeks of the ascetic face appearing darker than when living by reason of the white mitre placed on the head. A purple cassock set off the skirt of rich lace, the hands were gloved, and on one finger shone the Cardinal's ring. Words fail to describe the deep emotion awakened by the solemn and impressive scene, as streams of people of all classes moved slowly and reverently through the chamber.

THE PRINCE AND THE REPUBLICAN.

When the *Daily Chronicle* led the way by printing papers with an "inset" (that is, an extra page pasted in mechanically) a large gathering assembled one summer night in 1892 to witness the new process. In the midst of the proceedings, when a lull with the machines permitted another sound to be heard, the company were amused with the notification of the arrival of "Walker, London." Mr. Barrie's bright little comedy had been produced in the previous February, and in marched—not the author—but Mr. J. L. Toole, bubbling over, as was his wont, with geniality and merriment.

Another notable visitor was the Premier of New South Wales, Mr. George Dibbs, fresh from Australia. I had met this sturdy Colonial previously at the Savage Club, and in the course of a friendly chat he expressed the greatest admiration for the Prince of Wales. Dibbs, like Mr. Chamberlain, had first become noted at home for Republican views. At a large gathering at Warwick, Mr. Dibbs was presented to the Prince, by whom he was welcomed with much cordiality. Later in the day, just when Mr. Dibbs was feeling a little lonesome, the Prince approached him again and said, in the quiet affable manner which charmed so many public men, "I think I saw, Mr. Dibbs, that you liked a big cigar; will you take one of mine?" at the same time presenting his case. It was not, of course, the smoke, but the thoughtful courtesy and kindness of the Prince that captivated the stranger from afar. The world heard no more of the Premier's republicanism, and a very short time afterwards Mr. Dibbs accepted the honour of a knighthood.

"LLOYD'S" JUBILEE NUMBER.

Friends from many quarters combined to give the Jubilee Number of *Lloyd's* a character which may even now be called historic. One prominent feature was the introduction of a sermon. For this purpose I approached Dr. Benson (then Archbishop of Canterbury). After a little delay a telegram announced that his Grace would be at Lambeth Palace on a certain day. On calling, a young chaplain gave me a cordial reception; then led the way to the Archbishop. In the most kindly manner Dr. Benson listened, and during the discussion no single objection was raised to a Sunday paper. That obstacle was in my mind, because some time previously Mr. C. H. Spurgeon had made it an insuperable bar when I asked him to write a single article. In the end Dr. Benson promised to open the series by writing a special sermon, bidding me personally seek others, as "I should be sure to get on better with the Bishops than he would." The progress in that direction was most satisfactory, as was shown in the following paragraph in the *Athenæum*:—

"The Archbishop of Canterbury was recently approached by the editor of *Lloyd's News* with the view to the introduction of a short sermon in that journal. His Grace received the suggestion with favour, and, after an interview and correspondence with the editor, it has been decided to commence the series in the paper issued for the last week in November. The idea is a sermon of 500 words, the first of which will be written by the Archbishop of Canterbury; the Bishops of Bath and Wells, Ely, Ripon, Southwell, Wakefield, Sodor and Man, Lichfield, Peterborough, Rochester, Worcester, Bedford, Dover, Beverley, Southwark, Derby, and Barrow-in-Furness have already sent or promised sermons, and many more occupants of the episcopal bench warmly commend the editor's proposal."

With this feature from the Church assured I turned to the Stage, Henry Irving having some time previously promised that he would let me have something for the Jubilee Number. He kept his word by sending a delightful sketch abounding with kindly feeling, called "Black Spirits and White." Lord Brassey wrote a special paper on "Imperial Federation," then a comparatively new subject; Charles Williams dealt with the wars of the half century; Dr. Andrew Wilson with medical progress; Howard Evans with general politics. The whole band of "Idlers"— Jerome K. Jerome, Robert Barr, W. L. Alden, Eden Phillpotts, I. Zangwill, G. B. Burgin, and Barry Pain—made a joint contribution concerning "Looking Back"; George R. Sims and Henry Herman charmed the readers of fiction; John Northcott dealt with music; W. E. Church with art; and my son Arthur sent a characteristic sketch of an Opium Den in Australia. A page of journalistic history, with its many changes and contrasts, fell to my share.

RIGHT ROYAL TIME IN AMERICA.

Early in 1893—when the beneficial results achieved by the Jubilee Number were known—the proprietors handed me a cheque, accompanied by the offer of six months' holiday, thinking I might like to visit Australia. After my stay-at-home life, the idea of going away for half a year seemed too much to consider all at once; I therefore asked to be allowed to divide the time. In boyhood, Fenimore Cooper's romances inflamed me with the desire to see America. Here seemed an opportunity to realise my long-cherished dream. It was a good time from a journalistic point of view, as the Chicago Exhibition was in preparation, and excursions were being talked of. Starting from Liverpool in April, by the good ship *Arizona*, I had the happiness to enjoy "a pleasure trip across the Atlantic." Captain Brooks had made the passage 673 times, and was naturally full of experiences. He brought Irving and Ellen Terry back from their first season in the States, and took out Mrs. Langtry when she was starting to make her appeal to the Americans. Brooks was called by some the " smoke-room Captain," because he was fond of a little relaxation when the skies were clear and his vessel was in the open sea. He played a capital game both at whist and cribbage; we had many a contest together, even when the *Arizona* was rolling so that each card had to be held down as it was played. At night, on the least sign of fog, and whenever land came in sight, Brooks was another man—every inch a captain. Arriving in New York, there commenced for me what can only be called " a right royal time." Printing was studied in the great works of Hoe and Co., and the leading newspaper offices; the Lotus Club afforded hospitality; the theatres amusement.

WILSON BARRETT'S EXPERIENCES.

Crossing over to New Jersey, Wilson Barrett was found playing Hamlet, Miss Jeffries being Ophelia. The house, packed from floor to ceiling, very much resembled Sadler's Wells in Phelps's palmy days. On the Sunday morning I heard Dr. Talmage address the fashionable congregation assembled in his Temple, and then lunched with Barrett in Brooklyn.

Between the terrapin, clams, and other transatlantic delicacies, we exchanged confidences. The more one heard of Barrett's life story, the greater was the admiration for the unwonted pluck, endurance and energy of the man. Beginning with nothing, by dint of earnest labour he made a position as an actor. Turning then to management he achieved further success, only to find his savings swept away through misplaced confidence. The sum of £10,000 had been specially put aside as provision for his wife and daughters. Suddenly, when his wife was lying so dangerously ill that the least shock would have imperilled her life, Barrett learned that the investment in which he had trusted was a delusion and a sham. The lawyer to whom the money was confided was false to his trust. The blow came at a time when he had to bear its full weight in silence and struggle on. An unfortunate venture at the New Olympic ended disastrously—so badly, that on one occasion he was only saved from arrest for the taxes by the advances of a friend. Undaunted, Barrett laboured on, playing at his best in the higher melodrama, and then turning to authorship. Knowing the quarrel between Herman and Jones as to their collaboration in *The Silver King* (out of which both made a small fortune), the question was pressed on Barrett as to who first suggested the central idea of the innocent man thinking he had committed a murder. Barrett said he felt sure that this was Herman. As to the play he made light of their quarrels, saying that when they first brought it to him it was impossible for the stage. Only after he had personally made a large number of alterations and suggested many others, was it re-arranged in the form which rendered it so successful. The lunch with Barrett fell on St. George's Day, and the evening found me back in

New York attending Trinity Church, where the English residents make a point of assembling on this anniversary. With Royal Standards and Union Jacks adorning the church and a service designed to arouse patriotic feeling, it was a thrilling scene for any Britisher, though one could not agree with the Rev. Walpole Warren's fierce denunciation of Mr. Gladstone.

MEETING WITH PRESIDENT CLEVELAND.

After a day at Philadelphia came Washington; the feature there being an interview with the President. This was arranged by a private secretary staying in the hotel to which I went. Half-past eleven was the time fixed, and punctually to the minute my guide took me to the White House. On being told at the entrance that the President was in, he said, "Come along," and we walked up two blocks of stairs into a waiting-room. Then it was intimated that the President was receiving deputations, but without delay we passed on to the inner room. At the moment Mr. Cleveland was standing listening to a gentleman who talked very seriously: this afforded an opportunity for looking around. The apartment was square, with five doors. On either side of the one by which we entered stood deputations, half a score people, awaiting audiences. An engraved portrait of Washington hung near a couple of bookcases, while a fairly large table was piled up with letters, papers and books. Beside a handsome bouquet a single newspaper was noticeable. After the lapse of four or five minutes the President's visitor turned to leave, and my guide (cutting off both deputations) instantly advanced, saying that he had come by appointment to present an English editor on his way to Chicago. Mr. Cleveland smilingly shook hands, and his face lighted up as he mentioned that he had received quite a large party of Pressmen from England a few days before. The opening of the Exhibition was referred to as a great function, the President's manner becoming more animated as he expressed gratification at finding that foreign nations were taking so much interest in it. Various points were mentioned, Mr. Cleveland stating that he expected to reach Chicago some time on the Saturday previous to the opening. His manner throughout was not only courteous but affable; instantly affairs of State were put aside, and without a sign of being bored, he chatted in a bright and easy manner. Then, with wishes for a pleasant journey and a hearty hand-shake, the interview closed. Before leaving the White House my conductor led the way through the three private drawing-rooms, the State dining-room, and conservatories. Incidentally, as showing the stress of the Presidential labours, it was mentioned that during the two months that he had been in office, Mr. Cleveland had only enjoyed five or six hours' sleep daily. The practice of clearing up everything before he went to bed kept him engaged till three o'clock, and he was down again at eight or nine.

From the White House I passed on to the Treasury, where the monetary affairs of the nation are conducted. Of the 2,200 employees 1,000 were women, they being regarded as particularly adept in counting and checking the notes sent up by the banks. One woman, who had been engaged in this work for ten years, had only on a single occasion allowed a forged note to pass. Among the criminal stories was one considered especially smart. A lady having purchased a handsome shawl in a large store tendered a thousand dollar bill in payment. The firm, being a little suspicious, sent the note to a bank to be tested, and kept the lady waiting. On discovering the cause of delay she became most indignant, and refused to be pacified when the messenger returned with word that everything was correct. For a time the sale seemed lost, but later in the day, after the banks were closed, the lady reappeared, saying she could not shake off her fancy for the shawl. Apologies were duly tendered: she went off with her purchase and change for a thousand dollar note. On paying it into the bank next morning, the firm learned that a clever counterfeit had been substituted for the genuine note originally presented. The lady was never heard of again.

WHISKY FOR MEDICINAL USE.

At Chicago nothing could exceed the courtesy and attention paid to the English correspondents. The Exhibition was far from ready, but even in an unfinished state it afforded ample evidence of the magnificence that was revealed later.

One little incident showed the working of the Prohibition laws. In a new hotel near the Exhibition it was prominently announced that no intoxicating drink could be served even at meals.

Getting round the vast area of the Exhibition in the terribly muddy weather which prevailed was heavy work, and a little whisky appeared desirable. After being refused by one coloured waiter, another came up and said, "What is it you want?" "Well," we said, "if we cannot get a glass of wine or beer or something we shall have to shift our quarters." "Oh," he said, "if it is whisky you want, and will give me the order, it shall be on your table at dinner." The order was given, and at night there was a full-sized bottle with a chemist's label marked "For medicinal use, Ramsay's Superior Scotch Malt Whisky."

An invitation from Mr. Walter Harris to lunch at Victoria House drew me there immediately after the opening ceremony. At the entrance stood a City policeman (Atkins, 550), who testified his delight at seeing a visitor from Fleet Street by showing him every possible attention. Lord Aberdeen presided, and when the meal was finished, told me that the President had promised, if time permitted, to pay a visit to the Irish village. His lordship intended to follow the procession round the Exhibition, with a view to reminding Mr. Cleveland of his promise at the right moment. By request I carried a message with respect to this arrangement to Lady Aberdeen. The village, with its twenty-two Irish girls and four boys, was a bright and cheery place. A real blackthorn had been brought over for the President; a lace handkerchief and brooch for Mrs. Cleveland. During the time of waiting her ladyship was smiling and gracious, but had to submit to disappointment. The Earl ultimately came to

THE OLD ORDER CHANGED. 219

say that the President had not time for the visit.

At Denver people were greatly excited over two things—Mr. Bryan's candidature for the presidency and the silver question. Of course no encouragement could be given to the heresy of bi-metallism. At the smelting works, the largest in the world, the men worked in twelve-hour shifts. One of the proprietors, who hailed from Cornwall, was asked how he justified such long hours? He said the question had been raised and fully gone into; the proprietors offering to divide the day into three shifts of eight hours each, the wages being similarly apportioned. After due deliberation the men came back and said they would go on with the twelve hours. The wives, it was added, had really decided the question, saying they could not do with the reduced payment.

While staying at Denver a railway war was raging, rates being "cut" and "cut" down till it became possible to travel for any part of a distance of 400 miles through magnificent mountain scenery for a quarter—that is the equivalent of a shilling. Crowded trains were the natural result; ladies young and old turning out in large numbers to enjoy a cheap ride. This afforded plenty of company nearly all the way to Utah, the train running up and over its highest point, marked as 11,525 feet above sea level.

AMONG THE MORMONS.

A letter of introduction from New York secured me much attention and hospitality in Salt Lake

City. Everything was shown except the new Temple, which had shortly before been completed and closed to all but Mormons. I attended a Sunday service in the large Tabernacle where 5,000 persons received the Communion. An opening hymn was followed by a brief prayer, and then more singing. A blessing having been asked on the bread, some twenty young men bore it in baskets to all parts of the building. While this was in progress a preacher rose, announcing that he had been called upon without any notice to address them. This is the usual custom, there being no regular preachers at the Tabernacle, though Bishops conduct the services held each Sunday in the ecclesiastical wards of the city. The speaker—Mr. Penrose, editor of the *Salt Lake Herald*—enlarged on the need of light and truth in the world, invested Joseph Smith with the character of a prophet, and claimed inspiration for his followers. After a quarter of an hour he paused for a blessing to be asked on the water, which was then carried round in large tankards and distributed in two-handled mugs. Rising, Mr. Penrose spoke for another three-quarters of an hour. It was a bold address, without being more convincing than the arguments in favour of polygamy advanced to me by one of the Elders.

Proceeding westward, the delightful situation of San Francisco called forth unqualified admiration, and the place appeared outwardly far more English than the cities of the East. A brief steamboat trip to Vancouver's Island lives in memory by reason of the thrill experienced on landing under a flying Union Jack. The celebration of Queen Victoria's birthday brought out the Indians in full force and in their most picturesque array.

RETURN THROUGH CANADA.

Having resolved to return through Canada, I turned back by steamer to Vancouver. A letter of introduction from Sir Charles Tupper secured an immediate interview with Mr. W. C. Van Horne, president of the Canadian Pacific Railway (ofttimes called the "King of Canada"). He had arrived most opportunely, after a tour of inspection of the great line. Our conversation, prolonged till a late hour, ranged over the president's experiences with labour of all kinds, including Chinamen (of whom he spoke with great respect); and I had the benefit of his views on the condition of immigration, the opportunities offered to new settlers and the general prospects of the colony. Carlyle's gospel of work was never preached more earnestly than by Mr. Van Horne, himself one of the most earnest of workers. A note printed at the time is equally applicable to-day—"What Canada needs is men who will work with their hands on the land. Mixed farming promises the best results by diminishing the risks from frost, hailstorms, and other adverse influences that attend wheat growing; but to secure anything like speedy progress some capital is needed."

My journey included a trip of two hundred miles due north on a newly-formed branch line from Calgary to Edmonton. This north-west territory, then just being opened, gave every promise of the marvellous development which has since been witnessed. The few settlers it was noted "seemed resolute, confident and hopeful." They have since bridged the Saskatchewan river, and are bringing immense tracts of fertile land into profitable cultivation.

Amid the strangest collection of town names ever brought together in a railway guide, fancy lingers over one with peculiar fondness. Moose Jaw is a contraction of an Indian name, signifying literally, "the-creek-where-the-white-man-mended-the-cart-with-a-moose-jaw-bone." In the mountain town of Donald, having less than four hundred inhabitants, there were an Episcopal Church and three chapels, Roman Catholic, Presbyterian, and Unitarian. Calgary, at the foot of the Rockies, was a bright little town, marked out for expansion; Banff, with its natural hot springs, a delightful health resort; Winnipeg, a centre of vast possibilities. As time was passing rapidly it became necessary to push on by rail for nearly 1,300 miles. Despite the accommodation afforded by Pullman cars and sleepers, it was a wearing and wearying journey. Three days and two nights on the train made a restful period at the Clifton House specially welcome.

THE FALLS OF NIAGARA.

In my diary is this entry:—

"It is not in the power of language to exaggerate the transcendent splendour of the sublime Falls. I have admired one monarch after another among the snowy mountains; the lakes impress one as inland seas; and a sense of lonely grandeur makes the deserts speak eloquently to dwellers in crowded cities. But Niagara stands alone—supreme in might

THE OLD ORDER CHANGED. 223

and majesty, beautiful beyond compare, a glory of glories, marvellous in its overwhelming power—thrilling the spectator with thoughts that lie too deep for utterance."

The date of my visit was June 10th, and on proceeding to the engine-house just above the Horse Shoe Fall, I found it was the first day on which the electric power for the railway had been derived from a dynamo driven by water taken from the Falls. The arrangements for this appeared remarkably simple. Some hundred yards above the edge of the cascade a dam composed of double rows of timber, filled in with earth, was carried out about twenty feet into the main flow of water. This formed a channel nearly thirty feet wide at the mouth, narrowing to under twenty, and running for a hundred and fifty feet to the power house. Here, on account of the water falling fifty feet, a turbine wheel less than six feet in width was more than sufficient to drive the cars and provide electric light for the twenty miles of railway down to the Whirlpool. The waste water flowed into a tunnel which found its outlet under the Horse Shoe Fall.

A descent into the Cave of the Winds involved a spice of adventure, but it was not to be missed. Each visitor, male or female, has to lay aside every vestige of ordinary clothing and put on a flannel suit with oilskins over. A winding stair leads down to the rocks beside the Centre Fall, the smallest of the group coming between Luna and Goat Islands. There you enter on a long platform of wood, which, with many turns and windings, leads from rock to rock, sloping sometimes up and sometimes down, but giving an idea of safety through being well railed on either side. This is needful, as the mist sweeps in fierce gusts around, making it difficult—most difficult—to open one's eyes. At the suggestion of the guide I peeped through my bent hands at rainbows that formed a triple arch, and in one spot a complete circle. Next my back was turned to the spray, which came rattling down overhead with force enough to make my steps uncertain. Then in the midst of a strange murmuring, with the finest of vapoury mists driving around, and the sound of mighty waters ringing in my ears, my guide whispered, "Look up; you are now in the Cave of the Winds." The thrill was soon intensified when I had to step from the railed platform down to an open rock, with nothing to clutch at, where it was impossible to see, while the water from the fall came with a sharp recoil above my waist. It was a moment never to be forgotten. Though my guide assured me there was no necessary danger, a number of lives have been lost here. In the certificate which is made out for every visitor, the dimensions of the cave are thus given: 100 feet high, 150 feet wide, and 90 feet deep.

HENRY PETTITT AND HIS WORK.

On a cold night towards the end of 1893, I met Henry Pettitt at Drury Lane, and we chatted for some time at the little front bar of the theatre. *A Life of Pleasure* had enjoyed a successful run at "the Lane"; another of his plays, *A Woman's Revenge*, was drawing full houses at the Adelphi. Friends congratulated him warmly, while aspiring dramatists regarded his career with just a touch of envy. At times Pettitt was prone to express dissatisfaction with himself, and on this evening was more than usually gloomy. He told me his ambition soared far beyond the melodrama of the Adelphi; he yearned to write a play which could in some degree at least be measured with one of Sardou's. Thinking the depression was due to passing illness, I urged him to go home and rest; we parted never to meet again. For a week or so he was treated for brain fever, and curiously enough it was his lawyer who first suggested that the ailment was typhoid. Whether the mistake hastened the end no one can say; it came with terrible suddenness, as he passed away on Christmas Eve. Among the sharp struggles of early days the story of how he became a schoolmaster was told by Pettitt with deep earnestness. Things were desperate; it was a case of finding something to do or starving. A friend engaged in a large school told him a junior master was wanted, suggesting that he should apply for the post. "But I know nothing of teaching," said Pettitt. "Never mind that," urged the friend, "at least you look like a teacher." Very nervously, the tall, pale youth went to the school, and while waiting in the ante-room looked over a large map hanging on the wall. His eyes were fascinated by the letters Terra del Fuego; "The land of fire," he murmured to himself. On the head master appearing, Pettitt (still very nervous) talked of his shortcomings, and when asked to mention a subject in which he was specially weak, said "Geography." "Well, now," said the master, "if I were to ask you where is Terra del Fuego, what would you say"? "Oh," said Pettitt, "I should say it was there," instantly putting his finger on the exact spot on the map. "Well," said the master, " a young man who can do that is scarcely fair to himself in saying he knows nothing of geography." Other matters being settled, Pettitt was engaged, and thus bridged over the most anxious period of his life. School hours afforded time for writing. The popularity of one of his songs brought Pettitt into association with Paul Meritt. It was under the skilful guidance of George Conquest that these aspirants commenced their career as dramatists at the Grecian. They could not have found a better field nor a more helpful manager, albeit he adhered to the old system of small fees. Conquest backed up his own knowledge with a library of French plays. When any difficulty arose as to finishing a piece he would say, "What's the matter? Can't decide on a third act? Well, how does it run?" On being told, he would reach down a volume and point out the very scene the author required.

Another little story Pettitt told with much glee was in relation to a club gathering in New York, when he was twitted for referring proudly to an English street. The American, seeking to belittle everything in England, ended by saying sneeringly, "it had no streets more than a few yards long." When Pettitt had to speak again he asked if anyone had ever heard of Watling Street, which, starting in Dover, ran through Kent to London and thence on and on to Wales?

A BISHOP AND HIS INCOME.

In the autumn of 1893, the then Bishop of Wakefield sent me an account of the manner in which his income was spent. It was not printed at the time, at my request, but may be read with interest now:—

"At the last general election certain friends of mine, who went about canvassing (I won't say for which side), heard a good many strong things said about the income of the bishops. They were paid out of the taxes of the people, which was disgraceful; they ought to be divided up among the poor, which would at any rate do some good; they helped the bishops to live in luxury and idleness. Now, of course, it is only the ignorant who fancy bishops or clergy are paid out of rates or taxes. Not one penny of rates or taxes goes to any bishop or any parish clergyman. They are paid partly out of gifts in the shape of tithes, or land given in very ancient times, and partly by more modern and purely voluntary gifts. Now I am a bishop (which I suppose is not much in my favour) and I have done a sum in division by which I find that, if my income was divided up among the people of my diocese, it would give them exactly one penny per head per annum. As to luxury and idleness, there may be differences of opinion, but I am not fond of either myself, and I think a bishop who uses his income for idle self-indulgence is a disgrace to his order and a scandal to the Church. I am thankful to say I do not myself know such a one. I can't help thinking, however, it may correct some false notions if I try to give some idea of how a bishop's income is really spent. Well, my income as bishop is £3,000 a year. Now, the first thing I did when I was appointed to the bishopric was to dedicate one thousand a year to be given away in actual money, and then to make a resolve that no one connected with me should be any the better off by my having this income. I have children, but they will get nothing through my being a bishop when I die; I could not do this if it had not been that my father, who worked hard all his life at his calling, left me pretty well off. I should not blame a bishop who out of his episcopal income made some modest provision (by insuring his life for instance), for his family, only I had no need to do so. But what of the rest of the income?

Well, a bishop has to be always travelling about his diocese, going almost daily to this parish or that, and that costs a good deal. A bishop has to be receiving in his house all his candidates for ordination for four or five days at a time four times a year, and that is not done for nothing. It is true a bishop must keep a carriage if he is to do all the work looked for in these days; but he very seldom uses it for pleasure. It is true he must have a larger house and more servants than many, but he does not do this because he likes it (I should be much more comfortable in a smaller house and with two or three maids), but because he must be always ready to receive his clergy and to make his house useful for others. I can honestly say that far the greater part of my income, after putting aside the thousand a year for giving away in cash, is spent, not on self, but in the exercise of my office. I think bishops should try to live simple, unostentatious lives. They mostly do in these days. But I am quite sure of one thing, and that is that no other incomes in the land are spent so much for others, and so little for self, as those of the bishops."

DEATH OF MR. JONAS LEVY.

The oldest friend of *Lloyd's* and its founder—Mr. Jonas Levy—passed away in the summer of 1894. He was a link with the past in the fact that the fortune inherited by him was derived from farming the tolls around London. When the tollgates were disestablished the elder Levy was farseeing enough to put his money into shares of the London and Brighton Railway; these passed to his son Jonas, who was for many years vice-chairman of the company. A great lover of the drama, Mr. Levy was brought into connection with various literary clubs, the Reunion, Savage, Whitefriars, Urban, and others. For over fifty years he wrote the "Answers to Correspondents" for the paper, his training as a barrister qualifying him to deal plainly with legal matters. The best advice, of course, was to keep out of law as far as possible.

OSCAR WILDE'S RUINED LIFE.

Looking in at the Old Bailey on a Saturday afternoon of May, 1895, I just managed to squeeze my way on to the Bench as Mr. Justice Wills concluded his summing up at the second trial of Oscar Wilde. The calm judicial address left the question of guilt or innocence entirely to the jury. Gathering his robes around him the Judge stepped out, the prisoner was removed, the twelve men filed from the box, and the famous court, usually held under such strict control, seemed to throw off all restraint. The din of many voices rang in the air, and discussions of the most animated character were carried on in every nook and corner. It was at first thought, even by those who had heard the defendant go through his third course of perjured denial in the witness-box, that conviction was certain. As an hour went by without any sign from the jury, opinion grew divided. Some anticipated another disagreement, while a few cherished the idea of an acquittal. Minute by minute, watching the hands of the clock, the throng of spectators grew more and more excited. Art and literature have invested "waiting for the verdict" with many dramatic surroundings; they fall far short of the unspeakable pathos of the reality. If it thus thrills alike the anxious friends and unconcerned onlookers, what must the ordeal be for the one whose fate hangs on the result? The passing of a second hour deepened the impression of disagreement, only to be swiftly dispelled when the jury reappeared with the decision of guilty on all counts. A last despairing effort by Sir Edward Clarke to delay sentence was of no avail. The prisoner received the maximum punishment of two years' imprisonment with hard labour. As Wilde heard the sentence, he raised his right arm and gazed forward with a look of horror such as I have never seen on the face of any other man. It recalled one of those lurid studies of a lost soul pictured by the Belgian artist in what we know as the Wiertz Gallery. Although his mouth opened and his tongue moved, no sound reached the court. Yet another effort he made, while the anguish deepened on his torture-stricken face as he was gently turned towards the stairs and handed down from the dock.

During the period that Wilde was at Newgate I happened to visit Holloway, and was shown by the governor into the cell which Wilde had occupied while under remand. It was one usually devoted to prisoners in the first class, being double the ordinary size. Ink stains were plentiful on a small writing-table and on the wall behind it; a more uncommon and notable thing was that the cell reeked with perfume. After conviction (I learned from a medical friend) Wilde was very restless. On being locked in his cell for the night in the ordinary way, he paced up and down like a wild creature and at length rang his bell. When the warder appeared he asked for the doctor, but was told he had gone to bed, and he had better do the same. This pause only seemed to increase his agitation. After a while he rang again, declared himself to be very ill, and said the doctor must be sent for. Accordingly he came, when Wilde met him with the demand, " I can't bear this; you must give me something to make me sleep." Quietly, yet firmly, the doctor replied, " But you've got to bear it, and I shall not think of giving you anything. The sooner you recognise this the better will it be for you." Without another word the hopeless wretch bowed to the inevitable. Whatever his agony, he bore his suffering without complaint, and remained to the end of his sentence entitled to good conduct marks. A few years later the life of brilliant promise closed in poverty in a foreign land.

QUEEN VICTORIA FAVOURS THE EDITOR.

Queen Victoria's personal letter on the death of Prince Henry of Battenberg, in which the heart-sorrow of the Sovereign was revealed to her people, appeared on the morning after *Lloyd's* had won its prolonged fight for the million circulation. This fact—unprecedented in the history of a British newspaper—was deemed sufficient to warrant approaching her Majesty with a request for permission to print a facsimile of the Royal letter. At the outset I made a mistake in endeavouring to gain my point through the mediation of a friendly M.P. with the Home Secretary. Sir Matthew White Ridley's reply was delayed; then he wrote saying my application would be useless, as " he had already asked the Queen to allow him to lithograph the letter for another paper, and her Majesty refused." Once more arose the question whether

I should sit still or make a further effort. The old proverb "Nothing venture" pointed to action. Accordingly, late at night, a letter was addressed to Lieut.-Colonel Sir A. J. Bigge, the Queen's private secretary, begging him to lay my request before her Majesty. On reaching the office at noon next day there were inquiries as to what the Queen wanted with me. A telephone message, it appeared, had come through from Windsor Castle to the effect that my request was granted, but communication was lost before any details were added. A telegram dated 1.35 p.m. said: "Your application to reproduce Queen's letter is granted. Apply to Home Secretary, Home Office, who will hand over letter, but you must guarantee its safety and return as soon as possible.—BIGGE."

Needless to say, my steps were soon directed to the Home Office, but there difficulties arose. Both the Home Secretary and his private secretary declined to be approached, and during the hour of my waiting there was much telephoning to and fro between the Home Office and Windsor Castle. Then came a pause, which I relieved by going out to lunch. The return afforded no better prospect, and gradually it was extracted from one of the chief clerks that there was decided opposition on the part of the Home Secretary to giving up the letter. Ultimately a final answer was put off until next morning, the clerk privately intimating that the letter would not be obtainable in time for that week's issue. On returning to the office there was a second telegram from Windsor Castle, dated 4.25 p.m.: "Regret that I must ask you to cancel my telegram and letter of to-day, and permission

THE OLD ORDER CHANGED. 233

to reproduce Queen's letter must stand over for the present.—BIGGE." The letter referred to, which was as follows, did not come to hand till later:—

"*Windsor Castle. Feb. 21, 1896.*—SIR,—In reply to your letter of yesterday, the Queen has been pleased to grant your request for permission to print a facsimile of her Majesty's letter to the nation in your newspaper. I have sent you a message by telephone authorising you to apply to the Home Office for the original letter. Please understand that you must guarantee the safety of it, and that it is returned intact to the Secretary of State in as short a time as possible.—I am, sir, yours very faithfully, ARTHUR BIGGE."

It had been a most interesting day, and grew positively exhilarating towards the close, when I found a simple journalist concerned in this apparently subtle State duel between the Sovereign and one of her Ministers. Now, if ever, tact was needed to afford a hope of success. This must be the apology for printing the letter that was addressed to Sir Arthur Bigge:—

"SIR,—Permit me to thank you very cordially for the kindly readiness with which you laid my appeal before Her Most Gracious Majesty, and for the response thereto. It is unnecessary for me to describe my disappointment when, after three visits, and spending an hour or two at the Home Office, I was sent empty away. I bow most humbly and respectfully to the Queen's decision conveyed in your later telegram, and await Her Majesty's pleasure respecting the letter to the nation."

There the matter perforce rested until the following Tuesday evening, when a packet arrived by registered post with this letter:—

"*Windsor Castle. Feb. 24, 1896.*—DEAR SIR,—I beg to forward in a registered packet the Queen's letter to the nation which you have permission to reproduce in your newspaper. It is assumed that you will undertake to return the letter to me intact as soon as possible. I cannot help regretting that in applying for this permission you did not inform me of your previous communications on the subject with the Home Secretary.—I am, dear sir, yours very faithfully, ARTHUR BIGGE."

What had happened in the interval was plain. Royal letters addressed to the nation become State documents, and as such are kept in the custody of the Home Office. To save any further secretarial interference, even from a high officer of State, the Queen must have commanded the letter to be sent back to her, and then ordered it to be forwarded directly to me.

No time was lost in carrying out the wishes of her Majesty. In connection with a sketch of Prince Henry's career, it was noted that the Royal letter deploring his loss bore distinct traces of having been penned with tears. On the morning of its appearance in print papers were sent by request to Windsor, and brought forth the following acknowledgment:—

" Windsor Castle. *March* 1.—SIR,—I have to thank you for 100 copies of your paper which arrived here this morning. You have been very successful in the reproduction of the Queen's letter.—Yours faithfully, ARTHUR BIGGE."

I AM ORDERED TO THE MEDITERRANEAN.

A month later the *Referee* contained a significant announcement:—

" Our dear old friend, Mr. Tom Catling, editor of *Lloyd's*, has sacrificed something of health in scoring that million he is properly proud of. Under the doctor's orders he starts for

Gibraltar next Friday, and while in that quarter of the world will visit Malta, look in at Africa, and haply sample Spain and Italy on the way home. We all wish him speedy and complete recovery."

The reference to my health was unhappily true. During some building operations at the office in the April of 1895 my room was dismantled and a severe bronchial cold gripped me. "You ought to be in bed," said my doctor when I met and consulted him in the street; but that was not to be thought of. Summer relieved the attack, without getting rid of the mischief, I kept strenuously at work through the winter and spring: then came so near breaking down that a Mediterranean cruise was insisted upon. On board an Orient steamer I found myself in very cheery company, between Dr. Willis and Mr. McKendrick, the chief engineer. The doctor was constantly down upon the engineer for his narrowness of mind in regard to the saving of coal, and the latter aimed numberless shafts at the healing art. He clinched his remarks one day by launching the ever-effective story of the stranger who inquired of the Scotch boy in an out-of-the-way district as to the whereabouts of the medicine shop. The boy had never heard of such a place. Further inquiry and explanation led to his conducting the man to the village store, remarking that when anything was wrong in those parts they used whisky for men and tar for sheep!

The programme marked out for me afforded changes of scene that grew more pleasing as health gradually improved. A levanter—something worse than the most trying east wind at home—was blowing on the Rock, so the first P. and O. steamer to touch at Gibraltar bore me away to Malta. In the Antonio Gardens there, the pure air blowing over the island was sweetened with the rich perfume of orange blossoms, while golden fruit still hung upon the trees. Syracuse, being within a short steamboat ride, was too tempting to be resisted. On the return journey Granada revealed the glorious ruins of the Alhambra. It was there I saw my first bullfight, finding it nauseous and brutal, without being in the least entertaining. Tangier, with the district around recalling scenes described in Old Testament history, was far more novel and interesting. American tourists are not unjustly credited with rapid travelling. There being a weekly service of boats calling at Gibraltar, passengers from New York were enabled to stay off for seven days and go on by the next steamer. Two ladies, after a glance at the Rock, crossed over to Algeciras, proceeding thence by rail to Ronda and Granada. Returning next day, they caught a small boat from Gibraltar to Tangier; and by nice calculations were able to get back in time for their steamer, with the comforting reflection that they had accomplished a run through Spain and visited Africa in less than a week.

LABOURS OF SIR AUGUSTUS HARRIS.

My home-coming—usually one of the most enjoyable things associated with a foreign trip—was saddened by news of the serious illness of Sir Augustus Harris. Three days later he passed

THE OLD ORDER CHANGED.

away. If ever a theatrical manager could lay claim to the attribute of genius it was surely Harris. In 1877 he was playing the Boy in *Pink Dominos* at the Criterion; a year or so later he became acting manager for Edgar Bruce at the Royalty. In that post I well remember his gentle and courteous way of receiving Press folk. Down to October 19th, 1879, his name remained in the Royalty advertisements, and on November 1st he burst forth as lessee of Drury Lane. The daring of his even proposing to rent the national theatre was the talk of the clubs, and Harris told me afterwards that he was personally surprised to find himself in the position. The amount of money at his bank was infinitesimal, but after much searching he found a backer, whose faith and financial position enabled him to carry the business through. So hastily was the matter concluded, that Harris had nothing even in his mind for production. George Rignold entered on a short season with a revival of *Henry V.*, and at Christmas came the pantomime of *Blue Beard.* One of Harris's first acts on securing the theatre was to put himself on the roll of actors, in order to be eligible for the Drury Lane fund. " You never know what may happen," he said to me. " Look at the number of managers of Old Drury who have come to the Bankruptcy Court. The fund will at any rate provide me with bread and cheese."

When *Virginius* was produced we had a good laugh at the young actor-manager, because his dress as Icilius was so much richer than that of any other character in the play. On the last day of July, 1880, *The World* was brought out; after the success of that sensational piece, with its great raft scene, Harris felt himself safe. Having triumphed with drama in the national theatre, he turned his active mind to grand opera with equal success. I had the pleasure of enjoying his friendship throughout, and saw him under all manner of aspects:—In the theatre, when he conducted the rehearsals with untiring vigour; in private, after the plaudits of a crowded house had removed all anxiety concerning a new production; busily engaged in fulfilling the duties of sheriff; in the happiness of his own home; in club life; amid masonic surroundings, and on a sick bed.

Of the many rehearsals witnessed at Drury Lane, one specially comes to mind. The play was *Human Nature*, which has in it a stirring military scene. I was one of the very few in the stalls when Harris introduced me to my next neighbour, Colonel Kitchener. We chatted together for some time about plays and kindred subjects. As the battle scene opened it was arranged in the form of a square, surrounded by a low wall of Oriental pattern. The soldiers came at the wall with a springing leap and tumbled over on to the stage. Kitchener jumped up and cried, "No, no, that won't do." Harris, who was at the corner of the stage, immediately stood aside and told the players and troops to do exactly as the Colonel bade them. The scene thus revised became far more effective, and proved a lasting lesson to the young manager. Ever afterwards he strove to have all technical details in regard to the action and mounting of a play made as correct as expert judgment could render them.

In the early hours of one Sunday morning, I invited Harris into the Savage Club. On reaching the Savoy he said, "This is my birthday." Seizing the opportunity of offering good wishes, I soon had a bottle of champagne opened. A little group gave the old toast, "Happy returns and many of them." Harris shook his head and whispered to me, "I shall never make old bones." Any sadness was, of course, soon laughed off, but I thought of his words many times after. At certain periods Harris seemed to be carried away by his enthusiasm, and did not give himself a chance. The sharpest time of all, perhaps, came when he served the office of sheriff, as it meant his being called early, no matter at what hour he went to bed. Often he would dictate orders to his secretaries while hurrying through the morning bath.

During Harris's year of Mastership of Drury Lane Lodge (1887) Prince Ibrahim Hilmy was one of the initiates. As a compliment to the Master, the Prince gave a dinner at the Bristol Hotel, to which all the officers were invited. We duly assembled, but there was no sign of Harris. A quarter of an hour; half an hour; three-quarters; and a full hour seemed long in passing. Then it was decided to sit down. What had happened to keep the chief guest away no one could imagine. As we were nearly through the sumptuous repast —about a couple of hours after the time announced —in walked Harris. When the apologies and speeches were over he told me his story. In order to be ready he dressed quite early, and finding there was half an hour to spare threw himself on a couch, giving the servants strict orders to call him at the proper time. They called in vain, then let him enjoy his "beautiful sleep." No doubt it was better for him than the dinner, but he was naturally very angry.

If life is to be judged by what is put into it, rather than by mere length, Harris's career of forty-four years was more remarkable than that of any theatrical man of the nineteenth century. Down to the last he gave himself no repose, and his overwrought condition may be judged from his last words to Lady Harris, "Don't let anyone disturb me, I want a long, long rest." To attempt any review of the career of Sir Augustus would be to present a record of lofty intention and brilliant accomplishment. His early passing away was a deep grief to an exceedingly wide circle of friends and admirers, while the gap which he left has never been filled.

INCREASING THE MILLION CIRCULATION.

On the homeward journey from my first Mediterranean trip I tried to think of some fresh feature that would be serviceable for the paper. Science articles, treatises on natural history, biographies, records of curious customs, romances grave and gay, had enjoyed a good run, keeping the circulation well over the million all through the summer. Before landing from the steamer a light anecdotal sketch of the life of Queen Victoria was decided on, to mark the historic date when her Majesty would have reigned longer than the fifty-nine years and a hundred and ten days of George the Third.

Having to appear on the Sunday previous to September 23rd, 1896, there was little time for writing. All that could be done was to ransack every available source of information and to put the facts in chronological order, with a goodly sprinkling of illustrations. Printed as an extra four-page inset, which could be detached from the news, it greatly pleased the readers, sent the sale up thirty thousand, and taught me one more lesson.

In the Christmas number an equally light sketch of the career of the Prince of Wales appeared; its success was proved by the certified figures at the end of the year showing an average circulation of 1,053,923 copies.

Many questions as to "how it came about" have been put to me. My answer, "The Mantle of the Million is enough to cover us all," stands. "There is a tide in the affairs of papers" as well as of men. We caught it at the flood; one and all—from the proprietors to the printers, the editor to the errand boys—laboured together with a unity that I look back upon with the deepest satisfaction. United action secured the enduring triumph of over a million circulation.

It was the fulfilment of Alfred Bryan's prophetic picture in the first year of my editorship. *Moonshine* was then under the direction of Arthur Clements, an able journalist, who had made a sparkling diversion into the dramatic field by burlesquing Sir W. S. Gilbert. Editor and artist combined to prepare a cartoon that tells its own tale. "We must make it a Million" became an inspiring motto. Only one other feature of this composition calls for mention, the quotation from the fourth act of *Romeo and Juliet*, "How say you, Catling?" In the theatre Shakspere may have known a musician bearing the same surname as mine; but it would require a more than usually elaborate cryptogram to associate it with Bacon.

BLONDIN'S TRIUMPHS AND LOSSES.

Blondin, the wonder of his time, passed away early in 1897. When nearly forty years previously he proposed crossing Niagara he was declared to be mad. There was, of course, no means of raising a rope near the actual Falls; Blondin chose an equally dangerous spot above the Rapids, where the volume of water dashes between rocks of fearful aspect. Eleven hundred feet of rope were stretched from the Canadian to the American side of the river. To walk across called for skill and nerve in the highest degree, as a single false step meant a fall of one hundred and sixty feet and certain death. The world knows that Blondin passed over, not only once, but many times, occasionally carrying a man on his back. When Edward Prince of Wales witnessed this feat, his Royal Highness was invited to make the journey in the same way—an offer, of course, that could not be entertained. In the following year Blondin's appearance on a high rope stretched across the centre transept at the Crystal Palace created the greatest excitement ever witnessed there. Moreover, the engagement proved so successful financially as to give the shareholders a "Blondin dividend," which has not since been repeated. Only a few years

A PROPHETIC PAGE.

[To face p. 242.

THE OLD ORDER CHANGED. 243

before his end M. Jean François Gravelotte—Blondin being a name given him in childhood on account of his fair hair—paid me a visit. In the course of conversation mention was made of his losses in a wine business, and he explained that the unfortunate position was due to over-confidence in a manager. While Blondin had been thrilling the world with his exploits, care of the money that flowed in was left too much in the manager's hands. At length a shortage in the bank balance became known, and the hour of reckoning followed. It was then revealed that large sums invested in the wine trade had disappeared. Much money was lost beyond all question, and nothing was left but for Blondin to take over the concern in the hope of recovering anything that remained.

Years before Fred Maccabe, a single-handed entertainer, who was the first to go in for huge posters on the walls, told me a similar tale of loss through a manager. In his case thousands of pounds entirely disappeared, and late in life the unlucky little performer was left poor indeed.

PENNIES FOR THE ROYAL HOSPITAL FUND.

A happy coincidence enabled me to benefit the paper and simultaneously aid the Prince of Wales's Hospital Fund. When his Royal Highness announced the starting of the fund in connection with London's celebration of Queen Victoria's Diamond Jubilee, I had ready the commencement of a series of articles on "Our Great Hospitals." Two from my own pen dealt with St. Bartholomew's, the history whereof goes back to the reign of King

Stephen and the godly gifts of the Royal jester Rahere. The Prince of Wales having specially invited small subscriptions, *Lloyd's* appealed for a million pennies. Starting with 301,000 for the first week, the numbers steadily advanced. Just after the Queen's memorable open-air service in front of St. Paul's, the collection had reached a total of £3,646 13s. 4d. This meant 875,200 pennies, not quite what was aimed at, but still a worthy response from readers of the paper.

RESULT OF GETTING INTO PRINT.

The anonymous system of journalism under which I worked so long meant a quiet life. Directly one's name gets into the papers odd things are sure to happen. After I had acted as chairman at the forty-second annual dinner of Poplar Hospital, a letter reached that admirable institution from a poor lunatic in Leavesden Asylum claiming me as her son. After some incoherent references to money and to my being in the hospital through an accident, the writer said, "i was pleased to hear his name once more as he is my only son i have left and i came down here for a change of air to keep my food down and i like it very much he is a good son and i long to hear from him." In sending on the letter the Hon. Sydney Holland wrote across a blank page, "This is the way you desert your poor old mother! No wonder you were mad enough to accept my invitation to take the chair!" The temptation to recall one utterance at the dinner is too great to be resisted. It referred to a visit when the patients were enjoying cake and strawberries for tea in recognition of the honour conferred upon one of the benefactors of Poplar Hospital, Sir Donald Smith, just made a peer. In one ward some half-dozen young men, each with a broken arm, were actively carrying the dainties to those sufferers who were confined to their beds. A feeling of homelike comfort and friendliness pervaded all the conditions of the hospital. One aged fellow, who had been crushed by a huge block of mahogany, sustaining a broken arm and a fractured leg, whispered that on behalf of the young patients, as well as of the old ones, he was asked to say how much they appreciated the care of the doctors and the unceasing kindness of the nurses.

A THAMES TRAGEDY LEADS TO COMEDY.

A strange action against the paper, arising out of a tragedy, caused great merriment in a solemn London law court. On August 5th, 1897, the body of a man was found floating in the Thames off Carron Wharf, Whitechapel. It was evidently a case of murder, the perfectly nude body being tightly bound round with new rope. As the victim was over six feet in height and well developed, he must have been a remarkably fine figure of a man. After the remains had been buried as unknown, an Australian lady came forward expressing the belief that the dead man was her husband. Inquiries favoured this idea, and having resolved to try and unravel the mystery, an order for the exhumation of the remains was obtained from the Home Secretary. I then arranged with Dr. John Norton, medical officer of health for Westminster, to accompany the lady and a representative of the paper to Ilford Cemetery. In the early morning the coffin was secretly dug up, opened, and the body identified by the lady; the doctor agreeing that it corresponded with her description of the man, Moritz von Veltheim, to whom she was married eleven years previously at the registry office, Perth, Western Australia. A week or two after the record of the exhumation had been published came news from South Africa to the effect that Von Veltheim was alive and serving in the police force there. In addition to having to submit to the loss of a mistaken inquiry *Lloyd's* was soon after called upon to face a claim by the lady for damages of the most imaginary character. Though her information was entirely mistaken, she magnified its worth into hundreds of pounds, and by adding interest which she had paid on sums borrowed from other people, made her claim reach a total of over £500. When the case came before Mr. Justice Day in the mid morning he was in a most patient mood. The lady, who was fair to look upon and of attractive manners, talked and gossiped about her various journeys in pursuit of information; but the judge could not discover the slightest foundation for any claim. At last he asked the plaintiff if she had any witness. She named her solicitor, but he was not in court. As she assumed that he might have gone away to another court, Mr. Justice Day allowed time for him to be sent for, and search was duly made. Returning triumphantly with her solicitor he was duly examined, but could only relate certain details of interviews with Madame Veltheim. The Judge asked if she had any other witness, and she then expressed a wish for a reporter who had made some of the earlier inquiries for me to be called. Mr. Hales went into the box and the fun began. The lady questioned him as to what took place when they first met, what she had offered, and what he had promised from time to time at particular interviews. The plaintiff examined the reporter, and the reporter cross-examined the lady in a manner that made judge, counsel, and the entire court roar with laughter. This burlesque action went on until the time for luncheon arrived, when Mr. Justice Day quietly said, " No case; verdict for defendants." Nothing more was heard of the lady, and while the fate of Von Veltheim is known to all, the tragedy of the Thames which first brought his name before the world remains a mystery.

ARE DELUSIONS AN EXCUSE FOR MURDER?

Assassination, always a dastardly crime, appeared doubly wicked when William Terriss was struck down at the stage door of the Adelphi. For this deliberate and premeditated murder no shadow of an excuse was offered. At the trial three doctors agreed that the prisoner Prince was "suffering from delusions." The judge left the decision to the jury, and after half an hour's deliberation, the verdict was, " We find that he knew what he was doing and to whom he was doing it, but on the medical evidence we find that he was not responsible for his actions." Prince then passed to the luxurious retirement of Broadmoor, where more comforts are provided than he could have obtained by a life of steady industry. The views of many people on this question of the responsibility of so-called madmen were clearly set forth in the following letter written by Queen Victoria as far back as 1843:—

"The law may be perfect, but how is it that whenever a case for its application arises, it proves to be of no avail? We have seen the trials of Oxford and McNaghten conducted by the ablest lawyers of the day—Lord Denman, Chief Justice Tindal, and Sir William Follett—and they allow and advise the jury to pronounce the verdict of not guilty on account of insanity, whilst everybody is morally convinced that both malefactors were perfectly conscious and aware of what they did. It appears from this that the force of the law is entirely put into the judge's hands, and that it depends merely upon his charge whether the law is to be applied or not. Could not the Legislature lay down that rule which Chief Justice Mansfield did in the case of Bellingham,* and why could not the judges be bound to interpret the law in this and no other sense in their charges to the juries?"

From his retreat Prince sent me long communications. While unsuitable for printing they did not exhibit more delusions than are common with newspaper correspondents.

CONCERNING AUTHORS.

The study of literary people, though always deeply interesting, reveals strange contradictions. "Down with ego," shouted Carlyle; yet at another period (when writing his "French Revolution") he was shaking his fist at rich people driving through Hyde Park, exclaiming "None of you could do what I am at."

* Bellingham, the murderer of Prime Minister Perceval, was taken red-handed, tried, and hanged within a week.

An early letter by W. M. Thackeray throws some light on the commencement of his literary career in London. Written in March, 1840, it was addressed to "Jas. Vizetelly, Esq., 135, Fleet

My dear Sir—

That cursed paper took me eight days of my most valuable time. I put off other work to do it, and words for it I should have been paid immediately

The proofs of the Heads of the P. may stay or not as they like: if they don't dun me £10.10. on the 1st April I beg leave to back out of the concern altogether: and by all the gods will not write another line for the work.

Truly yrs
W M Thackeray.

Street." The penny post had just been introduced but there was no impressed stamp, nor any envelope. A sheet of notepaper, folded and addressed, was handed in to the office, the receipt for the penny paid being stamped on the outside. "Coram St.

1 py P. paid. Mr. 17." Whether the ten guineas demanded were forthcoming by the given date, or Thackeray carried out his threat to write no more for the "Heads of the People," I am unable to say. That he quickly found a better opening is certain. Twenty years later, 135, Fleet Street again came into notice—in the imprint of the *Daily Telegraph.* The paper was started in the Strand, and continued to be published there until the 23rd of October, 1860. This was on the eve of the development of the rotary presses that made the wonderful progress of newspapers possible.

Dickens, Thackeray, Ainsworth and a host of novelists of their time not only wrote to order, but turned out copy with the printer's devil waiting at their doors. A succeeding generation wished for more freedom. When I asked Mr. Rudyard Kipling for a story he answered (as the reader will see) by saying that he found it "impossible to guarantee work in advance without damaging its quality." " Q." failed to send a short story for the required date. In apologising, he said, "Please believe that in writing up to time I am incorrigible. Any attempt to do it makes other people mad and me miserable."

On the other hand, nothing pleased some of the lady writers so much as getting a plentiful stock of orders. One popular novelist rejoiced in having commissions for stories totalling considerably over half a million words.

Hall Caine has always wielded a most prolific pen, which reeled out copy by the yard. This sometimes made it impossible to follow the order of his chapters. One such instance brought a groan

THE OLD ORDER CHANGED. 251

from the author, but, after my explanation of the exigencies of space, he wrote:—

"I had no thought of complaining; it was merely that in the instalment last week I had been working up from the

> Arundel House
> Tisbury.
> Wilts.
> Friday. 20/7/94
>
> Dear Sir:
> I am in receipt of yours of the 19th inst & in reply can only say that if I had a tale of the length you need by me I would send it. As it is I find it impossible to guarantee work in advance without damaging its quality
>
> Very Sincerely
> Rudyard Kipling

first line to the speech anent the curl that I felt like an actor who is within sight of his best effect when the curtain is rung down on him. But no matter! With best thanks for your very friendly letter,—Yours very truly, HALL CAINE."

MY LIFE'S PILGRIMAGE.

This shows that, as far back as 1892, thoughts of the stage were beginning to run through the author's mind. In another letter he wrote, "I am returning the proofs of 'Cap'n Davy's Honeymoon,'

I will send it if you will pay £50 for first rights

remain faithfully yours,
Ouida

with best thanks for the care and real intelligence with which they have been read in the printing house." I record this with special pleasure as a tribute to the readers who worked with me during a long term of years.

Ouida's bold, running hand was unmistakable; no author before or since made a tale extend over so many sheets of paper. She sometimes relied on an agent, and at others tried to make her own arrangements, asking (as in this instance) three times the rate of payment which she could command for the first serial rights of a short story she had ready.

Joseph Hatton told me that he once received a commission from America to secure a batch of short stories by particular writers, James Payn being one of them. When Payn was approached he said he had no story by him, and declined to promise one. His stand-off attitude was so decided that Hatton wished to drop him out of the list; the Americans, however, insisted, and ultimately Payn was paid a hundred pounds for a short story. A fortnight later Hatton was intensely amused at receiving a letter from Payn, asking if he wanted another tale, as he had a couple ready to submit!

George Linnaeus Banks was a thorough Bohemian, who delighted to be known as "The Poet of the People." He could throw off some telling verse relating to political or other topical subjects, and was a ready speaker at discussion halls. Poetry of that order, however, did not lead to money-making. After being married for eighteen years, his wife turned from practical work to novel-writing, and achieved some deserved success. Banks once told me with much glee of his returning home from a club after the summer sun had risen and finding his wife sitting by an open window looking on to a small suburban garden. She had sat up to finish her story of "The

I have had a hard fight — but I have won, & won alone — I have no one to share either the profit or the fame — this time. If all is well in London — I shall be a free man in a year — ready to begin the world afresh once more.

With the kindest of good wishes dear Cathay believe me

THE OLD ORDER CHANGED. 255

Manchester Man." Taking up the manuscript, Banks read the last chapter, then turned and said, " My dear, you have written a really great story. Now you shall have the whole of the bed to yourself; pray go and enjoy a good sleep. I will rest here."

Wilson Barrett returned to London, rejoicing in the success of *The Sign of the Cross*, of which he was the sole author. He wound up a long letter to me with the page which is reproduced.

You must not judge any paper by the first number. In the summer of 1879, G. R. Sims had an interest in a new periodical called *One and All*. The early reputation achieved by "Mustard and Cress" in the *Referee*, backed up by some bold advertisements, led the public to expect much from the novelty. In the afternoon of the day that *One and All* appeared I met Sims in Fleet Street in high glee. The demand had been most gratifying and, said Sims, "If it only keeps up to the record of the first number, my living will be amply provided for." The second number told a different tale; the paper dwindled; and ultimately died. The young editor learnt his lesson, and made up for any disappointment by founding two plays on the plot of the serial he had written for *One and All*.

The inheritance of a great name is not always of benefit to the possessor. Tom Jerrold told me that he tried to depart from his father's dramatic and literary pursuits, studying horticulture and gardening under Sir Joseph Paxton. When, however, the son of Douglas Jerrold sought an engagement, or suggested the writing of articles on gardening, he was invariably met with the query,

"What the dickens do you know about gardening?" And no amount of argument sufficed to get over the difficulty.

Any bother about a title was very troublesome and a waste of time. On receiving a serial story from John Strange Winter with the title "Justice," extra caution was demanded; an important volume bearing the same title by Herbert Spencer having just been issued and extensively advertised. A letter to the philosopher brought this courteous reply:—

"64, Avenue Road, Regent's Park, N.W. Sept. 11, 1891. Sir,—I shall not raise any objection to the use of the title 'Justice' by Mrs. Stannard, provided that in all the advertisements it appears with the words 'a novel' or 'a story'; thus 'Justice : a Novel,' or 'Justice : a Story.' Of course in the serial publication in your paper the confusion of title would be of no consequence; but it might lead to some misunderstanding in the re-published form of the work, in the absence of the explanatory words. I consent, therefore, on condition that these explanatory words are inserted.—I am, faithfully yours, HERBERT SPENCER."

SIXTH STAGE.

THE PROFIT AND PLEASURE OF TRAVEL.

The Holy Sepulchre at Jerusalem—Wedding Feasts at Tiberias—Damascus and Baalbec—Jews at Richon le Zion—Pleasant Hours with Mr. Sankey—Mr. Gladstone's Last Crossing—My Mistaken Identity—Bismarck's Death First Published in London—Honours for Mr. Henniker Heaton—Notes on Freemasonry—The Loss of Mr. Herbert Lloyd — Lunch with Mr. Swinburne — Mark Twain—My Circus Adventure—From Fleet Street to Khartoum—Flogging Egyptian Prisoners—"Touch and Go" in the Soudan—Where Gordon Fell—Welcome back to London—French Goodwill to English Visitors—Service on a City Committee—One Man Among Two Thousand Women—The Passing of Queen Victoria—Algeria and the Sahara—Coronation of Edward the Seventh—Sea Trips and Their Attractions—My Contempt of Court—The Charms of Southern Spain—The Release of Mrs. Maybrick—Lord Kelvin's Kindly Act—My Jubilee on *Lloyd's*—Side Lights on the Savages—A Martyr of the Law—The Honour of the Bar—The Author of "Moses and Aaron"—The Czar's "Bloody Sunday"—My Great Loss—Irving: The Man and the Actor—A Grand Reception in Austria—Tracing Long Lost Relatives—The Sadness of Farewell.

THE HOLY SEPULCHRE AT JERUSALEM.

THE taste for travel awakened by the tour through America and Canada increased as the benefit of my Mediterranean cruise began to be felt. From that time it became my aim to seek a holiday as early in the year as possible, and to make for warmer climes. Rome, even at the time of the Carnival, was disappointing on the festive side; still nothing can mar the interest of its memorial ruins. The charm of Naples, the marvel of Pompeii, and the wonder of Vesuvius fill the imagination; while Venice remains unique among the manifold attractions which Italy offers.

No tour it has ever been my lot to make, however, so lives in memory as that of the Holy Land. Beyond some excitement over the landing at Jaffa, there is little at the outset to strike attention; the rail winding its way up to Jerusalem awakens modern rather than ancient ideas. The squalor of the city is most depressing. Traditions clustered around the great Mosque, the whole Temple area, and even the Church of the Holy Sepulchre are for a time bewildering. A little investigation, however, tends to remove many difficulties, especially in respect to the Sacred Tomb. Mrs. Alexander's hymn, "There is a green hill far away, without a city wall," must not be understood to mean far away from the city. Dean Stanley pointed out that "there is in the Scriptural narrative no mention of a mount or hill, and there is no such name as 'Calvary.'" The passage from which the word is taken, Luke xxiii. 33, is merely the olden translation (calvaria) of what the Evangelist calls "a skull." This was written years before Miss Gordon made known her illustrious brother's idea as to his having found "the true Calvary" outside the present city. Such a notion is opposed to all that we know respecting the changes which occurred during the many sieges of Jerusalem, and it may be repeated with confidence "if the Church of the Holy Sepulchre does not cover the real spot, it is idle to seek for it elsewhere." Despite the picturesque and imposing appearance of Jerusalem, with its castellated walls thirty-eight feet high, manifold mosques, minarets, convents, churches, and other striking buildings standing out from the slopes of its four hills, the site is a small one—as is proved by the fact that I walked round the outer walls in less than an hour. From the Mount of Olives the view over the city, with the Dead Sea in the distance bordered by the hills of Jordan, is an inspiring sight. Bethany and Bethlehem near at hand are but villages. A long day's journey to Hebron shows much of the country, but is disappointing, as the Mosque there remains closed against all save royal visitors.

When the Sermon on the Mount was preached Galilee embraced many cities and a large population; now you may ride for hours without meeting more than a few wandering Beduins, who are inclined to beg a little food. Capernaum, scene of many "mighty works," lies buried, and only the name reminds us of Bethsaida. Hill and plain are left well-nigh deserted: yet the whole region kindles the belief that one day there will be a return to its old fertility and usefulness.

WEDDING FEASTS AT TIBERIAS.

Although marriage is so differently regarded by the varying population, the wedding feast forms an important feature with all classes. A Mahometan may divorce a wife whensoever it pleases him, but as a bride he takes her home with much show of rejoicing. A Beduin wedding party passed on the shore of the lake as I crossed it, gay singing being mingled with rapturous shouts and the firing of many guns. Of the marrying of a couple of Greek Christians it is possible to enter into more detail. The bridegroom went down from Nazareth to wed a maid of Tiberias, accompanied by half a score friends on horseback. At night the festivities commenced with a double ceremony, the males, to the number of a hundred, crowding into a single room to hold small lighted candles while the bridegroom was shaved; the bride being similarly attended by her own sex for adornment after her preliminary bathing. High jinks followed, professional singers and dancers being engaged to perform whenever the fun showed signs of flagging. Each new visitor was greeted with a shrill chorus of welcome, for which he was expected to bestow a small gratuity on the singers. Cigarettes and drinks were handed round. These compliments soon became overwhelming, small glasses of aromatic liquor being followed by larger quantities of arrack—a rank spirit that burns the mouth and throat. When the proffered glass was courteously declined (through an interpreter) the one who offered it said he would drink my health and to all Europeans. Everybody evinced the kindest disposition, and I was specially favoured with an invitation to accompany my wife to the house where the female feast was in progress some distance away. A shrill and rattling chorus welcomed us. At the moment some kind of incantation seemed in progress; the bride, decked in bright colours, and wearing many necklaces, strings of coins, and gold braid, stood swaying with closed eyes, between two huge decorated candles held by women. Very speedily I was pushed forward through the densely-packed throng of women and young children to be presented to the bride, and the prettier young attendant, known as "the maid of the bride." After they had mounted a kind of throne songs and dances followed—each dancer simply posturing on a space a yard square. This feast, it was said, would go on all through the night. Next day I was early at the church, the wedding being fixed for three o'clock. The bridegroom in an adjacent room quietly smoked till the bride was brought up on horseback. All through the elaborate ceremony, which occupied a full hour, the crowd kept up a constant babble; but the two priests did not show the least impatience. When at length all was over, the bride, entirely hidden by a pink veil, was led to the back of the church to receive congratulations from female friends (who ultimately bore her away on horseback) while the bridegroom was kissed on each cheek by the men. We had met several times, and he came up to me with an attitude that implied readiness to receive my salutation; I could not force myself beyond a handshake and hearty good wishes. At nine o'clock the following morning a numerous procession set out with the wedding party for Nazareth, the city being reached in the evening. The bride was kept closely veiled, and would not be permitted to join her husband until after another night's revel with her female friends.

DAMASCUS AND BAALBEC.

Damascus, founded (according to Josephus) by Uz, great-grandson of Noah, has been famous all through the ages; and having outlived the assaults of Jews, Assyrians, Persians, Macedonians, Romans, Saracens, and others, is still, even under the Turk, the busiest and most active city open to the tourist in Syria. In every way it is a place of abiding interest; full of the bustling life of to-day and abounding with records of a momentous past. On the slope of one of the hills Adam is said to have lived; and Shakspere adopts the story that it was there Cain killed his brother Abel. The names of Abraham and David are linked with the olden city; where centuries later the famous Caliph Haroun Al Raschid flourished and Mahomet was a camel driver. Going or returning the tourist can stop midway over the Lebanon hills and drive from Mallaka to Baalbec. There, in regarding the remains of ancient temples dedicated respectively to the Sun, Jupiter, Baal, and Venus, wonder and admiration swallow up all other feelings. By what means did Phœnician giants rear the vast stones to their positions? They lie there over sixty feet in length with the four sides, each measuring thirteen feet, so perfectly squared that, though no cement was used, it is impossible anywhere to insert so much as a pin point. The most modern of the Temples belongs to the second century, while the mists of antiquity enshroud others. Yet the outlines are so marvellously preserved that one can walk round and mark the elegant proportions of each majestic edifice, gaze on the lofty columns which remain as evidences of past grandeur, and find on every side relics of the finest artistic decoration for capital, frieze and ceiling. The staircase of one tower exists, and along with three gigantic subterranean passages is a small one in the Temple of Jupiter, which makes plain the method within reach of the priests for "working the Oracle." Just under the place where the statue stood are holes communicating with a secret chamber that was only reached by a person crawling from a hidden entrance.

JEWS AT RICHON LE ZION.

"What of the Jews?" has often been asked me. In and around Jerusalem it must be said that they do not show to advantage, appearing to lack any idea of industry or cleanliness. In other places, however, a common notion that the Jews will not work was shown to be altogether unfounded. Twenty years before the period of my visit the locality of Richon le Zion might have been described in the words of Isaiah, "Sharon is like the wilderness," wild dogs ranged in the wilder grass growing in the sand, and there was no other sign of life. Through the generosity of Baron Rothschild a beginning was made, and I found nearly eight hundred Jews zealously working, having brought thousands of acres of land under fruitful cultivation. Only one or two families were English, the majority being Russians and Germans. Previously to settling there many had been engaged as merchants, bankers, and in other commercial pursuits, so that they had little or no practical knowledge of tilling the soil. An entry from my diary may be quoted:

"Richon le Zion was described to me as an effort to enable every man to reap the fruit of his labours, and to found a home on his own land. Each plot is valued at a certain price, and can be paid for in a longer or shorter period, according to the success of the settler, without any addition whatever in the shape of interest. Vines have been largely grown, and almonds and oranges are rapidly coming on. The well-kept gardens and vineyards are arranged between avenues of quick-growing palms; and early in February roses and geraniums were blooming freely in the open air, peas and broad-beans were over a foot high, asparagus was ready to cut, and lettuces and radishes abounded. Eucalyptus trees, which have been largely planted, flourish in the rich soil that lies beneath the sandy surface, and already tower far above the tiled roofs of the two-storied houses which are the common form of residence. They are for the most part detached, and offer many comforts. Fair roads are being made, and already there is an effort to light them with public lamps. The situation of this smiling landscape under a bright sun, with blue sky overhead, was beautiful in the extreme. A fresh breeze blew from the direction of the sea, while as I sat in the open enjoying a cup of tea newly made by one of the kindly settlers, there could be seen towards the east the mountains of Judæ white with the snow which had fallen that morning."

A party of Russian Jews who landed at Smyrna, under the stress of unemployment, were supposed to have been converted. All went quietly for a while; then they began to murmur. According to my informant they seemed to regard Christianity as a kind of freemasonry, and demanded to know when they were to be entrusted with the "secret." They had read the twenty-fifth Psalm, and the third chapter of Proverbs, interpreting the "secret" referred to therein as some tangible information, which as converts they were entitled to demand.

PLEASANT HOURS WITH MR. SANKEY.

In the return journey my passage was taken from Beyrout on a French steamer, which called at Constantinople and Athens. On board I found Mr. Ira D. Sankey hurrying away from Syria owing to the news from America of coming war with Cuba. Many friendly conversations were the result of this meeting. Being invited to assist in arranging an English service, I appealed to the purser, who said there would be no objection if the passengers were agreed. Proceeding to question all who spoke English, one young man raised a smile by saying, "I have no objection, if my father wants to conduct a service on board the ship." It was not at the time known that he was a son of Mr. Sankey. There was no opposition, and thirty-four gathered together in the cabin; two Frenchmen most courteously stopping their game of cards and retiring. Many familiar hymns were rendered with deep feeling as we passed through the Dardanelles, but Mr. Sankey's remarkable power was best displayed before crowded audiences in the largest halls. During the evening the great mission work of Mr. Moody was discussed, and Mr. Sankey told me how he was led to join him.

When the two first met in 1870, Sankey was known as a voluntary singer at Sunday School gatherings. Being thirty years of age, married, the father of two children, and well placed in a Government office with an assured position, he had no thought of entering the ministry in any form. Very soon after hearing Sankey sing, Moody said to him, "You will have to come with me." The suggestion met with no encouragement, and a direct offer was declined. When further pressed, Sankey sent word that Mr. Moody would readily find a far better singer than he was. Mr. Moody acknowledged that he could find several better singers, but not one to sing as he wished, to move masses of people as Mr. Sankey did. There the matter rested for some months, Mr. Sankey's family and friends being entirely opposed to his throwing up his prospects in life. On the other hand Mr. Moody (who had been noted for his energy when dealing in boots and shoes at Chicago) was persistent in his appeals. At length he prevailed on Sankey to spend a week with him. Before that week was out the Secretary of the Treasury had received Sankey's resignation, and henceforth the two men laboured together with all their energies.

Samos, where we landed, is famous for its wine, which is of the muscat flavour and very sweet. "Wine for girls," said a native. When a flask was produced, several members of the party declined to take it, on the plea that they were teetotallers. Mr. Sankey, although an earnest advocate of temperance, had no such narrow view; and together we sampled the wine of the country, washing down the nuts and raisins that were offered us by the friendly islanders.

The manifold changes involved in a trip of this kind may be understood from the fact that I was nineteen nights at sea, travelling in eight different steamers, landing and returning at various places in fifteen small boats. More than eighty hours were spent in fourteen trains, including one night in a sleeper; carriage drives occupied more than a hundred hours, and shelter was found in thirteen separate hotels.

MR. GLADSTONE'S LAST CROSSING.

Among the fellow passengers encountered crossing the channel on the way to Dover was Mr. Gladstone. He looked worn and ill as he passed to a private cabin, leaving the care of his wife to servants, with the result that she slipped and hurt her leg rather badly in stepping down from the railway carriage. A quick passage made the home-coming enjoyable, but it was reported soon after that Mr. Gladstone said to a friend, " You see in me the most miserable man in the world." Suffering cruel pain from the disease which had seized on his face, and no doubt feeling that the end was approaching, the condition of the great statesman was at that time most pathetic. Loving hands and skilful scientific treatment did all that was possible for the illustrious patient; but three months later his prolonged and noble career came to an end at Hawarden.

MY MISTAKEN IDENTITY.

Another incident of this channel trip was my being mistaken (not for the first time) for a distinguished public man. As I moved along the deck of the steamer a young lady, sheltering between the funnels, gleefully exclaimed, " How do you do, uncle?" My look of amazement was followed by the gentleman with her adding, "Good morning, Sir John." On my disclaiming both title and relationship it was said, "If you're not Sir John Aird, you're Mr. Catling." A little chat brought the explanation that the gentleman, who met me some years previously in America, had since married a niece of Sir John Aird, and was thus able to correct the mistake into which his wife had fallen. The confusion began long before.

"Sir John, I shall be pleased to take wine with you," was shouted at me across the hall of Freemasons' Tavern in the year 1892.

As I looked up Dr. Lennox Browne exclaimed, "That's not Aird," and the matter ended in a laugh. But it proved to be the first of many similar mistakes.

With a very pleasant little Press party, I journeyed to Cornwall for the opening of the South Western line to Bude. As we rode slowly on a trolley over the new-laid rails the foreman of works and others said they could never look at me without thinking that the chief of the firm which had made the line was with them. At the hotel, when the numbers of the rooms were distributed, I was left out, the chambermaid saying, "Sir John will know his own room, won't he?"

Quitting the Uxbridge-road Station rather hurriedly one day, a workman, who had evidently some appeal to make, approached me murmuring, "May I speak to you, Sir John?" When I shook my head and passed on, his look of disappointment was plainly mingled with incredulity.

While waiting for a train at San Remo a

gentleman, raising his hat, said, " Have I the honour of speaking to Sir John Aird ? "

On various occasions when visiting the Reform Club, the welcome from members has been, " Good evening, Sir John."

Writing in the *Illustrated London News,* James Payn remarked, " I once had a double who gave me considerable inconvenience, but it is hardly necessary to say I made a few guineas out of the resemblance." Advantage of this kind never fell to my lot ; though, when staying in the South of France, friends assured me that anywhere from Nice to Mentone I could obtain goods on credit in the name of Sir John Aird. Yet the resemblance was in no way complete.

Just previous to the American line resuming the running of its steamers after the Cuban War, a luncheon was given on board ship at Southampton. On that occasion I was called upon to respond for a toast which had been proposed by Sir John Aird, and no one thought of our being in any way alike.

BISMARCK'S DEATH FIRST PUBLISHED IN LONDON.

A notable instance of the way in which electricity sometimes fits the exact requirements of a newspaper was afforded when Bismarck passed away. The Prince was known to be very ill, consequently his biography was duly kept ready in type. Midnight passed without any definite message being received, and the paper went to press. Before printing commenced momentous news arrived. Dr. Horrovitz, correspondent of the *Daily Chronicle* in Vienna, had looked in at the central telegraph office there. Finding the clerk in charge was a friend he remained chatting, and thus heard of Bismarck's death from a message which was being sent through on its way to the Emperor William, then yachting in Norway. It was not until some hours afterwards that the news was made known in Berlin. The correspondent instantly despatched a telegram to London, and it came into the hands of a smart youth, who speedily passed it on from the office of the daily paper to my son. Through this combination of fortunate circumstances *Lloyd's* was two hours ahead of every other paper in the world in announcing the great statesman's death.

HONOURS FOR MR. HENNIKER HEATON.

A Canterbury pilgrimage in the spring of 1899 awakened far-reaching reflections. The honorary freedom of the ancient city was conferred upon a native of Kent, who had devoted all his powers to linking the world together by means of Imperial Penny Postage. In company with Mr. Henniker Heaton there travelled from London the Rev. Dr. Taylor, Master of St. John's College, Cambridge; Sir William Peace and Sir Julian Salomons, Agents-General for Natal and New South Wales; Sir John Gorst, Mr. Walter of the *Times*, Mr. W. L. Thomas of the *Graphic*, and myself. The popular member was most cordially welcomed by the Archbishop, the Mayor, and other authorities; the roll of freedom being enclosed in a rich casket made of oak taken from the Cathedral. After the official proceedings the company moved to St. Margaret's Hall for the inevitable luncheon. Prior to sitting down townsfolk and visitors mingled freely together, the wife of the Archbishop being notably gracious. Dr. Temple, departing from the custom of his predecessors, who resided at Addington, had just moved into a new house in the diocese. Wishing to have this fact recognised Mrs. Temple, as she shook hands with some local ladies, said smilingly, "We are neighbours now, aren't we?" At table the Archbishop referred to his schoolmastering days at Rugby, telling with great glee the well-known story of the boy who, complaining of the ill-treatment of his tutor, asked his father to appeal to the head master, adding, by way of postscript, "Temple is a beast, but a just beast." His broad views were shown in the attitude towards temperance. The Archbishop abstained in order that he might consistently preach teetotalism to others, but was liberal minded enough to provide for those who thought differently. When entertaining or giving a semi-public dinner at Lambeth Palace, wines were placed upon the table along with minerals and other drinks.

The Canterbury crown for Mr. Henniker Heaton was quickly followed by a similar honour from the Corporation of London, the City Freedom being presented with due ceremonial in a casket of gold.

NOTES ON FREEMASONRY.

The 19th of April, 1899, is marked with a red letter in my Masonic Calendar; it was the date of the following letter:—

" United Grand Lodge of England. Dear Sir and Brother, —I have received the commands of the Most Worshipful

Grand Master to acquaint you that his Royal Highness purposes to confer on you the rank and dignity of Past Assistant Grand Director of Ceremonies. I am to ask you to be good enough to favour me with an early intimation of your acceptance of the distinction, which will be announced at the Grand Festival, to be held in this building on Wednesday, the 26th inst., at 5 p.m.—I am, dear sir and brother, yours fraternally, E. Letchworth, G.S."

I thus had the honour to figure as one of twenty-five brethren on whom Past Grand Rank was conferred to mark the completion of the twenty-fifth year of the Grand Mastership of the Prince of Wales.

Freemasonry is not a subject concerning which any disclosures are to be made. Douglas Jerrold's humorous comments, put into the mouth of Mrs. Caudle, were my earliest lessons. A story (reprinted in *Lloyd's*) of Pope Pio Nono being expelled the Order attracted attention. Under the name of Mastaï-Ferretti he was initiated in 1826 under the old Scottish rite of the Orient, at Palermo. After being crowned Pope and King, the same Mastaï-Ferretti cursed his former brethren, and excommunicated all Freemasons. For this act he was called to account, and failing to send a reply or offer any vindication, a decree of expulsion followed, being signed by King Victor Emmanuel, Grand Master of the Orient of Italy.

The effect of this excommunication was felt in England; the Marquis of Ripon on becoming a Roman Catholic resigned his position as Grand Master. What at first seemed to be a misfortune resulted in the Prince of Wales succeeding to the position, thus bringing about the modern development and extension of the Order in so many beneficent ways.

My admission into the craft was due to Augustus Harris, in the newly-formed Drury Lane Lodge. On March 9th, 1886, P. Cremieux Javal, H. H. Morell Mackenzie, Louis Hervé, and Thomas Catling were initiated by Joseph Parkinson, acting Master, in the absence of the Earl of Londesborough. Before the year waned I was actively at work as one of the founders of the Savage Club Lodge. The distinction thus came to me of being installed as Master within three years of my initiation. It was with no little nervousness that I advanced from one position to another, but the brethren were always most kind. The list of entertainers at my installation banquet will show how the Savages rallied in support of the Lodge:—J. L. Toole, Edward Terry, James Fernandez, Walter Clifford, Deane Brand, Ben Davies, Courtice Pounds, Harry Nicholls, Herbert Campbell, John Radcliffe, McCall Chambers, Herbert Thorndike, Lovett King, Geoffrey Thorn, R. Ganthony, John Le Hay, Alfred Moore, Charles Bertram, W. Nicholl, E. J. Odell, Franklin Clive, Schartau, J. Kift, W. Ganz, Theodore Drew, Edward Bending, and Willie Wright, with the band of the Grenadier Guards, conducted by Lieut. Dan Godfrey.

Electoral contests in Grand Lodge, when zealously waged, were apt to excite feeling, especially as there was only the one office of Treasurer to be filled. The open polling was therefore wisely abolished in favour of voting papers being sent in prior to the date of the election. It was in 1889, I think, that the old order was followed for the last time. Candidates were nominated in Grand Lodge, and the voting immediately followed. There was nothing to be said against either of the two worthy masons who were to be brought forward, but clearly both could not get in. As I moved to select a place midway in the hall, my good friend J. H. Matthews, the chief scrutineer, said, "Well, I'm sorry for you this time, Catling." "What's the matter now?" was my query. "Why," said he, "you haven't got a ten to one chance." "Any way we are going to have a run for our money, and it will be for all we're worth." In due course Lord George Hamilton, the First Lord of the Admiralty, proposed George Everett, addressing himself chiefly, I noted, towards the Grand Officers on the dais. Speaking as W. M. of the Savage Club Lodge, on behalf of Edward Terry, my appeal was made to the general body of Masons crowding the hall. Before the votes were counted Terry had to run away to act. An hour or two later I carried to his theatre the gratifying news that he had been elected Grand Treasurer by a majority of more than 200—840 to 617 votes.

On my subsequently reaching the chair of Drury Lane Lodge it was a delight to find John Northcott Master of the Savage Club Lodge. The occasion was happily commemorated in Alfred Bryan's cartoon.

It has been my privilege to attend notable gatherings in historic places, first among which must always be placed the consecration of the

JOHN NORTHCOTT AND MYSELF.

Sketched by Alfred Bryan.

[To face p. 274.

Rahere Lodge, in the summer of 1895. The great hall of St. Bartholomew's Hospital, with its records of beneficent kindness to the sick and suffering, carried the mind back through more than seven centuries to the gentle-hearted founder. As each phase of the impressive ceremony proceeded, the wider loomed the influence of Freemasonry. The Grand Master (then Prince of Wales) and the Crown Prince of Denmark were on the dais, with the Earl of Lathom as Consecrating Master, Lord Roberts, S.W., Lord Skelmersdale, J.W., the Dean of Gloucester, Chaplain, and Dr. Godson awaiting installation as First Master. It was a memorable scene in London's oldest hospital, princes and peers, warriors and statesmen, churchmen and city merchants, mingled with humbler brethren. Well was it for the chaplain to remind his hearers that "Masonry belongs to the Court and the camp, to the great centres of commerce, to the scholar's study, to the cottage of the artisan, but its true home is where it may best assist and comfort those that mourn and are in need." In a prosaic age we do well to cherish ideals, especially those which embrace lessons of life and death as pure and lofty as those of Freemasonry.

Rather more than three years later it fell to my lot to correspond with Lord Kitchener and arrange a special lunch in his honour, on behalf of Drury Lane Lodge, of which he was one of the founders. The warrior brother expressed a wish to remain a subscribing member, and greeted all who were introduced to him with a hand-grip they could not readily forget.

THE LOSS OF MR. HERBERT LLOYD.

By the passing away of Mr. Herbert Lloyd on May 12th, 1899, I lost a sincere and generous friend. He was one of the four kindly brothers to whom the father had left the direction of his great properties. Delicate from his youth upward, Mr. Herbert Lloyd had sought the benefit of life in warmer climes. He spent a number of years in South Africa, chiefly devoted to astronomy, subsequently visiting Australia and making holiday in Egypt; all in vain, as he died in his forty-second year. In every relation of life his gentle manner, genial spirit, and constant consideration for others won the highest regard. Always looking upon the bright side, despite his constitutional weakness, he made himself beloved by all who were privileged to know him. A letter bubbling over with good humour, written in response to a little present sent for his wedding, is before me, vividly recalling the cheerful smile of a good man who truly "wore his heart upon his sleeve," and ever sought to make others happy.

LUNCH WITH MR. SWINBURNE.

With a view to obtaining a poem from Mr. Swinburne, negotiations were opened with Mr. Watts-Dunton. Writing from "The Pines," Putney Hill, he sent a kindly invitation to lunch, courteously adding directions for reaching the house with the greatest ease. On arriving, in company with my old friend W. E. Church, a few minutes before the appointed time of 1.30, we were warmly welcomed. It was a beautiful July day, with Putney looking its best. Mr. Swinburne was out for his usual morning walk. Pending his return the business in hand was talked over. Any idea of asking the poet to write was out of the question; some compositions, however, were admitted to exist in manuscript, and it was thought that Mr. Swinburne might be induced to revise one for publication in the way desired. Suddenly the outer door opened and the poet came bounding into the hall, with a noisy bustle which seemed to be understood as an indication that he was ready for lunch. In a very few minutes the meal was on the table, and after a cordial greeting the party of four sat down. Mr. Swinburne's bearing was marked by a simplicity which rightly belongs to a man in his own home. If conversation languished to some extent it was by reason of the afflicting deafness under which the poet laboured. Having finished his bottle of beer, he turned from the table to some new books which had come in that day. A marvellous change came over him; all seriousness instantly disappeared. One volume, which had been eagerly expected, contained references to the poet's schooldays. As he raised his head and pointed these out to Mr. Watts-Dunton, the flashing eyes and exalted expression made him appear as one transformed. A French critic once described him as "the most extravagantly artistic being to be found upon the earth." The genius of his higher life was undoubtedly linked with a lower homely nature, and I count myself fortunate to have caught glimpses both of the man and the poet at this brief meeting. But the poem never came to hand.

MARK TWAIN.

An invitation to the famous American humorist brought forth the following kindly reply:—

> Hotel Krantz
> Vienna, Feb. 25/99
>
> Dear Sir
>
> I very much wish I could do that, but my engagements & occupations are such as to put it out of my power
>
> With many thanks to the Society for the honor done me by their invitation,
>
> I am Sincerely Yours
> Mark Twain

ADVENTURES WITH A CIRCUS TROUPE.

The Court Circular of July 19th, 1899, announced that Queen Victoria witnessed a procession of Sanger's, which comprised upwards of 150 horses, six elephants, several camels, and a number of birds and wild beasts. It was a great day for "Lord George," and in addition to pleasing the Sovereign enabled a party of Pressmen to enjoy an outing at Windsor. The invitation sent to the papers offered "every facility for making sketches or notes before, during, and after the procession." First we sat down to a substantial meal, surrounded by the pomp of the great travelling circus. It was there intimated that all who cared were welcome to take part in the procession. A few held back, the majority readily accepted. The show was of wondrous diversity. "St. George and his Seven Champions" were succeeded by Richard the Third and Queen Elizabeth. From Egypt came the Khalifa with gunboats of the Nile, a triumphal car represented India and its Nobles, while others were devoted to the Colonies. Exactly what part I was supposed to fill must remain unknown. In a varied robe of many colours, and wearing a kind of Druid crown, my identity was entirely concealed, save for the beard. Royal weather favoured the display; three times the procession passed slowly before the Queen, Sanger being then presented to her Majesty. This was the occasion on which the old showman, after declining a cheque, received a silver cigar box that was a far greater joy.

With the opening of the circus my crown was laid aside, but not the new dignity it conferred.

As a professional I was warmly received in a region of the Castle; one introduction followed another, and endless yarns were spun of a showman's wandering adventures. From first to last it was a notable evening, abounding with surprises, and casting a flood of light upon the inner circle of Court life. As a journalist often doomed to disappointment in seeking this knowledge, I recognised and almost envied the advantage enjoyed by so humble a professional as one who had represented an imaginary king in a circus pageant.

FROM FLEET STREET TO KHARTOUM.

My holidays were mostly arranged in a hurry. Looking in at Messrs. Cook's City office early in January, 1900, to inquire after anything fresh, the offer was made, "We'll book you to Khartoum if you like." "What about coming back?" I asked. "Oh! you shall have a return ticket." Thereupon the firm undertook to make out an itinerary; a few days later a cheque for something over a hundred and fifty pounds was handed in for the trip from Fleet Street to Khartoum and back. All that remained for me to do was to make sure of a cab from home to the station. Once started it was easy to race across France, skim over the Mediterranean, and be in Cairo within a week. From that point a different state of things prevailed. It was the year of a specially low Nile, and the first tourist boat stuck on a sandbank for thirty-eight hours. This necessitated taking train from Luxor to Assouan in order to catch a second boat for Wady Halfa. A second stoppage, when the boat rested on another bank for forty-three hours, upset all calculations. The train from Wady Halfa ran once a week; it started on Thursday night, and we arrived on Saturday morning. Faced by the necessity of waiting nearly six days, twelve out of the thirteen passengers who had booked for the trip were scared off; I alone remained. Wady Halfa was then a place of five or six thousand inhabitants, mostly Berberines and Soudanese, with a sprinkling of Greeks, Armenians, and Syrians. The one hotel, although unfinished, provided comfortable quarters. Its proprietor was a Greek, the manager a German, his wife French. For four days I was the sole visitor and the only Britisher in the place. The rest in this quiet corner of the desert, with its fresh breezes and glorious sunshine, was delightful. Gordon's people (as he called the Soudanese) were always interesting, and I amused them greatly when wandering under the oleanders which lined the principal thoroughfare.

During one lonely ramble I came upon an Egyptian medical department, receiving a most kindly welcome from the officers. We sipped coffee together, and as some knew a little English, chatted over passing events. The prison doctor told me he had charge of 250 convicts, many of whom were murderers and thieves of the worst description. Two were to be flogged that afternoon. One was to receive twenty lashes for making unfounded charges against officials of the prison, the second ten for stealing an orange. When brought out, the first man was nervously anxious for his punishment to begin; but he had to wait, with gleaming eyes, while the doctor felt his pulse, and applied the stethoscope to his breast. Then a further delay ensued in order that the other prisoners might witness the scene. As they filed up, each man in chains, their eager eyes seemed fastened on me. Some score of soldiers kept the ground, and besides a couple of hundred convicts there were as many natives as onlookers. Three chairs were brought out, a cushion being politely placed on mine, between the doctors.

The apparatus was simple—three cross-bars on two uprights securely fixed on a stand. The first prisoner stepped on this, and while his head was held well forward over the top bar by one warder, two others firmly gripped his arms. His skin was lighter than many around, but it changed to a livid pink and then a dark purple as the thongs of the cat descended. After ten lashes had been given a fresh warder stepped forward, and, by letting the blows fall a little lower on the bare back, made the poor wretch quiver, though he uttered no cry nor showed the least sign of fear.

A feeling of pity for the second man could not be resisted, considering his offence, but this passed when I saw that his punishment was lighter than the thrashing which used to be commonly inflicted on juvenile offenders in my schoolboy days.

WAR NEWS IN THE DESERT.

A mile and a half from my hotel, beside the Nile, report said, there was a military camp, with five British officers, an equal number of civilians, and one English lady. Not having seen a war telegram for several days I wandered to the camp thirsting for news. The officers were away, and an Englishman in the telegraph department said there was nothing fresh to tell me. My journey looked like being fruitless, when an orderly brought in a closed telegram. Breaking the envelope, the official read it with evident satisfaction, but said, "This is marked 'private.'" We then talked for a few minutes as to my journey, the delays on the Nile, and my wish to get to Khartoum. After reading through the telegram again, the official said, "Though this is marked 'private' there cannot be any harm in an Englishman knowing its contents." He then read out the surrender of Cronje and his entire force to Lord Kitchener at Paardeburg. This cheering information, which reached me at such an opportune moment, was imparted on the afternoon of Shrove Tuesday, the very day on which the surrender took place.

"TOUCH AND GO" IN THE SOUDAN.

The publication of exaggerated accounts of reverses to British arms in South Africa had a profound effect throughout Egypt, and brought the Soudanese regiments at Omdurman to the verge of revolt. Evidence of trouble first appeared by the passing of some half-dozen Soudanese officers through Wady Halfa. From my window I saw them early one morning taken on board a Government boat under a guard of thirty-two soldiers. It was whispered that they were on their way to Cairo to be tried by court-martial, on the charge of endeavouring to induce the native troops to rise against the British.

On reaching Khartoum and mentioning what I had seen, the matter was talked of more openly, as all danger was over. After the battle of Omdurman resulting in the flight of the Khalifa, Kitchener offered his Soudanese prisoners the opportunity of entering the British service. They accepted on condition that rations were provided for their women. Each soldier acknowledged a wife, and the majority also looked after a sister, a mother-in-law, a cousin, or an aunt. For a time all went smoothly, but after Lord Kitchener's departure signs of disaffection became visible in Omdurman. The women chattered among themselves, saying the English were getting the worst of it in the Transvaal, and they were not going to be kept under and be treated like children. They followed up their grumbling by attacking and injuring two British officers in the open street. The men of one regiment began to lose their ammunition day after day, and when called to account, seized their arms. Matters were growing serious. "It was touch and go" were the words used to me in respect to the crisis when the men of the discontented regiment were ordered to parade at a given hour. Some of the officers had grave doubts whether native troops would obey. To meet any emergency the Seaforth Highlanders were assembled at the same hour on a gunboat stationed opposite the Omdurman gate, with the avowed object of being taken down the Nile for a picnic. Arms and ammunition were ready on board, and the officers did sentry duty ashore to signal the least sign of mutiny. It was a matter of anxious concern for the time being, but happily all passed off quietly,

THE AUTHOR IN THE NILE DESERT.

SOUDANESE WAITING FOR THE TRAIN.
A Snapshot at Khartoum in 1900.

the Soudanese giving up their arms. The gunboat, however, was not moved throughout the day, the picnic of the Highlanders being postponed.

Subsequent inquiry traced the trouble to certain Egyptian officers, and it was the principal offenders who came under my notice on their way under arrest to Cairo. Four of them were ordered to be dismissed from the service, one reduced to the ranks and subsequently discharged with ignominy, one placed on the unattached list, one severely reprimanded and placed at the bottom of the roll of officers. In confirming the judgment of the court-martial the Khedive notified, as a warning to would-be mutineers, that any future offenders would not escape so lightly.

Although the Soudanese troops had proved themselves faithful, arrangements were at once made for dividing the force. This involved providing a special train or boat to convey the many female followers of the men. Hours before the time for starting, the women, with all their belongings bound up in bundles, assembled on the river banks and there accompanied the monotonous beating of the tom-toms with weird chants and strange cries. The proceedings were singular and amusing enough, as good order prevailed. I moved freely and alone amidst the natives of Omdurman, just as safely as at home.

In Khartoum, only beginning to rise from its ruins, things were different. There had been several murders, in which the native police were implicated, and tourists received many warnings. No hotel existed; we were lodged on a gunboat, which had come down from Fashoda swarming with mosquitoes. The weather grew hotter day by day, until the thermometer registered over a hundred degrees in the shade, one result being a prodigious thirst. No discomfort, however, could destroy the supreme interest of the place.

WHERE GORDON FELL.

An opportunity to attend Sunday morning service in the new palace of the Sirdar was seized with alacrity, because it took me to the spot where Gordon fell, after his heroic defence of the city for 387 days. Mr. Gwynne, a good type of the zealous missionary, preached briefly, watch in hand. In a subsequent talk with him he spoke of the near future, when he hoped to labour among the heathen tribes above Fashoda, and to that end was taking lessons in their language, from the water-carrier of the Khalifa. My letter of introduction from Charles Williams led up to an invitation to lunch from Lady Wingate and a subsequent pleasant chat with the Sirdar. From him I received confirmation of the account given in his book as to the way in which Gordon met his death—not fighting in the streets, but calmly facing fearful odds in his own palace. Deep regret was felt at the time that this ruined palace was not preserved as a shrine, instead of being uprooted by Lord Kitchener for the building of a new home for the Sirdar. With Oriental people the tomb of a hero becomes an enduring shrine; that of the Mahdi was a feature of Omdurman.

WELCOME BACK TO LONDON.

By forsaking the river and taking to the rail my return was accomplished in twenty-three days,

THE GATE OF OMDURMAN.

Photographed from Gunboat on the Nile.

RUINS OF THE MAHDI'S TOMB, OMDURMAN.

[To face p. 286.

THE PLEASURE OF TRAVEL. 287

while the outward journey took thirty-nine. The trip was rounded off by a little incident that called forth a humorous sketch. I reached home on the night of one of Dalgety Henderson's Bohemian concerts and was able to put in an appearance. G. R. Sims had taken the chair at my request and subsequently wrote:—

"Four months ago when this concert was arranged, Catling said to me, 'If you take the chair I will support you.' A couple of months later he went forth to the battle plains of Egypt, and in the distraction of travel, dates and other things were wiped off the mental slate. Sitting one afternoon in the courtyard of a high official of Khartoum, he picked up a paper which the official had left on the table. It was the *Referee*—The missing link in the chain of memory was instantly supplied. The wanderer in Khartoum remembered that on March 29 he had to be a Bohemian in London. He consulted authorities and ascertained that by travelling night and day he could just do it. He left Khartoum that night, and never halted or paused until at 7 o'clock on Thursday, March 29, he stepped out of the Continental Mail at Charing Cross. He left his luggage unclaimed in order to avoid delay with the Customs, dashed across London in a hansom, leapt with a harlequin bound into evening dress, sprang into the cab which he had kept waiting, and made his triumphal entry into Freemasons' Hall, exactly as the hour of nine was chiming from a neighbouring church. It was a grand deed—a splendid example of our proud boast that an Englishman's word is his bond. The brother soldier of the pen had travelled night and day, four thousand miles, to keep his appointment with DAGONET."

FRENCH GOOD-WILL TO ENGLISH VISITORS.

As the result of a visit to the Paris Exhibition of 1900 an opportunity was afforded of showing good-will towards the French people in a way that was at once warmly recognised. *L'entente cordiale* had not then been thought of, and it vexed me to find a London morning paper depreciating the Exhibition as "a failure." After glancing at a few features of the brilliant show my article said:

"Before starting, on my way, and in Paris, I had read and heard of ill-feeling towards English people. From first to last nothing of the kind was visible, nor did I meet with a single Englishman who spoke of anything but being received with the greatest courtesy and kindness. . . . An international Congress of Pressmen was meeting in the Exhibition, and nothing could have exceeded the efforts of M. Victor Taunay, and the French members associated with him, in welcoming journalists from all parts of the world."

This tribute to the nation and its truly great Exhibition, which appeared on the Sunday morning in London, was next day fully reproduced under the heading "Les Rapports Franco-Anglais" in *Le Matin*, of Paris.

SERVICE ON A CITY COMMITTEE.

New experiences of a very pleasant kind came with service on the Lord Mayor and Sheriffs' Committee for the City of London. It devolves on the Lord Mayor Elect to name twelve members, while the Sheriffs nominate six each. Alderman Frank Green was advancing to the civic chair; the Sheriffs already in office being Alderman Vaughan Morgan and Mr. (now Sir) Joseph Lawrence. The connection of the last-named with newspapers and printing led to my being invited to serve. Many meetings were held at convenient hours, easy-going methods prevailed, and everything passed off most pleasantly. The committee enjoys a great show of authority, but rarely departs from precedent, or resists the overruling influence of permanent officials. No matter how quaint may be the methods of the past, even to the verge of pantomime, they survive untouched by the manifold changes of centuries of progress. In the olden days of candles and torches, illuminating the Guildhall required such elaborate preparations that it was accompanied by a special "lighting-up dinner." Gas and electricity have rendered the work superfluous; the dinner still takes place.

Lord Mayor's Day is a costly business for the three citizens who share the expenses—half being paid by the Chief Magistrate, and the other half in equal portions by the two Sheriffs. Despite earnest efforts to economise, backed up by the examination of innumerable details, we found it impossible to carry out any appreciable retrenchment. If the forms, ceremonies, and hospitalities of a municipality so deeply rooted as the City of London are to be maintained a liberal outlay cannot be avoided. Though smoking is now freely indulged in at public dinners both great and small, tobacco remains barred at the Lord Mayor's banquet.

Seating the guests requires much deliberation, especially when royalties are present, and some curious tales were told by officials. Arriving rather late on one occasion, when the company had assembled, the old Duke of Cambridge looked down at the chair reserved for his use, then blurted out, "I'm d——d if I'm going to sit there." Explanations were tendered with all possible suavity; it took some little time to soothe the Duke, but in the end he gave way and took the vacant chair. On another occasion distinguished guests at the top table, finding themselves rather closely packed together, quietly pushed out a chair. Prince Henry of Battenberg, arriving soon after, could not find a seat in the place marked on the plan. No one moved, and he was compelled to appeal to an official. Every position had, of course, been assigned in strict order of precedence, and official authority was invoked to move the guests closer together so as to replace the chair. Turning round before he sat down the Prince said "Thank you; they are very cruel to me."

ONE MAN AMONG 2,000 WOMEN.

During a great conference of women-workers at Brighton in the autumn of 1900, I was specially anxious to secure some of the leaders as contributors. With that end in view a visit was paid to the famous seaside resort, and the preliminaries promised well. Lady Aberdeen displayed great interest in the idea, and when her ladyship was announced to read a paper I wanted to hear it. There was, however, a bar, as only women were to be admitted to certain specified meetings, and this was one of them. Naturally, it intensified my wish to be present. The first step needful was to buy a season ticket. Having allowed the meeting to begin, my daughter went up to the door and inquired of the lady on guard whether her father could be admitted. The response was, "Yes, if he has a ticket." Whereupon, I was promptly inside the Pavilion. Before a seat could be reached another charming young lady dashed up, exclaiming, "You mustn't come in here." My answer was simply, "But I am in; surely you won't turn me out." I promised to squeeze myself into the most obscure corner, and quickly secured a resting place against the outer wall. There I had the satisfaction and advantage of hearing several questions treated in a thoroughly practical manner. Two or three speakers aired ultra-sentimental views with regard to slum life, and were disposed to think that every ill in that direction could be removed by the State. Then up rose Mrs. Fawcett, and with clearness of thought and forcible expression scouted the idea. It rested with the women themselves, and not the State, to first deal with this slum question; an hour's good elbow work would suffice to transform many a slum tenement into a clean and wholesome dwelling room. On subsequent days I met a number of ladies concerned in the conference, and expressed a hope that forgiveness was accorded me for intruding into the meeting, where amid two thousand women I was the only man. "Oh, yes, I saw you," was the comment of each one.

THE PASSING OF QUEEN VICTORIA.

No incident throughout my career so deeply moved all classes of our far-reaching Empire as the passing away of Queen Victoria on the threshold of the twentieth century. Three days before the end Her Majesty, by living beyond the eighty-one years and two hundred and thirty-nine days of her grandfather, George the Third, became the oldest

Sovereign in English history. Then the record of the prolonged and glorious reign was overshadowed by death. An event of such import naturally aroused the energies of the Press, bringing out some of the best and worst features of modern journalism. One correspondent, dissociating himself from the throng around the gates, waited quietly in the office; he there heard the first intimation of the royal decease, and was enabled to despatch the momentous message to Fleet Street some minutes in advance of any of his colleagues. Personally, I wish to repeat most sincere thanks to the Venerable Archdeacon Sinclair for kindly coming to my aid on that occasion with a special sermon. A touching sketch of the Queen's life ended with this vivid sentence :—

"She left the world an example of a sweet, true, pure, wise and courageous woman, who guided an Empire to unparalleled heights of prosperity."

With the following week came the royal obsequies, carried out with stately dignity in the presence of a nation of mourners. From an Admiralty steamer I watched the solemn procession between lines of battleships from Cowes to Portsmouth. As the yacht bearing the Queen's remains moved over the water, nothing disturbed the calm serenity of the beautiful February afternoon save the hollow echoes of the minute guns and the puffs of smoke seen from each vessel as the firing proceeded along the line.

It may be permissible to record that the funeral number of *Lloyd's* reached a circulation of 1,462,202.

ALGERIA AND THE SAHARA.

Great historical events, both ancient and modern, were recalled by a tour from Tunis to Algiers. Though by no means fulfilling the promise of "Sunny Algeria," it presented a rare succession of novel scenes and natural wonders. As visions of Dido and Hannibal and Astarte arose, I stood appalled amid the long-buried ruins of Carthage, with only a church and a museum as evidences of life, where once flourished the greatest city of antiquity. Perched on its rocky height of nearly a thousand feet, Constantine is still a thriving place; Fort National (the pride of the Third Napoleon) remains a military station. In order to understand the Sahara, it is needful to remember that the desert is not an immense plain of loose sand, dotted here and there with green oases, but comprises two main divisions: one a rocky plateau, the other a vast depression of sand and clay. So far from being waterless, there are numberless springs and streams which flow in many parts, making them marvellously fertile. Shut in by mountains, the desert here and there rises high, and in other parts dips below the level of the sea. Biskra, with an elevation of a little over three hundred feet, lies in a happy medium position. It is here that the French have reared a new holiday city, "far from the madding crowd," with hotel and other arrangements that secure a fair amount of comfort. Close at hand is a veritable Garden of Eden, while an hour's drive into the desert enables a visit to be paid to Sidi Okba, the most original and strongest-smelling native village it has ever been my lot to encounter. In the English Church of Holy Trinity at Algiers I found a tablet to Mr. Edward Lloyd, in recognition of his being "the first to show the value of Alfa fibre for the manufacture of paper." There was a time when this esparto looked like becoming a source of permanent profit to the Spaniards; but the demand stopped on wood pulp coming into use. The most interesting excursion in the district was to the Trappist Monastery of Staouëli, where a hundred members of the antique fraternity were living in seclusion from all womankind. Their vow involves silence and abstinence from every kind of animal food. A richly-stocked poultry yard provoked inquiry, when it transpired that in cases of sickness many indulgences were permitted. At the entrance there was a "guest chamber," beyond which no female visitor was allowed to go; there they had to remain while the men were taken round by a kindly brother.

CORONATION OF EDWARD THE SEVENTH.

Precedent so largely governs Court ceremonials that it is always worth a journalist's while to look up any records of the past that may be available. When the coronation of King Edward the Seventh was finally fixed to take place on a Saturday, I decided to act as my own correspondent. History showed that great changes had taken place in respect to the three Sovereigns crowned in the nineteenth century. Despite the poverty of his country in 1821, George the Fourth resolved to outshine all previous monarchs. The King, with waving ostrich feathers surmounted by a black heron's plume, was enormously overdressed; and every part of the proceeding was overdone. At the close of the ceremonial in Westminster Abbey, before the disrobing was completed, the peers and privileged people darted away to Westminster Hall for the banquet. At the close a most startling scene was witnessed. The instant the King left there was a rush to the royal table, and a "general snatch" at the forks and spoons. Even the ornaments were broken up and appropriated in the wild scramble. In the national records the cost of this reckless orgy figures for a total of £243,000.

Ten years later William the Fourth abolished the banquet and was crowned at a cost of only £50,000. Victoria's coronation day was marked by popular rejoicings on all sides—a fair in Hyde Park, a royal procession through the streets, and fireworks—the expense whereof reached £70,000.

Coming so soon after the illness of the King, the crowning of Edward the Seventh and Queen Alexandra was followed with deep anxiety by the whole nation. Every effort was made to shorten the ceremonial without divesting it of historic pomp and pageantry. Repeated rehearsals helped to quicken the action, and by the abandonment of the sermon, with other changes, a full hour was saved. The gradual assembling of the brilliant throng within the ancient Abbey, the stately processions of King and Queen, the solemn religious rites, formed scenes of unequalled splendour and magnificence. When the entrancing music ceased, a moment of deep silence preceded the thrilling outburst from the excited assembly, "God save King Edward!" As the echoes resounded there came a blare of trumpets, the roll of many drums, and the sound of distant guns.

Of the grandeur of the spectacle there could be no question, but as I looked at the gorgeous adornment of the vestments of the clergy, archbishops, and bishops vying with each other, the feeling would creep in that they resembled George the Fourth in being "enormously overdressed." To meet the cost Parliament voted £100,000, and £70,000 for the entertainment of Indian Princes. There was later a supplementary vote of £25,000.

SEA TRIPS AND THEIR ATTRACTIONS.

While there is naturally great liking for the gigantic steamboats of modern days, many a small steamer, carrying only a very limited number of passengers, affords a vast amount of pleasure. One most enjoyable trip took in Gibraltar, the Moroccan ports of Tangier, Casa Blanca, Mazagan, Mogador, and the Canary Islands. Landing at each port afforded many glimpses of life and character. However familiar may be the description of a place, there is always something fresh to be discovered with one's own eyes. In another year I formed one of a small party bound for Malta and Alexandria. The stay in the latter port afforded time for a week's run to Cairo, and during the seven weeks' holiday there were forty fine days. One day claims a record for itself, as the steamer with engines going at half-speed was labouring in a heavy gale from early morning till after midnight. It was on the outward journey, just after a good crossing of the Bay of Biscay. Pitching and straining badly, as heavy, dangerous seas flooded the decks, the ship had to be kept with its head to the gale, making but thirty miles during the whole day. It was a time of trial and extreme discomfort, not free from danger; but no one of the dozen passengers showed the least trace of nervousness or anxiety. The trouble was soon over, leaving only a deeper impression of the skill, courage, and endurance of the officers and crew engaged in our merchant service.

MY CONTEMPT OF COURT.

Contempt of court has been developed into a powerful weapon for lawyers in this twentieth century. Its secret uses were recently condemned by high authorities in the *Times*. My experience would throw further light on the danger if the whole truth could be told; but that is too often the last thing sought after in a court of law. All through my life it was the constant endeavour, while doing one's duty to the paper and the public, to give law and lawyers as wide a berth as possible. It was entirely against my will that in 1903 I appeared in one of the High Courts, with several legal gentlemen engaged on my behalf, to "show cause why I should not be committed to prison for contempt of court." The alleged offence was publishing an article on a murder case. As the man was caught with a smoking pistol in his hand and said "I know quite well what I have done," the case was clear enough, and could not have been prejudiced by what was printed. The two Judges on the bench, however, would admit no mitigating plea. Their long harangues, which scared my daughters sitting at the back of the court into the belief that they were going to lose their father for a time, had the opposite effect on me. Such lectures I thought heralded dismissal with a reprimand; but that overlooked the one important aim of the law to secure costs. It was no great surprise to be fined fifty pounds and ordered to pay the costs.

Before their Lordships left the bench I took out a cheque book and prepared to write, whereupon the Master smilingly said, " This is a ready-money court, Mr. Catling." A friend had therefore to be called on to take the cheque across the street to the Union Bank. Pending his return I was conducted by the tipstaff, in company with my solicitor, to a private room below the court. It was small and scantily furnished. A black cat lay cosily coiled up in front of a fire, on which somebody's dinner was steaming in a stewpan. Bank notes were quickly brought back, handed over, and a receipt for the fifty pounds being given, the proceedings ended.

What of the prisoner whose case was declared to have been prejudiced? At his trial counsel adopted what the paper had said would probably be the plea. It was urged that at the time he committed the offence the man was insane and not responsible for his actions. The jury returned a verdict of manslaughter, and instead of being hanged, the prisoner was sent to penal servitude for twenty years. That was the public side, but by no means the whole story of my contempt of court.

THE CHARMS OF SOUTHERN SPAIN.

One of the prettiest round trips which Europe offers takes in many picturesque districts of Southern Spain. Starting from Algeçiras, on the bay of Gibraltar, the train runs through cork woods up to Ronda, the scene of numberless brigand exploits; thence Malaga on the Mediterranean coast and Granada, famous for all time for the richness of its Moorish ruins, are readily reached. Cordova rejoices in a cathedral of many columns; it was formerly a mosque second in its proportions and adornments only to the Kaaba of Mecca. Seville pleased me most; the April sunshine was as glorious as in Egypt, the air as warm and genial, without the sudden decline of temperature at eventide. The orange groves, radiant with golden fruit, seemed endless; on every side flowers in profusion made the gardens a succession of scenes of natural beauty. For the Semana Santa, or Holy Week, processions and ceremonies are provided on the most imposing scale; an attraction so great that hotel accommodation can only be secured far in advance, and then at double the ordinary rates. When Byron praised "Cadiz—sweet Cadiz" he was thinking of the allurements of its women. Spanish grace is still as undeniable as it is fascinating. Reared almost in the midst of the sea, the city occupies a position of unusual charm. Hotels and mansions faced with white marble give marked distinction to its squares and streets; but the unsavoury odours make me remember it as smelly Cadiz.

THE RELEASE OF MRS. MAYBRICK.

News was wont to travel very slowly in London. With the increasing demand for papers, and the multiplication of telegraph and telephone offices, facilities for gathering information have been enormously increased. Science and improvements in machinery have worked marvels for the Press; but even now occasional openings occur for human ingenuity. Nothing helps so much as a wide circle of good friends. It was a friendly message that pointed the way to a notable sensation at the beginning of 1904. Four days after the event there came this note:—" F. M——k went to a refuge last Monday, and not a paper has got hold of it yet." Definite as was the statement, the work of verifying this important item demanded delicate handling. Any attempt to put the question openly would have ruined the whole business; official answers on such occasions get as near to lying as makes no difference to the reporter. Ordinary rules had to be set aside to guard the secret; no outside aid could be invoked; yet it was imperative to secure confirmation from the prison. How and in what manner a trusty member of the staff carried his inquiries through need not be told. Suffice it that *Lloyd's* on Sunday made the first announcement of the release of Mrs. Maybrick on the previous Monday. The plain circumstantial statement so startled the Press that more than one important London daily paper obtained some sort of official authority for at first denying it. American correspondents who had been eagerly watching and waiting for the news were aghast. All the world knows that *Lloyd's* report proved to be true to the very letter.

LORD KELVIN'S KINDLY ACT.

There is a saying on the Riviera that "Men go to Nice to amuse themselves; to Cannes to be married; to Mentone to die." It is not the place that kills; you can have a very good time anywhere between Hyères and Bordighera. My stay at Mentone in 1904 was specially happy; at the Hôtel des Anglais I found a pleasant party—Sir Christopher Dyer, from Kew Gardens; Mr. Stewart, an ex-M.P.; Mr. Hamilton Edwards, the journalist; and Mr. Spencer, a friendly iron merchant, among them. Whist had not then given place to bridge; a quiet rubber shortened the evenings and led to many familiar talks. One day I was sitting with Mr. Stewart when Lord Kelvin arrived at the hotel. Much has been written of the frank and kindly face of our great scientific peer. Here surely was a kindly act, for at fourscore he had come over from Cap Martin expressly to see the old fellow-student whom he had not met for forty years. They sat in close converse for some time, and Mr. Stewart afterwards told me something of their boyhood days. When William Thomson moved from his birthplace in Belfast to Glasgow University he was only a little over ten years of age, but knew more mathematics than the other students of sixteen and upwards. All through life he combined sweetness of character with commanding knowledge, fully realising Huxley's saying, that " gentler knight ne'er broke a lance."

MY JUBILEE ON "LLOYD'S."

It was in the somewhat depressing calm of Ajaccio, near Bonaparte's birthplace, that meditation on my fifty years in Fleet Street began. The crossing from Nice to the small Mediterranean island was as comfortless as any twelve hours at sea could well be; while Corsica in no way fulfilled anticipations awakened by the poetry of Mrs. Barrett Browning, or the brilliant romance of Mr. Merriman. Neither "odorous valleys," "soft air," nor the wild figures of vendetta were encountered. Wandering freely about the little township—through squalid lanes as well as broad avenues and open squares—not a single armed man was seen. A journey of thirty miles by rail to Vizzavona, followed by rambles amid the pines in sight of the snow-clad summit of Monte d'Oro, the notorious bandit region of Bocognano, confirmed the peaceful impression of the population of what had long been known as "The Isle of Unrest." In defiance of the historic record of Madame Bonaparte's house being burnt, the room in which the future Emperor was born is still shown. Though the building, furniture, and surroundings have undoubtedly been changed, the locality in which the Corsican family grew up is one to awaken mixed memories of their after greatness and littleness.

Appended to a brief record of this holiday in the Riviera was the personal note:—

"With the issue for the present week I complete fifty years' work on *Lloyd's News*. As editor for the last twenty years it has been my happy privilege to see the paper constantly growing in favour with the public, and my fervent hope is to remain the faithful servant of the readers and the proprietors for some time longer."

Jubilee through the ages has been defined in various ways; always in association with rejoicing. I gratefully recall incidents of that happy time. One, in which my fellow-workers showed their kindness and good will, was thus reported by the *Westminster Gazette*:—

"Presentations to journalists, like those to other individuals, are, no doubt, common enough, but that of a Chippendale writing cabinet made to Mr. Catling on Tuesday was quite out of the ordinary, inasmuch as it was given by the editorial, composing, and reading staffs of *Lloyd's Weekly News*, in celebration of the Jubilee of Mr. Catling's connection with the paper, 'to mark their appreciation of his qualities as chief and friend.'"

Congratulations from my brother Savages came with the following letter from the esteemed Hon. Secretary:—

"MY DEAR CATLING,—The Committee of the Savage Club, taking advantage of an auspicious anniversary that has just occurred, desire to celebrate your long membership and service by entertaining you at dinner as the guest of the Club on Saturday, the 30th inst. George Byron Curtis has promised to preside, and only your consent is necessary to complete the arrangement. Let me offer my own congratulations to a dear old friend on attaining his professional half-century, and possessing the confidence and regard of more and more admirers with every year that passes. Yours, very sincerely, ED. E. PEACOCK."

Curtis, then editor of the *Standard*, presided over a large gathering of Savages and friends. Charles Morton, whom I had known from the early days of the Canterbury, telegraphed from the Palace Theatre :—

"Sincere congratulations to Mr. Catling on his Jubilee. He is catching me up fast, but I am determined to keep the lead."

An extract from *Lloyd's* records a still brighter episode :—

"The Editor was on Tuesday the recipient of a massive silver bowl bearing the inscription, 'Presented to Thomas Catling, Esq., by the proprietors of *Lloyd's News*, as a mark of friendship and esteem, and in grateful recognition of fifty years of devoted service to the paper, 1854—1904.' A graceful addition to the gift was a brooch— an opal set with emeralds and diamonds—for Mrs. Catling, the formal presentation being made at Mr. Frank Lloyd's Croydon residence. The guests included, besides Mr. and Mrs. Thos. Catling, Mr. and Mrs. Arthur Lloyd, Mr. Harry Lloyd, Mr. and Mrs. Alfred H. Hance, Mr. and Mrs. T. T. Catling, and Mr. F. W. Bayliss."

The kindness and generosity of Mr. Frank Lloyd and his brothers went far beyond the bowl, which is one of my cherished possessions. No words can adequately express the gratitude of myself and my family.

SIDELIGHTS ON THE SAVAGES.

The Savage Club, like so many British institutions, has grown from small beginnings to a great company. Aaron Watson and J. E. Muddock (Dick Donovan) having dealt with its history in two recent volumes, my jottings will be confined to incidents of a personal character. At the outset, as the members wandered from one tavern to another, it mattered little whether the subscription of five shillings was paid or not. Even when I entered the club, in its fifteenth year, there was considerable laxity. From the Gordon Hotel the Savages in 1874 removed to Evans's. It was there in the following year that the first organised attempt at an entertainment was made possible by the committee deciding to hire a piano. The annual dinner at the Criterion was another sign of expansion. Ash Wednesday was selected on account of the theatres being closed, thus enabling the dramatic members to attend. For the first time evening dress was demanded, despite severe protests from the ultra-bohemians. H. S. Leigh, author of "The Carols of Cockaigne," defiantly appeared in a frock-coat.

Since January, 1876, when I was appointed one of the honorary auditors, I have continued in office, being re-elected each year. Accounts of a very varied character have thus come under notice, the first being submitted by Charles Millward, most generous of treasurers, who could never find it in his heart to strike an old member off the roll. Millward might be designated as a many-sided man. While conducting a somewhat large business as a monumental mason, he wrote a number of pantomimes and contributed a weekly letter, full of bright gossip, to the Liverpool *Porcupine*. It was of Millward that H. S. Leigh told the rather cruel story of a visit one Sunday morning, when he found him sitting on a tombstone finishing a pantomime for the Adelphi. New quarters having been taken at Haxell's in the Strand for a rent of £300 a year, it became needful to keep a much closer eye on the receipts. Among the entries of the time is a note from Henry Irving promising to pay up his arrears at an early date. The obligation was faithfully discharged, and he remained a Savage to the end of his days, although he rarely visited the club.

American papers have contained accounts of the Prince of Wales's easy freedom in a velvet smoking suit, offering his cigar-case to whomever came in his way. Every statement of this character is pure invention. His Royal Highness first met the members at the twenty-fifth anniversary dinner in 1882. As the Prince entered Willis's Rooms he looked round with a smile of recognition, and then shook hands with Henry Irving, Sir Francis Truscott, Mr. Sydney Hall, and George Grossmith. After a few brief speeches had been made His Royal Highness was elected an honorary member. A varied entertainment was rattled through for a couple of hours; the company then, at a little after nine, adjourned to the Clubhouse in the Savoy. Before leaving the Prince said "he had rarely, if ever, spent so enjoyable an evening." In the following year another royal visit was paid to the club, when Mr. Melton Prior showed sketches and lectured on the Egyptian campaign. After taking supper the Prince presided over a smoking concert, when high-class music was plentifully sprinkled with comicalities: Charles Townley's "Moses and Aaron," and "A Bathe at Eastbourne" by J. E. Soden, greatly tickled the royal chairman. The club clock stopped, leaving the hours unmarked as they sped lightly away till midnight. As the cheers which greeted the recital of G. R. Sims's

"Lifeboat" by James Fernandez ceased, the Prince rose and said, "Brother Savages, if we stay all night I don't think we can improve upon what we have just heard; therefore we will adjourn."

A menu, headed by clasped hands holding the flags of England and France, reminds me of an international incident as far back as the summer of 1881. Somers Vine, who had been closely concerned in both visits of the Prince of Wales, carried through arrangements for a Savage Club reception at Boulogne. It was in every way successful, and did at least something to establish good relations between the two countries.

Some simple rhymes invite quotation because they express the real spirit of the club, and have been preserved on the menu used when Augustus Harris was in the chair.

> Here at this board each man's a brother,
>   And though our virtues may be few,
> Each does his best to help the other,
>   And be to Savage instincts true.
>
> Here men by work and worth we measure—
>   Each has his own appointed task—
> Pursuing pence for public pleasure,
>   With pen or pencil, lyre or mask.
>
> Though some would make the world ideal,
>   And only play the dreamer's part;
> We have to recognise the real
>   In this, our Brotherhood of Art.
>
> Without this union life would moulder;
>   But strong in concord let us stand,
> Bohemian braves, to shoulder, shoulder—
>   All workers in our Savage band!

As I look back over the records of the many true Savages with whom it has been my privilege to foregather, note the interest shown in the club by King George, as well as his royal father, and remember the illustrious visitors, a cordial echo must be given to the wish expressed on a recent occasion by Sir Charles Wyndham, "Long may the Savage Club continue to be a free royal exchange of thought and affection, where wit encounters wit, fancy stimulates fancy, and heart opens to heart."

A MARTYR OF THE LAW.

The story of Adolf Beck furnishes the most crushing condemnation of every branch of our legal administration, from the policeman on his beat, through the whole line of detectives, superintendents, experts, doctors, solicitors, counsel, up to the Home Office. Here was a man—an alien living in our midst—suddenly arrested on the word of a loose woman in the streets, hurried from court to court, tried and condemned to seven years' penal servitude. Frauds and thefts of the most mean and despicable character had been reported, but no single article was ever traced to Beck. An ex-policeman and certain women of the "gay" class were brought forward to swear to his identity, but others who declared that he was "not the man" were kept back. There was ample knowledge that the real culprit was a Jew; a single medical examination would have shown that Beck was not; the tainted evidence of the women was held to be sufficient, and he passed into penal servitude in 1896. During the weary heartbreaking years that followed, the unhappy prisoner never ceased to declare his entire innocence. Again and again his petitions were sent up to those in authority, but they never reached the Home Secretary.

Liberated in July, 1901, Beck made his unhappy case known to George R. Sims. Then commenced what judges and lawyers so violently condemn, Trial by Press. After many interviews and the careful sifting of Beck's whole story, I followed up the good work begun by Sims in an article showing that justice could only be reached by an official inquiry. Of course no one moved; Beck, however, continued to declare his profound faith that one day his innocence would be made known. When, a year later, he was again arrested for a similar series of robberies from women, his few friends were aghast and Authority triumphed. Yet something awakened a doubt in the mind of Justice Grantham; after Beck's second conviction in 1904 he deferred sentence until the next sessions. Before this arrived the actual perpetrator of all the mean thefts, dating back from 1877, had been arrested. Beck's entire innocence was then established beyond question. It is idle to call this a miscarriage of justice. After searching investigation the Government report said he "was convicted from evidence on which everything that told, or might be thought to tell, in his favour was excluded; his case was never tried." Despite the scathing condemnation, there followed the extraordinary recommendation that more lawyers were needed at the Home Office. A little common sense, inspired by a real desire for justice, would speedily have arrived at the truth. Happy in the clearing of his good name Beck cherished no bitterness, though the horrors of prison life could not be forgotten.

THE "HONOUR OF THE BAR."

Will lawyers ever try to live up to their boasted "honour of the Bar"? A distinguished statesman, speaking from inner knowledge, only the other day pronounced the Bar to be "the most dubious and disagreeable of all professions." Another authority says, "the one great principle of the English law is to make business for itself. There is no other principle distinctly, certainly and consistently maintained through all its narrow turnings." Dr. Johnson, in his first dictionary, defined justice as "the virtue by which we give to every man what is his due." It would be well if this could be inscribed in letters of gold over every judgment seat. When a French judge answered the appeal of a prisoner on trial for her life by saying "For the honour of the law I protest," he only acted in accordance with his legal training. Why is it that a man who conducts his own case is said "to have a fool for his client"? "Counsel do not ask questions for the benefit of the jury" was said in court quite recently; and complaints of "inaccuracies in summing up" are growing painfully prevalent in appeal cases. Too many judges are only lawyers on a higher level, requiring to be reminded that justice is demanded from them. When a county court judge makes the open avowal "I have often won cases that never ought to have been brought," he shows how much is wanting. A lawyer proved to have supported a speculative action with exaggerated and absolutely false statements escaped with a judicial lecture that turned the whole proceedings into a farce for all save the unfortunate defendants who had to pay the costs.

According to a Scotch barrister there is "a code of honour among adulterers" as well as thieves. "What is honour?" asked Falstaff dubiously. "A word. What is that word, honour? Air. A trim reckoning ... I'll none of it, honour is a mere scutcheon." Personally I have no legal grievance whatever; but looking at the matter from a literary side, there is a temptation to remind lawyers of Lady Teazle's query to Joseph Surface, "Don't you think we may as well leave honour out of the argument?"

THE AUTHOR OF "MOSES AND AARON."

Charles Townley (the Geoffrey Thorn of later days) began his career as reporter on the *Islington Gazette*, when Sir Edward Russell was writing leaders and preparing for the wider journalistic flight which has carried him to honour and fortune in a provincial town. As Charles developed, his versatility stood in the way of any marked success in one direction. We met on the *Hornet*, when he was scribbling comic biographies of classic heroes, directing the make-up of the paper, and showing a French artist the kind of caricature portraits required for London. In this his preliminary sketch was often more effective than the Frenchman's drawing; but there was no demand for such work. Making sure of bread and butter from journalism, Townley wrote several comic songs, "Moses and Aaron" proving a great hit. Geoffrey Thorn was assumed as a stage name when pantomimes were turned out for several theatres year after year. Townley (who had acquired local celebrity by his writing as "The Merry Villager") meanwhile kept his eyes open for any appointment that might be going in Islington. At length he became superintendent registrar, which insured a comfortable income. Charles, however, remained faithful to his first love, and stuck to journalism to the last. As a traveller I do not think he ever went beyond Margate. The sketch which is reproduced came in a letter, and gives his original idea of the Alps.

THE ST. PETERSBURG MASSACRE.

The Czar's "Bloody Sunday" in St. Petersburg enabled me to give a forcible illustration of the advantages of electricity for newspaper purposes. Fifty years previously it took ten days for news to struggle through from the Crimea; in 1905 messages from the Russian capital reached London in as many minutes. Anticipating trouble, I arranged with Reuter's Agency for a series of special telegrams during the day. By this means a full story of the savage massacre was presented in an extra edition of the paper. In point of time St. Petersburg is rather more than two hours ahead of

GEOFFREY THORN'S IDEA OF THE ALPS.

[To face p. 312.

London. As the chief firing took place between eleven and four in the day, by five o'clock *Lloyd's* had three columns of telegrams in type. No other paper made an effort, and the special edition, with its exclusive account of the sanguinary scenes, created a deep impression. Street sellers in the calm of Sunday evening met people coming out of church, and found a ready sale. A friend told me that he watched one man in Islington, who gradually advanced the price as his limited stock diminished. From twopence the paper went to fourpence and then sixpence; all sold readily. As the man pocketed the last coin he leant against a lamp-post, and a tear was in his eye. Was he mourning over the fact that such a profitable line of goods had come to an end, or lamenting his lack of courage in not speculating in another quire?

MY GREAT LOSS.

Truer friend than John Northcott never fell to the lot of man. When we first met both were commencing a newspaper career. As time rolled on the struggle which gives such interest to the Battle of Life served to draw us closer together. Our several duties at first lay wide apart; that mattered not, for the friendship was as real as it was enduring. Northcott's gentle nature more than atoned for my rougher character. The course of events ultimately made us fellow-workers in the same firm; and in Masonry and Club life we were together. Through all the companionship was a delightful experience for both. No shadow rests upon the memory of this good and true companion of my early manhood. His sudden breakdown and gradual fading away proved a loss so bitter that even now I dare not trust myself to write upon it. The sorrow is too deep for words.

IRVING—THE MAN AND THE ACTOR.

It was at the bar of the old Albion tavern, hard by Drury Lane, that I first gripped the kindly hand of Henry Irving. From the time that we there clinked the homely pewter, and pledged each other in a draught of ale, a friendly confidence drew us together on many occasions.

The greatness that came to Irving later did not spoil him in the least, nor mar his deeply-sensitive nature. A wonderful glimpse of that sensitiveness, illustrated in so many generous ways, was afforded during a charming day with him at Margate. Talking of his early years, Irving recalled that when quite a small boy he was sent from London to stay with his Aunt Penberthy at Hayle, in Cornwall. Having had sixpence given him, he bought a smart whip, and on arriving ran merrily up to his aunt, showing his new treasure. Mrs. Penberthy (who had a small boy of her own), instead of displaying the least sign of pleasure, said sharply, "You might have bought Johnny one." So deeply was Irving's gentle heart stung by this utterance that he never forgot it. Though more than half a century had elapsed, there was a painful break in his voice as he told me the simple story.

Sir Henry's small dinner parties were arranged with the most thoughtful regard for his guests, and

8 January 1905
17, STRATTON STREET,
PICCADILLY. W.

Dear Hiram Corning —

Greetings & every good wish.

I should be delighted if you could give me the pleasure of your company to Dinner at the Reform Club on Sunday next — 15th at a ¼ to Eight. All old friends.

Sincerely yrs
Hy Irving.

he wrote the letters of invitation. In January, 1905, Clement Shorter, J. M. Bulloch, Nicol Dunn, Austin Brereton, and George Spencer Edwards were present at the Reform Club. One of the number, through fear of gout, dare not touch the port, which the host had specially selected. The old English waiter paused before pouring it out, as with bated breath he whispered " '47." This led Sir Henry, in a tone of gentle remonstrance, to exclaim, " Never mind its age, give us some wine."

On his return from a holiday—the longest he had ever taken—early in September of the same year, I spent several hours in Stratton Street. Before, during, and after lunch Irving went over many details of his career without the least reserve. Reaching London the day before by the Great Eastern Railway, he walked through Old Broad Street, and said he looked round the spot where his parents lived, and he first began to labour. I introduced this fact into the sketch prepared for the commencement of his jubilee year, but Sir Henry struck it out in the proof, with the comment, " Not worth mentioning—only five weeks and no salary." Throughout the interview it became painfully apparent that the strong man was breaking down. Through life he had enjoyed excellent health. On one occasion I heard Toole say, " Nothing is ever the matter with Irving." Being asked the cause of Northcott's death I said " Heart trouble." Irving, although showing signs of continuous suffering, repudiated the idea that anything was wrong with his heart. " They call it emphysema," he said, in reference to his own difficulty in breathing. Whatever may have been the inward suffering, he bore it bravely and without flinching to the end.

Much has been written concerning early predictions of the actor's future greatness, but no authority can be found for them. Mrs. Calvert has recently told the truth clearly by saying, "Irving was just a pleasant, intellectual young man, with no special suggestion of power." Talking of the Vaudeville days at my last interview, he said several bookmakers were hovering about the new theatre. One of them asked his assistance in sending a son to Marlborough College, and Irving wrote to the headmaster. The introduction proving successful, the grateful bookmaker offered to build the actor a theatre; but, said Irving, "the thought of becoming a manager, much less a theatrical proprietor, had never entered my head. All I looked for was a good engagement, with the best salary to be had." Yet the turning point of his career was to come within a year. While *Two Roses* was running, and he was regarded as a comedian, his thoughts aspired to tragedy. To test his powers he one Sunday evening startled a theatrical gathering by seating himself in a chair and reciting "The Dream of Eugene Aram." James Albery was of the party, and he created amusement by wanting to know what became of the boy referred to in Hood's poem. There was much after-talk concerning the recital, and its repetition at a public benefit performance deepened the impression. Still, no one imagined what was in the player's mind. His pursuit of Colonel Bateman for an engagement at the Lyceum looked like a gigantic blunder; and when he found his opportunity with the performance of *The Bells* its success came as a profound surprise to the manager and every member of the company.

Of Irving's subsequent career and the strenuous labours by which he became head and front of the stage it is unnecessary to say anything here. He not only delighted the audiences of Britain and America, but won their affection and admiration by the sweetness and charm of his manner. Old friends were never forgotten, and in private converse he displayed far more modesty than usually pertains to the profession. The difficulties which had to be overcome for his make-up as Napoleon in *Madame Sans-Gêne* he described in a way that created roars of laughter. Discussing Shakspere one evening, he said to me with evident consciousness of deep meaning, "I can't play Othello." In 1879, at the close of Chippendale's benefit performance, I made my way to Irving's dressing-room with the view of getting a few reminiscences from the old actor. He admitted it was true that he carried proofs from Sir Walter Scott to his printers, but would add no word of explanation. He had taken his farewell, and wished to have nothing further to do with the stage. It would please him best not to be reminded of it in any way, here or hereafter. "What!" said Irving, "you don't mean to say that you won't let them hear you in the next world! Why, if they'll only let me go on playing Hamlet I shall be happy." That sentence revealed the real feeling of the man. In opposition to all the advice of his relatives, and despite the chilling comments of friends, he had resolved to devote his life to acting. It was no mere

LYCEUM RECEPTIONS.

choice of a profession. His whole nature thrilled with the desire of embodying dramatic ideals, and every thought was devoted to studying the means by which success could be won. His inner meaning found expression later when in lecturing he said:—

"How engrossing the fascination of those steady eyes, and sound sympathies, and beating hearts which an actor confronts as he steps upon the stage to work out in action his long-pent comprehension of a noble masterpiece! How rapturous the satisfaction of abandoning himself, in such a presence and with such sympathisers, to his author's grandest flights of thought and noblest bursts of emotional inspiration!"

The receptions which followed memorable nights at the Lyceum were the most fascinating ever held in a theatre. When they fell on Saturday nights, it was needful for me to get my notice completed and in print before joining the party. Though this made me late, it meant freedom to stay to the finish and enjoy the merry talk and contrast of experience in which Irving, Toole, and a small coterie of intimates delighted. It was indeed a time to "sip the foam of many lives." William Tinsley in his "Recollections" thus refers to one such scene, after the hundredth performance of *The Merchant of Venice*:—

"I stayed until about four o'clock in the morning, and then left with my old friend, Mr. W. S. Johnson, for his house in Regent's Park, and after a gossip there for a time, made my way to King's Cross to catch the first train for home. On my way I purchased a copy of the Sunday morning edition of *Lloyd's News,* and found that it contained a list of the guests and reports of most of the speeches that I had heard spoken less than three hours before on the Lyceum stage."

A more singular incident comes to my mind of

an early morning in 1883, just prior to Irving's departure for America. The huge gathering had melted away and only a few of us were left. As we moved towards the private entrance in Burleigh Street someone whispered "There's some girls there." No notice was taken of this, but directly Mr. Irving appeared in the open doorway three or four young women exclaimed simultaneously "God bless you, Mr. Irving!" then darted away as fast as their legs could carry them. Inquiry confirmed the belief that they were thoroughly respectable folk, who, moved by simple admiration, had waited for several hours after midnight just to catch a last glimpse of the favourite actor and bid him God-speed on his journey to the great Republic.

It may be well to anticipate inquiries respecting these and other festive entertainments on the part of managers by saying they were not accepted without question. At a very early period Joseph Knight discussed it with me, and it was agreed that if you were on such terms of personal friendship with a manager or actor as would entitle you to offer him hospitality in a club, there need not be any harm in your being a guest in his theatre. Such courtesies did not lead to corruption or undue influence. An opportunity of showing this occurred during the dark days of 1899, when a few pressmen had the gratification of arranging a little outing for Sir Henry and his two stalwart managers. The party foregathered in my home, when I was able to call attention to a bust by Mr. Jackson sent me in 1875. "Ah," said Sir Henry, "they used to tell me that was a capital piece of work and a good likeness." A set of the "Irving Shakspere," which I had received from his collaborateur, Frank Marshall, also attracted his notice, and therein he inscribed his name. From Brixton a couple of open carriages drove us round the heights of Norwood to the Queen's Hotel, and there at an oval table we sat down—Sir Henry, Bram Stoker, Henry Loveday, Richard Butler, G. Spencer Edwards, I. Seaman, John Northcott, and myself. All formality was abandoned, and it had been arranged that though the board blazed with flowers, there should be nothing higher than the cruet. So we faced each other; the talk of that delightful evening, overflowing with anecdotes and brightened by manifold experiences, becoming general. The fleeting hours sped only too rapidly, but the impression left by the gathering was one of deep satisfaction to the journalists who had the honour of acting as hosts.

Why actor-managers should be so widely condemned has always been a puzzle to me. Surely Phelps's eighteen years at Sadler's Wells ranked with the greatest Shaksperean events of the nineteenth century. Charles Kean's record at the Princess's must also be given a conspicuous place. Both worked with untiring zeal and for limited salaries. In my last talk with Irving the question of salary arose, and he told me that at one period he offered Mr. Forbes Robertson an engagement at three thousand pounds a year; but that actor was not able, owing to other arrangements, to accept it. Charles Kean's private account-book was in Irving's possession, and it showed that thirty pounds per week was all that was put down for his salary; a similar sum being allotted to Mrs. Kean.

Then, as now, salary was a momentous consideration. I remember dear old Mrs. Keeley telling me that the happiest day of her life was when her daughter came to say she had been engaged for the Haymarket for the same salary as herself—twenty pounds a week.

A GRAND RECEPTION IN AUSTRIA.

Soon after the opening of the Austrian Travel Bureau in Piccadilly, an excursion to Vienna proved too tempting to be resisted. When Bonaparte crossed the Alps in mid-winter all the world wondered; here was an offer to breakfast in London and dine the next day in the beautiful capital of Austria. The journey of a little over eleven hundred miles was memorable for its many-sided views by the way. Once within the Alpine region every peak, from the lowest foothill to the higher ranges, many thousands of feet above, was snow covered. Adown the slopes the dark green leaves of myriads of pine trees were flecked with white, while nature's mantle shrouded the deep valleys. The city, with half-melted snow dropping from roof tops and blocking the roadways, was at a disadvantage; but the warm welcome of the Austrians made amends for all. Ours was a pleasant little party, consisting mainly of Press folk, with Mrs. Humphry and her daughter Pearl (now Mrs. Adams) as the chief ladies. Dr. Karl Lueger, the famous burgomaster, led the way with a dinner at the Rathaus, which equalled any royal reception it has been my lot to witness at home or abroad. Friendly speeches were exchanged, and before leaving I was handed a letter, which being translated ran thus:—

"Allow me to inform you that at the ball of the Town of Vienna I shall introduce you to His Imperial Highness Prince Ferdinand. I beg of you, therefore, to appear in time in the ball-room with the secretary, Dr. Rudolf Bibl, who has to arrange the presentation. With the expressions of the highest esteem I sign myself yours, KARL LUEGER, Burgomaster."

This ball, given in aid of the poor of the city, is a great event of the year. For it the vast hall, which accommodated thousands of people, was richly adorned; each staircase and landing being transformed into a garden of choice flowers. On a central dais were grouped the wives of ambassadors and ladies of the nobility. The Archduke Ferdinand (heir to the throne) represented the Emperor. After watching an opening dance, the Prince addressed himself to each lady in succession; and then received those whose names had been passed for presentation. In an affable and pleasant way he said he was glad to welcome an Englishman who had been led to visit Austria and see something of the country for himself.

The more I saw the greater seemed the charm, as Semmering, Salzburg, Innsbruck, Botzen, Meran, Trent, Rovereto, Arco, and Riva came under notice. Historically famous, the Semmering Pass is an ideal mountain resort. Resting some three thousand feet above sea level it remains throughout the winter covered in snow, which neither falls nor scatters after the manner of the heavy flakes known in England. For the most part there is an absence of wind, and then it is a delight to be out in the sun, breathing the pure air, watching the sports, or admiring the moving and wonderful pictures that burst upon the sight at every turn. One morning, when a gentle breeze blew lightly on the outer edge of pines, the frozen snow was wafted softly away in a glittering shower of icy gems. The thermometer registered twenty degrees of frost; yet it did not strike cold either when bustling about on foot or being driven swiftly over the snow-covered roads in sleighs.

The railway history is of peculiar interest, since it dates back to 1854, when the Emperor Francis Joseph (then a young man of four-and-twenty) made the first trip on the line. It was the earliest mountain railway in the world, and as such continues to be the special pride of Austrian engineers. The winding track involved the building of 15 tunnels, 16 viaducts, and 129 bridges : yet the work, which occupied six years in completion, was so effectually carried out that the line is still in excellent condition, after fifty years' heavy traffic.

TRACING LONG-LOST RELATIVES.

Inquiries for long-lost relatives, which brought many family romances to light, grew out of a pathetic occurrence in America. A young Englishman going into a small town was accidentally drowned on the day after his arrival. On overhauling his effects a local photographer found two portraits, one of an elderly woman. With the kindly intention of discovering the dead man's relatives, he copied these photographs and sent them to *Lloyd's*. What followed was told in the next issue :—

"Last week there appeared a brief account of the drowning of a young Englishman, sent us by Mr. Wheeler, photographer, of Richford, Vermont, United States. There was no clue to his identity, save that he had stated the night before that his name was Henry Preston, and spoke of living near Holborn, London. After the lapse of two-and-a-half years from the fatal occurrence on June 28th, 1874, Mr. Wheeler wrote begging us to publish particulars for the sake of easing the minds of his friends, if possible, and enclosing copies of two worn photographs. The letter was printed in *Lloyd's* on Sunday, and Monday morning brought the sorrowing mother of deceased to our office with facsimiles of the portraits. The young man had been in America for about a year before his death, the sudden news of which was a great grief to his mother and other relatives. But they expressed their heart-felt thanks to the American gentleman who took so much kindly trouble to send the information."

Towards the end of the same year came a letter from Chatham Island, New Zealand. The writer, who signed his name William Adams, described himself as an orphan boy between fourteen and fifteen, and asked for help to find his step-mother. He said, "I was born in Keninton (*sic*), and my own mother died when I was very young. After the death of my mother my father married a woman named Mrs. Scott, who was very good to me." From the rest of the letter it appeared that there were seven in family, and after a time husband and wife fell out and separated, the father taking the young boy away with him to New Zealand. Mr. Adams was accompanied by a woman, who ill-treated the lad, and he ran away from them in Auckland. This inquiry was speedily answered by the step-mother and sister of the orphan boy.

Another inquiry was received in the following year from Calvinia, South Africa. The writer said, "Would Mr. David W. Adams, who resided at 35, Upper John Street, Hoxton, like to hear of his eldest son that left in the ill-fated barque Verulam? Not having heard of my family since 1871, I am very anxious." This was signed "S. Aubrey Adams." Relatives in London promptly came forward, and it was subsequently discovered that this S. Aubrey Adams was brother to the William Adams who wrote from New Zealand with the view of discovering his step-mother.

As years passed inquiries became so numerous that it was resolved to make them a regular feature. From the first, the motive was sympathetic, nothing being charged for inserting inquiries. Many of the leading Colonial papers rendered assistance by generously reprinting inquiries.

Again and again relatives were brought into touch with one another after long periods of silence. An Ealing resident sought for news of his brother, whom he had not heard of for sixty-two years and believed to be dead. The emigrant was in reality living at Condobalin, New South Wales.

Another remarkable inquiry, contained in a letter from Toronto, ran thus:—

"It was my misfortune when an infant to be kidnapped about the year 1858 from a very highly respectable family living somewhere near Manchester. The people I was brought up with emigrated to Toronto. I was always led to believe I was their son. In 1902, when my adopted father was on his death-bed, he motioned me to him, and then said: 'You are not my son. Your name is——.' A violent fit of coughing seized him, and in a few minutes he had passed away, carrying the secret with him to the grave."

Through the publication of this letter the writer's relatives were found.

Two sisters who had vainly sought each other for thirty years proved to be living less than a mile apart in London, and a brother and sister, after hunting for each other for thirty-five years, discovered that they were separated, not by a continent, but by the distance from St. George's Road, Southwark, to Edmonton.

A Staffordshire man made inquiry for three brothers, and news came that all were living within twenty miles of Sunderland. And forty years had elapsed since the four met!

A woman inquired for her brother who left home in 1891 and of whom nothing had been heard since. Long after a letter was received from the man. Writing from New Zealand, he said that he had returned to England in 1894, 1896, and a few years subsequently, and made futile efforts to discover his relatives. One day, when in the heart of the New Zealand bush, a mate of his came to stay in the camp, bringing with him some books and old newspapers, including a copy of *Lloyd's*. While the long-lost brother was reading the jokes in that paper he was called to assist in gathering some firewood. When he returned, and was trying to find the place where he had left off reading, he saw his name in the next column.

A clerk in the post office corresponded concerning

a brother, a civil engineer, who eleven years before had emigrated to New York. The writer stated that the missing relation was devoted to violin-playing. A few months afterwards the brother in London received the violin from a farmer in Wisconsin. The player had been unfortunate, taken to itinerant playing, and had died in the house of the farmer, who said he had not the heart to keep a family relic.

THE SADNESS OF FAREWELL.

Like most changes in my Pilgrimage, retirement came suddenly. The strain of many years had weakened my health, and the offer of rest under most kindly conditions was made in so generous a spirit as to command ready acceptance. As was said in my farewell address, however, "After long association with the ever-growing power and advancement of *Lloyd's News*, it is impossible to pass from the manifold activities of editorial life without more than common sadness." I could but tender most sincere and heartfelt thanks to the proprietors, to the army of distinguished authors who had been contributors, to my loyal fellow-workers on the paper, and to the wide circle of pressmen who had dealt so generously with my career. After serving for nearly fifty-three years, my labours on *Lloyd's* were brought to an end on the last day of 1906.

SEVENTH STAGE.

RETIREMENT AND REFLECTION.

From My Fellow Workers—Welcome from the Whitefriars—Dinner at the Trocadero—First Days of Rest in Rome—Bosnia and Herzegovina—The Art of Deception—A Great Writer's Sad Career—Friends Among the Doctors—Press Congress in Berlin—Help for the Journalists' Orphans—Seeing the Midnight Sun—In the Depths of a Mine — A Run Through Portugal — Looking Back — A Few Black and White Artists—Theatres and the Press—The Journalistic Calling.

To be freed by the striking of the last hour of 1906 from all necessity for further labour was an experience so novel as almost to bewilder the mind. The meaning of my whole life had been looking forward—ever forward. Though the frame was weakened, the brain still beat steadily, making it impossible to sit down suddenly and feel that the working days of my Pilgrimage were over. Though associations with the office had come to an end, the influences around were of the most soothing character. Mr. Frank Lloyd closed a long letter by saying:—

"Let me wish you and yours a very happy New Year, and thank you from the bottom of my heart for your devoted services to *Lloyd's*; for the kindness and real consideration which has always characterised your relations with every member of the family, and, for the matter of that, with every member of the staff, and with all who have been brought into contact with you through a lifetime. The severance of our intimate business relations is a real grief to me, but I earnestly hope that a trip into summer climes and a cessation of active business will greatly help your health, and that I may long have the pleasure of claiming you as one of my oldest and truest friends. Yours ever sincerely, FRANK LLOYD."

One other expression of good will may find a place:—

"MY DEAR TOM CATLING,—I feel that I must write at once and let you know how sincerely I hope that you are carrying with you into the well-earned leisure you have decided to enjoy a plentiful stock of health and good spirits. God bless you, old friend, and keep you hale and happy in your 'otium cum dignitate' for many a long day to come. Don't go round the world all at once. We shall want to see you at frequent intervals, to keep the legend of good fellowship in Fleet Street blowing among the chops and steaks, to say nothing of the tobacco-smoke. Yours always sincerely and gratefully, GEO. R. SIMS."

FROM MY FELLOW-WORKERS.

With the dawn of the New Year there came a touching tribute from my fellow-workers, who assembled at St. Bride's Institute to say farewell and to make a presentation of silver. Mr. Neil Turner, the manager, presided, and in the course of a sympathetic speech said they "viewed my retirement with genuine sorrow and unfeigned regret." He then read the address:—

"THOMAS CATLING, Esq. Dear Sir and Friend,—On the occasion of your retirement as the honoured and distinguished Editor of *Lloyd's Weekly News*, after fifty-two years of ungrudging and unceasing service, we felt it impossible to let you go from us without some recognition of the appreciation and esteem in which you are held by every worker, from the

RETIREMENT AND REFLECTION. 331

highest to the lowest, connected with the paper. As a result we now ask you to accept this Address and the Piece of Plate with which it is accompanied. In offering it we cannot forbear pointing out that under your able direction, in the face of enormous opposition, *Lloyd's News* has so steadily grown in influence and circulation that it now occupies the premier position amongst the weekly newspapers of the world. Such a result must naturally fill you with pride and satisfaction when you reflect upon it, and we are proud to have been associated with you in its attainment. We bid you a regretful good-bye, and heartily assure you that in leaving us you carry with you our most sincere and affectionate regard. Live long; enjoy your well-earned rest; and the blessing of God be with you. Jan. 1, 1907."

A few words from W. E. Church and Stuart Robertson, with my earnest thanks, ended the talk. In shaking hands with James Jagelman, the energetic chief of the composing room, and the others present, I found only one (Alfred Mead) who had worked shoulder to shoulder with me picking up type.

WELCOME FROM THE WHITEFRIARS.

From the other side of Fleet Street came a touching and kindly invitation to become an honorary member of the Whitefriars Club. As the brotherhood includes a large number of leading journalists, the tribute was specially pleasing to one who years before had regretfully retired through failing health. Some club notes remind me that "among the early Friars were Tom Hood, William Sawyer, Joseph Knight, Barry Sullivan, Thomas Archer, Ashby Sterry, Godfrey Turner, William Black and Charles Gibbon." Of these good Fleet Street penmen, whom I knew so well, only Ashby

Sterry remains. The long-time secretary, J. Farlow Wilson, bearing the burden of eighty years, is the dignified father of the body. Next in my love and remembrance stands William Senior, from whom I hope one day to have a lesson in golf. The club now includes men like Sir Carruthers Gould, Clement Shorter, Arthur Spurgeon, and Sir William Robertson Nicoll; with a long array of other earnest workers in literature, science, and art. A night with the Friars, when they are entertaining a distinguished guest, is an occasion of great and lasting interest.

DINNER AT THE "TROCADERO."

Of the wider tribute from journalistic friends it is difficult for me to write in adequate terms; refuge must therefore be found in quotation. The committee comprised:—

"Lord Burnham (*Daily Telegraph*), the Chairman; Lord Glenesk, *Morning Post;* Lord Northcliffe, *Daily Mail;* Sir William Treloar, Lord Mayor; the Hon. Harry Lawson, *Daily Telegraph;* Mr. Frank Lloyd, *Daily Chronicle* and *Lloyd's News;* Mr. John Boon, Exchange Telegraph Company; Mr. W. F. Bradshaw, Reuter's Agency; Mr. Richard Butler, *Referee;* Mr. A. G. Gardiner, *Daily News;* Mr. Arthur Lloyd, *Daily Chronicle* and *Lloyd's News;* Mr. Harry Lloyd, *Daily Chronicle* and *Lloyd's News;* Mr. John M. Le Sage, *Daily Telegraph;* Mr. W. T. Madge, *People;* Mr. John Moore, Central News; Mr. Ernest Parke, *Morning Leader;* Mr. Edward E. Peacock, *Morning Post;* Mr. C. Arthur Pearson, *Standard;* Mr. S. J. Pryor, *Tribune;* Mr. George A. Riddell, *News of the World;* Mr. E. Robbins, Press Association; Mr. William Senior, *Field;* Mr. G. Stole Thomas, *Daily Graphic;* Mr. J. E. Woolacott, Chairman of the London District Institute of Journalists; and Mr. Robert Donald, *Daily Chronicle* (hon. treasurer)."

RETIREMENT AND REFLECTION.

At the outset a wish was expressed that the testimonial should take the form of a presentation portrait, painted by a distinguished artist, and first shown at the Royal Academy Exhibition. In accord with this desire I called at the abode of Mr. Sargent, but the artist was out, and not expected back for some time. The walk home led to the abandonment of any idea of a picture. I found that a little gathering was looked for, to secure which a request was made that Lord Burnham would agree to a dinner, and honour the company by presiding. His lordship's ready assent drew together a memorable company at the "Trocadero." The House of Commons was represented by Mr. Henniker Heaton and Mr. T. P. O'Connor; art by Sir James Linton and Yeend King; the drama by Bram Stoker and Harry Nicholls; science by Gordon Salamon; the City by the Lord Mayor. In a delightful speech, Lord Burnham proposed my health. Looking to a newspaper record, I find that my reply closed with the following passage :—

"In the name of my wife, who will be charmed with the artistic and beautiful service of plate that I am taking home to her, of my daughters, who, I believe, even now are delighting themselves with the music of the new piano, and myself, I have to thank you, my lord, Mr. Frank Lloyd, and all my friends, for your overwhelming kindness—a kindness to which I can lay no claim whatever, but which will never be forgotten by me, and, I believe, will live long in the journalistic memory of Fleet Street."

The *Daily Telegraph* said truly : " The musical portion of the programme, which was arranged by Mr. Landon Ronald, was of superlative merit.

The artists were Mr. John Coates, Mr. Jean Gerardy, Mr. Harold Bauer, Mr. D. Ffrangcon Davies, Dr. F. Byrd Page, Signor Costoleri, and Mr. Frederick Upton." Pressmen to this day assert that the banquet provided by Joseph Lyons was one of the choicest and most dainty they ever sat down to.

FIRST DAYS OF REST IN ROME.

As the most hopeful way of beginning the new life, without any settled duties, my steps were turned abroad. It was a pleasant task to take my two youngest daughters to spend Easter in Rome. Under the glorious Italian sky we rambled round the many points of special interest which the Eternal City offers; extended our tour to Florence and Venice, revelling in the artistic treasures of both cities. As we grow older we are driven to number our friends by the mournful record of those that are lost. During the week in Rome the *Times* brought me a double grief. First I read that my brother James, who was present at the farewell dinner, had passed away; next that Alfred Hance, the manager with whom I had worked for over thirty years, was dead. While slowly recovering from a serious illness he had been cruelly assaulted and robbed within sight of his own door; the shock proving too severe for his enfeebled frame. An inquiry being demanded, the verdict was "murder by some person or persons unknown." Truly a grievous end for one who had striven to lead a gentle life, avoiding injury to a single fellow creature.

BOSNIA AND HERZEGOVINA.

Within a month of my return there came a fresh temptation. When Bosnia was first mentioned for a holiday tour friends were disposed to be more jocular than helpful; and the addition of Herzegovina upset all seriousness. Quoting a recent traveller's description of these provinces as " Savage Europe," some offered presents of deadly weapons, while others suggested increased life insurance. Nothing of the kind was needed. Under Austrian rule the two provinces, so long misgoverned by Turkey, have been won over to civilisation, without displacing the native population. Situated on both banks of the Miljacka river, and enclosed on three sides by lofty mountains, the city of Serajevo presents an imposing appearance. The heights and hilly parts are mainly occupied by Mahometans, who have nearly a hundred mosques, while the Christian inhabitants have settled in solid buildings reared in the lower parts of the town. Besides ample provision for elementary education, there are art schools and technical institutions of a thoroughly practical kind. Ancient and modern costumes appeared strangely mixed in the street life. Top-hats were worn alongside the fez; some women covered their faces, and wore full baggy Turkish trousers, while others were quietly dressed in European costumes such as might be worn any day in Regent Street. Mostar, the capital of Herzegovina, though less advanced, shows signs of moving in every direction that makes for peace. This was the aim of Lord Salisbury when at the Berlin Conference he proposed placing Bosnia and

Herzegovina under the control of Austria. How well the mandate had been obeyed was apparent to the English party with which I travelled over the State railways from the Adriatic.

THE ART OF DECEPTION.

From early boyhood conjuring always had a great fascination for me. I derived additional amusement from watching the growth of particular tricks; an extinguisher used by a conjurer named Jacobs would now appear the clumsiest contrivance for the disappearing trick. Professor Anderson's early use of electricity in table-rapping feats was recalled by the death of Charles Bertram in 1907. When I first knew Bertram he was practising card tricks hour after hour behind the bar of a tavern in Garrick Street. It is only by inexhaustible patience and the employment of every known means to render the fingers supple that cards can be manipulated so as to deceive the closest observation. Privately, in the Savage Club, Bertram performed some of his tricks slowly for me to see how the top card was withdrawn and placed at the bottom or in the middle of the pack. After I had watched this he would then perform the trick rapidly and in a way not to be detected, though I knew actually what to look for. A little experience with Lord Lister completely mystified Bertram. After performing what Bertram called one of his simplest tricks—so simple that every time he was afraid of being detected—Lord Lister turned to him and said, "I have seen you do that before, Mr. Bertram; I thought it was electricity then, now I am sure of it." I am led to think that brainy men are in many affairs of life the easiest possible to deceive. After watching Mr. Stuart Cumberland's thought-reading exhibition with Mr. Hall Caine at the Haymarket Theatre, I said to Cumberland that he seemed to have an easy task. Cumberland, who in private substituted "muscle-reading" for "thought-reading" said he did not lead Hall Caine at all, he was simply dragged along to the particular spot in the dress circle where a pin had been hidden. Few people remember that Mr. Maskelyne came out as a plate spinner, keeping rows of plates spinning on a large table and never allowing one to fall. I formed one of a small committee of inspection on his first appearance in London, when he told me that for many hours every day for eight months he had practised this one trick. I sat with Messrs. Maskelyne and Cooke in their cabinet and managed to curl myself up into the box out of which Mr. Cooke used to escape, yet I can offer no suggestion as to the way in which the tricks are carried through, any more than could a man in the back seat of the gallery.

A GREAT WRITER'S SAD CAREER.

The passing away of David Christie Murray in the same year set me thinking over the mournful career of this acute journalist, brilliant story-writer, and able speaker. I knew him intimately for a number of years, and read with deep sorrow his gloomy reflections at the age of sixty. "The air is thick with the shadows of regret," he wrote. "Life was one constant vicissitude, an unfailing series of ups and downs, of jolly, happy-go-lucky rejoicings with comrades who were equally careless with myself, and of alternating spells of hardship. 'Literature (said Sir Walter) is an excellent walking-stick but a very bad crutch,' and so in truth I have found it all my days." Murray having thus lifted the curtain on his own life, I may be forgiven for pointing a moral. The unhappy writer learnt nothing either from prosperity or adversity. Yet he never failed to find a friend whether in the heights or depths of fortune. One day he told me with much rejoicing that he had made over £2,000 in the previous year. Being much interested in the prices of fiction at that time, I made close inquiry, and found that he was under the mark by two or three hundred pounds. Nothing of the kind ever happened again.

As years passed the spells of hardship became more and more frequent; one trouble followed another. With a view to escaping the pitfalls of London, he set up an establishment in the country. Things went smoothly enough till certain payments were overdue; then came the crash and a sudden change of address. A more severe crisis drove him out of the country. Poor Murray! it looked as if his drifting would bear him right away. No; after prolonged absence he one morning reappeared in my office, a figure of abject depression. As he represented himself, he had reached "Despair's Last Journey." Many a time and oft he had been stone-broke, but never so helpless as now. "My dear Catling,' he said, "I haven't a halfpenny, and don't know where to raise one." Then we fell talking as to what could be done. Murray offered to write anything I wished; his name he feared would be a bar with any publisher; so I should have the copy anonymously and could use any name that pleased me. We did not do business on those terms. A little quiet talk soothed Murray; he went away with a sovereign for pressing emergencies, arranging to come again in a couple of days. Meanwhile he was to prepare an outline for a serial story, and I promised to study the position with respect to his name. Before meeting again I was talking over business with Mr. Frank Lloyd, and mentioned Murray's unhappy position. On putting the question "Should Murray's offer of a cheap story be accepted or not?" Mr. Frank Lloyd said, "If Mr. Murray will write you as good a story as he has done before, pay him what his work merits." The arrangement which came out of this was honourably observed on both sides; the tale was a good one, and rightly appeared with the name of its author, who never after said a word about abandoning it. In later years a sad depreciation was seen in some of Murray's work, though at times there were brilliant flashes of the older and higher method. He could not be got to write far in advance; one story which opened with a magnificent first instalment gradually weakened so much that characters had to be incidentally referred to in proof in the endeavour to keep up a continuous interest. The final instalment, which only came to hand at the last moment, was utterly disappointing. It was so bad that when Murray came with another proposal, I had to remind him of what was, in a literary sense, a failure. "Oh dear," said Murray," "you would not blame me if you knew where that story was finished." It was known to me that another home, furnished on the pernicious and inexcusable hire system, had been swept away; what followed only came from his own confession, that he had completed the tale in the infirmary of Wandsworth Prison!

FRIENDS AMONG THE DOCTORS.

Dyspepsy, the fiend that has tortured so many sedentary workers, made my life miserable in the summer of 1908, bringing other troubles in its train. Earlier in the year I had tried the Riviera and sampled Switzerland, in sight of the splendour of Mont Blanc. Relief was not found abroad, by the sea, or in the country. Wellnigh despondent, I returned home on August 1st, and had the good fortune to come under the care of Dr. Sandford Arnott, who was doing duty for a friend away on holiday. With a serious face he ordered me to keep in bed, and for the first time in my life I obeyed the direction. A few days' careful treatment wrought a wonderful change; one bad symptom after another disappeared, and at the end of a fortnight I was able to rest my head upon a single pillow, breathing with an amount of comfort that had not been enjoyed for years. Dr. Arnott laid me under a deep debt of gratitude, which will ever remain with me, though my joy is saddened by the reflection that I am shut out from further help at his hands. We parted as the best of friends; it is the mysterious binding force of medical etiquette that bars the way.

One of my earliest friends was a fine old doctor

RETIREMENT AND REFLECTION. 341

of the Abernethy type, who did much good in Clerkenwell fifty years ago. Many stories were told of the abruptness of Leonard Goddard, but no one doubted his medical skill. His advice in the upbringing of a family was invaluable. The beneficial uses of hot and cold water were insisted upon; also the trial of simple home remedies before calling in the doctor. I never heard anyone more eloquent in the contempt of "physic." In the sixties I was welcomed in his surgery on a Sunday morning to talk over the newest books. These days, when so many things have been made free by the State, would have angered him sadly, for he held firmly to the old saying "What you get for nothing is nothing worth." Yet in practice he was most reluctant to send out his bills for service rendered. For ten years I had the benefit of Dr. Goddard's assistance without receiving any account, or having a word said on the matter. It was only after my pressing for the settlement that he made a very moderate charge.

In club life it has been a pleasure to meet many medical men, including two notable doctors like Sir Benjamin Ward Richardson and Sir James Crichton-Browne. The latter is still with us, always ready to further any good cause, and to uphold the glory of Shakspere against all comers.

It was at the sick bed of a penniless journalist, who in the belief that he was dying had sent for me, saying he would like to shake my hand before passing away, that I first met Dr. R. Fitzroy Benham. The doctor, at the close of a hard day's work, had driven several miles to see this poor patient. Timely aid soon put him on his feet, and he went on reporting for many years. As I became better acquainted with Benham, numerous other instances of his kindness to the sick and suffering were discovered. It is my firm belief that he was actuated throughout by the most benevolent intentions. Yet his life resulted in martyrdom. By seeking to establish a local hospital in Kensington without adequate support, he excited the bitter opposition of his professional brethren. A serious mistake was made in the choice of a building; law proceedings ensued, involving debt and other troubles; some critics objected to the name of the Queen's Jubilee Hospital; others to the insufficiency of its arrangements. Benham struggled on under every adverse circumstance, for many years devoting time and money to the cause on which his heart was set. He gave himself no rest, and the result was a complete breakdown, followed by long wearying illness and premature death.

PRESS CONGRESS IN BERLIN.

In company with an old colleague (Joseph R. Fisher), Arthur Walter, James Baker, and other delegates of the British International Association of Journalists, I journeyed by one of the magnificent boats of the Hamburg-America Line to Hamburg, on the way to Berlin. In Germany we found on all sides and amid all classes the greatest friendliness. Officially the arrangements gave marked importance to the Congress, and were designed to afford the greatest pleasure to the visitors. In his report our honorary secretary well said:—

"The scene in the Chamber of the Reichstag when the first sitting of the Congress opened was a magnificent one. Here

RETIREMENT AND REFLECTION. 343

in this hall, where so many fiery debates, involving serious matters for the welfare of the German people, have been fought out, were gathered the representatives from twenty-one nations of the Press parliament. Herr W. Singer, of Vienna, occupied the president's chair, and near him were Herr George Schweitzer, the German president, and M. Taunay, the French general secretary, and on either side the bureau representatives of the various nations. There were present also, in recognition of the importance of the gathering, the Prussian Ministers Von Rheinhaben, Von Moltke, Dr. Reseler, and the Secretary of State for Foreign Affairs, Von Schoen, as well as Under Secretaries of State and members of the Reichstag.

"In the afternoon the Chancellor, Prince Von Buelow, gave a reception in his historic residence, and the scene in the forest garden, beneath the rooms in which the Berlin Congress was held, was full of animation. The Chancellor chatted with representatives of the varied nationalities, and then, standing at his garden door, gave an important speech."

The discussions in many languages were devoted to upholding the dignity of the Press, and securing as far as possible unity of action and liberty of thought. After Berlin there followed an excursion to Frankfort and a delightful day at Wiesbaden.

HELP FOR JOURNALISTS' ORPHANS.

A small committee of London journalists, desirous of aiding their own orphan fund, agreed to the publication of a special volume. Lord Burnham's name sufficed to secure influential support; plans were laid and estimates obtained. The volume proposed looked promising, but how was it to be carried through without a penny of capital? Being altogether devoid of the persuasive method required for a good beggar, I could not see the way out. One day, however, the plan and the wish behind it were explained to the Hon. Harry Lawson, with a blunt earnestness that led him to look me straight in the face and say, "You want some money?" "That is exactly the position," was the reply; whereupon he took up half a sheet of notepaper, and in his father's name wrote down a generous contribution towards the cost of production. From that moment the work went forward, Lord Northcliffe, Mr. Moberly Bell, Mr. Frank Lloyd, Mr. Arthur Pearson, Mr. Kennedy Jones, and Mr. Ernest Parke sending further aid. Pictures were gathered by Mr. M. H. Spielmann, from the President of the Royal Academy, and other distinguished artists. For the literary matter Mr. Walter Jerrold was always at hand as one of the readiest of helpers in securing poems, essays, stories and other papers from leading authors. All who were applied to, even when compelled to decline, wrote so kindly that editing "The Press Album" became a labour of love. When the question of production arose, Mr. John Murray showed his sympathy with the orphans by volunteering to bring out the book free of any publishing charges. As the result of the effort a thousand pounds have been added to the capital fund, enabling the annual allowance for each orphan to be at once increased.

SEEING THE MIDNIGHT SUN.

More novel than agreeable must be the estimate of a trip to the North Cape in 1909. Hammerfest, the most northerly town of Europe, famous for its constant odour of cod-liver oil, was wet, muddy, and depressing. The people, as everywhere throughout Norway, were kindly and obliging, the link with home being established by an excellent telegraph service. Off the famous cape on the evening of July 2nd the outlook was desperately bad, cold and rainy, with a strong wind blowing up a heavy sea from the icy north. There was no more chance of seeing the sun than on a November night in London; neither moon nor stars could be distinguished in the blackness. One of the most foolish of everyday things is grumbling at the weather; on sea or land we have to take it as it comes. More rapidly than anyone could possibly have anticipated, the next day brought a marvellous and exhilarating change. Rain no longer fell, the clouds rolled away, out shone the sun on a silvery sea, lighting up every snow patch on the peaks and hills of the placid fjord. The captain cheerily foretold a fine night. As hour after hour passed—eight, nine, ten, eleven o'clock—without the least waning of the light, all on board were eagerly watching for the fulfilment of their wish to behold the sun at midnight. That was the supreme object of the long journey into the Arctic Circle. The reality as far exceeded expectation as it baffles description. Photographs of groups and near objects were as readily taken on the upper deck as on the clearest day; neither twilight nor shadow marred the solemn beauty of the sun gleaming white on the northern horizon. "There was no night," and consequently no signal for going to bed, a thing to marvel at, but it upset the succeeding day so considerably that no one desired a repetition of the experience.

IN THE DEPTHS OF A MINE.

During a holiday in Cornwall an opportunity opened for seeing the famous Dolcoath tin mine. I take the record thereof from my daughter's diary:—

"When Mr. Arthur Thomas, the courteous manager, whispered that we might go down, the first feeling was one of delight. On being told, however, that it meant putting on men's attire and the costumes were produced, we began to tremble, mentally at least. The dress consisted of trousers and coat of thick corduroy cotton stuff and flannel shirt. After a moment's hesitation we plunged boldly into them. The maid then brought us our headgear—a hard metal hat, to be worn over a white linen cap. We put them on rakishly, not to say becomingly, but that would not do. We must take our hair all down, screw it up tight, and cover it with the linen cap. Not daring to admit any desire to shirk it we went on. After a good laugh at each other's appearance we ventured into the open, where, of course, a snapshot was instantly insisted upon."

On reaching the shaft, the writer says:—

"The first sight of the 'gig' gave us a real shock. A rough sort of lift, measuring about two feet square and thirteen feet high, was divided into two tiers. Mainly made of iron, it just fitted the little black hole we were to go down. My sister and I flattened ourselves at the back of the lower tier, one of the overseers acting as guard in front. My father and a medical friend were directed to the upper floor, which they reached by going up a ladder and then crawling along a platform that left no possible room for standing upright. Thus we packed ourselves in, three on each tier."

The downward journey for near three thousand feet occupied about five minutes, the darkness,

IN MINERS' DRESS FOR DESCENDING DOLCOATH.

[To face p. 346.

RETIREMENT AND REFLECTION. 347

clanking of chains, and rushing of water making it seem much longer. Nothing happened; the exploration below, however, served to increase our admiration of the splendid heroism of miners, who are always ready to risk their lives to save others.

More romantic was an incident which subsequently happened to one of the party. My medical friend was Dr. W. A. Chapple, who had practised in New Zealand for twenty years, and been a member of the Legislature. Without any settled plans in England he must have been looking round, for just as the last general election was coming on I heard of his going to Scotland for a week-end. His stay was somewhat extended, with the result that he returned M.P. for Stirlingshire. The electors are to be congratulated on their choice, for to great personal charm Dr. Chapple adds clear views concerning the social and economic questions of the time.

His success recalled a former visit to Scotland, when I travelled with another earnest Liberal, Mr. A. C. Morton, and joined him in making inquiries respecting "Home Rule All Round." Since then seventeen years have passed, and the question is still being discussed. Mr. Morton meanwhile journeyed on to Sutherland, and has been twice returned to Parliament by that Scottish constituency.

A RUN THROUGH PORTUGAL.

The quiet, easy courtesy of all classes of the Portuguese did much to make a tour in the spring of 1910 pleasant and profitable. For the workers, especially the women, who go almost universally barefoot, there was deep sympathy, though few seemed to invite it. What Byron said of Cintra, that "it contains beauties of every description, natural and artificial," is true of much more of the country. The beauty, however, so far as man's handiwork is concerned, belongs to the past. Whether one has to speak of the ancient Moorish fortress, old-time castles, cathedrals, palaces or convents, admiration must be qualified; their glories have faded, if not passed away. My disappointment was in some measure due to the weather, for there is no more certainty of finding spring sunshine in Portugal than there is in Algeria or Cornwall. One day at Mont Estoril showed the glory of the southern coast; but Cintra was cold and wet, Lisbon swept by heavy rain-storms, Coimbra gloomy and uncertain. A charming interval enabled a bullfight to be seen in the capital. Altogether unlike the Spanish fights, the Portuguese show, with some fine horsemanship, was enjoyable. In their play with the bull the men showed great dexterity, and an element of real fun came in when the bull leaped the barrier and chased his tormentors.

Historically, Braga, standing in the port-wine district, dates back to the Romans. It is a busy, bustling place; but has no attraction beyond that it leads to Bom Jesus. This wonderful church is perched on a lofty hill, approached by broad flights of steps, with landings or platforms on which are reared shrines containing life-size coloured groups of figures representing scenes of the Passion. The view from the mountain is superb. For picturesque effect, indeed, it far surpasses Bussaco, though the

RETIREMENT AND REFLECTION.

scene of Wellington's famous victory over Massena is the one satisfactory holiday resort in the land, seeing that it boasts a well-managed and palatial hotel.

In moving about the country one heard nothing but gloomy anticipations of the future. There was some pity for the young King, but violent denunciation of the corruption of the governing party.

LOOKING BACK.

As an old resident of South London I am tempted to quote a sketch of Dulwich from "Hone's Everyday Book." In 1824, the writer, on reaching "the summit of the Five Fields," exclaimed:—

> "Heav'ns! what a goodly prospect spread around
> Of hills and dales, and woods, and lawns, and spires!

"This is a fairy region. The ravished eye glances from villa to grove, turret, pleasure ground, hill, dale; and 'figured streams in waves of silver' roll. Here are seen Norwood, Shooter's-hill, Seven Droog Castle, Peckham, Walworth, Greenwich, Deptford, and bounding the horizon, the vast gloom of Epping Forest."

Long years ago I guided a few friends along the path of these Five Fields to the Greyhound, where we frolicked and dined. Dulwich still has its charms, though the tavern has disappeared and the Fields can no longer be traced. It is idle to lament the picturesqueness of the past. Where one family lived in luxury, five hundred now find comfortable homes, with the advantages of ready means of transit, good sanitation, fine open parks, and Tate libraries scattered around.

Now that George the Fifth occupies the throne I may recall one of his Majesty's earliest speeches, delivered on the stage of the Surrey Theatre. It was to help a most deserving charity that Prince George crossed the river on a cold day in the middle of December, 1892. After inspecting the Royal South London Ophthalmic Hospital the Prince and party moved to the theatre for the purpose of a larger public meeting. The proceedings were simple and entirely sympathetic, the Duke of Cambridge and the Bishop of Rochester being among the speakers. Professor Malcolm M'Hardy, whose energy had done so much to secure the completion of the new hospital, was warmly complimented by the Prince. Ladies in the pit had taken their opera glasses, and it was noted that his royal highness showed unmistakable signs of nervousness, though whether this was due to the novelty of his position or the cold no one could guess.

When a young grandson in the uniform of a scout asked if I had ever met his famous leader, the answer was "Oh, yes." During his service in the Matabele war Baden-Powell acted as correspondent of the *Daily Chronicle*. On his return I met him in the office, and in talking over varied experiences in South Africa he said that on one occasion his life was saved by a knowledge of skirt dancing. Misled by the apparent quiet which prevailed around a native kraal he approached too near the entrance. In an instant he found himself the target of many warriors, who darted into the open. Instead of attempting flight in a direct line Baden-Powell remembered the lessons he had

RETIREMENT AND REFLECTION. 351

learned for a charity bazaar, and, with the whirling motion of an expert skirt dancer, got safely away.

The club land of Fleet Street rests under the shadow of a loss, which defies explanation and is the more regrettable because it cannot be made good. At the beginning of 1899 the *Athenæum* printed this paragraph:—

"Genial and erudite Sylvanus Urban would not fail to rejoice in the groups which Mr. W. Maw Egley has recently completed for the club-room of the Urban Club in Fleet Street, a composition of small whole-length likenesses, highly finished, and almost photographically faithful. There are not fewer than forty-nine portraits in this extremely laborious and well-considered composition. An assembly of the Club gave the artist an excuse for his picture; accordingly the members are placed at the well-known tables, and Mr. Catling, the chairman of the evening, stands up, hammer in hand, as if about to address the company, which comprises Messrs. J. Coleman, W. E. Church, C. Cruikshanks, H. S. Ashbee, B. F. Stevens, A. H. Hance, and Alban Doran, as well as the artist himself, Sir H. Irving, Dr. Phené, and Sir J. Crichton-Browne."

Through the intervening years the painting has been carefully preserved. One morning this summer it was missed from the frame. Examination showed that the canvas had been cut from the wood backing over which it was stretched. The exact date of its disappearance cannot be fixed, nor can any adequate motive be suggested for such a mysterious robbery. Apart from the Club it can be of small value.

A FEW BLACK-AND-WHITE ARTISTS.

In the days of *Judy* and *Moonshine* John Proctor's cartoons ranked with the most famous of political pictures. It cannot be said that they were always free from bitterness, albeit the genial

Scotch artist had no touch of ill-nature in his whole composition. When Johnny heard of my retiring he said, "You have had the luck of it." On my asking "How?" he replied, "Why, I have been at work longer than you have, but I never had the luck to find a firm to last for fifty years." Proctor's stories were the delight of clubland, and his old companions wish him the brightest of days in his Surrey retreat.

Alfred Bryan began most nervously, and remained to the end of life one of the most retiring of men, moved neither by ambition nor the hope of gain. He declined a flattering invitation to join the artistic staff of *Punch* and refused engagements for papers that would have paid him four times the amount he was receiving from the smaller sheets that encouraged his early efforts. That was his idea of loyalty, and nothing could induce him to depart from it. His success in portraiture was as great as his method was remarkable; he never put pencil to paper for a preliminary sketch, contenting himself with a close view of his subject.

Just the opposite principle was pursued by the brilliant and indefatigable Harry Furniss. Though a marvellously rapid worker, he never lost an opportunity of fixing an intended subject in his sketchbook. I have acted as his screen in the lobby of the House of Commons while he furtively made a few strokes that secured the characteristic form and features of a member. Slight as these might seem, they afforded just the assistance required to give full effect to the artist's finished drawing. One of the bright illustrated letters he was wont to send his friends is reproduced, showing what

RETIREMENT AND REFLECTION. 353

"My dear Catherine,

I think it would give me greater pleasure I assure you. But unfortunately there is another Grand old man & his claims are for his own in these matters.

could be accomplished with a few strokes of the pen.

A touch of genius has rightly been accorded to Phil May, too soon lost to the world of art. Poor Phil! he used to smile with that irresistible roguish twinkle in his eye and say, "No whisky, no picture." Drink—foolish drinking at the wrong time—I fear had much to do with his early collapse. Oh, the pity of it; for no blither spirit, no more hilarious companion has ever crossed my path. Phil May's yarns of his American trip brimmed over with fun. He tried to be a match for New York hospitality, and tried in vain. One night he closed a festive bout by saying he must go to bed. Escaping on this plea he ascended the lift and reached his room. There a fresh temptation overcame him; he changed his clothes, was taken down by a lift in another part of the hotel, and falling into the arms of the crowd he had left shortly before, was received with a shout. Making a night of it took far too much out of him. Once only I travelled a short way with May. We met at Drury Lane, holding conference at the little bar in the front of the theatre. I was bound for the Savage Club, and on hearing this Phil said: "I'll come with you." At the start it was agreed that we should diverge for a minute to make an inquiry at Covent Garden. The minute was a short one, for my companion insisted on moving forward, when he found the theatre closed and no bar open. A few quick steps took us to the market, where Phil cried "Halt"; he could not pass the Hummums. Half-a-dozen good fellows, all associated with the stage, were found at the inner bar. Hospitality given and returned made the merry moments fly only too rapidly; Phil May, with his quaint fancies and flashing replies, was the life of such a convivial gathering. When at length a fresh start was made our way lay down Southampton Street, some firmness having to be shown in resisting an invitation to just "look in" at the corner hotel. Knowing the perils of the Strand, the highway was crossed at a rush, or there would have been no escaping Romano's before we reached the home of the Savages. It was not a question of craving for drink, or inability to pass open doors; at each place named Phil knew he would break into a party of friends; his whole existence on such occasions yearned for companions to whom he could cry, "Come, rejoice with me." His great talent was linked with weakness so human as to make us remember him with Robert Burns for his work, and not for any failings.

Tom Merry turned out a large number of clever sketches. Whether a caricature, a cartoon, or a whole sheet of portraits was required, Tom seemed equal to any occasion. Yet his life was a prolonged impecunious struggle; when health gave way the end came with sad and mournful suddenness.

In Tom Browne appeared an artist of altogether different type. Ability became the ally of steady industry, success in one direction quickening his ambition to reach the fulfilment of higher aims. Always a student he laboured earnestly, the while showing a capacity for business that ensured ample comfort for himself and family. His charming personality made him popular in all circles. A sturdy territorial, fond of horse exercise, Tom seemed marked out for a long life, when his promising career was cut short by the development of a deadly malady.

THEATRES AND THE PRESS.

Few things in Merrie England have passed through more changes than the amusements of the people. The attitude of the Press in relation to it has been equally variable. In the eighteenth century one London newspaper paid as much as £200 a year for early intelligence of what was to be presented at the theatres. It was then a custom towards the close of one night's performance to announce what would be played on the following evening.

The nineteenth century saw the development of another curious custom: newspaper proprietors printing their own press tickets, with which some dozen or more persons were sent to a theatre each night. These tickets, of course, were not always honoured, and sometimes led to odd mistakes. The editor of one paper told me he had been in the habit of supplying a friend with tickets for a particular house, and he became so well known that when, on a special occasion, the editor himself appeared he was promptly put out as an impostor. This system was in use when I commenced in the sixties. Charles Mathews and Benjamin Webster at length protested against it, and it gradually fell into disuse.

Only a few first nights possessed any attraction. If I asked a friend to accompany me the inquiry

RETIREMENT AND REFLECTION. 857

would be, "It's a first night, isn't it?" "Oh, yes." "No, thanks, I'll wait and see what it is about before I go."

Of the old managers whom I knew, John Douglass and Nelson Lee were two splendid examples. With them both a "man's word was his bond." Douglass told me that he never had but one dispute with an actor, and that was on the single occasion when the man would insist on having a written agreement. Margate was the Mecca for actors in those days. On one occasion, while waiting at the railway station, a star came up and asked with some surprise if Douglass was going third class. "Why,' was the frugal manager's response, " there isn't a fourth, is there?" Another John succeeded his father, and with the aid of brother Richard made the Standard more than locally famous by a succession of spectacular pantomimes and romantic melodramas. Some of the latter were adapted from popular tales. Even after his Drury Lane successes Andrew Halliday disclaimed *writing* melodramas, being wont to say they were "built up." A proof of this occurred when Sir Walter Scott's *Fair Maid of Perth* was in preparation at the Standard. At the rehearsal of a particular scene all the actors came to a stand, for the "cues" were missing. John Douglass, as the adapter, described what ought to be done, but the actors shook their heads. It soon became clear that there was a gap somewhere, which involved confusion. The parts were then gathered up and placed in Douglass's hands. They had not been entirely written out, according to old custom, but consisted in many places of pages cut from the printed story. The adapter had simply drawn a pencil mark down the side of the passages that were to be used, and handed the volume over to the prompter to get copied out. In doing this with scissors and paste, the fact that some of the dialogue appeared on both sides of certain pages was overlooked, with the result that when one side was stuck down the other was lost to sight. An angry exclamation from Douglass, on making discovery of how the blunder occurred, was followed by an order to get another copy of the tale. As there was not one in the theatre, the rehearsal for the time ended.

Actors are so absorbed in the advantages of their respective parts that they appear to be bad judges of plays. Buckstone, after being in low water, was buoyed up by the assurances of his company that Athol Mayhew's *Mont Blanc* would prove "another *Overland Mail*," and when it failed he became sadly dejected. David James told me that at the final rehearsal of *Our Boys* he asked Miss Larkin, "Well, what do you think of the play?" "What can I think, Mr. James, but that it will be the greatest failure you have ever had." It ran for 1,200 nights. *A Message from Mars* appealed so little to Herman Vezin that after rehearsing for some time as the Messenger he abandoned the part, and thus slipped out of a brilliant success.

The illusions of the stage appeal to players in very different ways. I remember Miss Marie Litton, a clever actress, who made a conspicuous hit as Rosalind, and died too early, telling me her experience. Appearing under Mr. J. A. Cave's management as a boy in a sensational play, she had to be lashed to a plank which, when set in motion, would be drawn towards a circular saw. Although she knew the scene was only an illusion, with no real danger, she said it always made her sick, and the feeling returned long after at the mere thought of it.

E. P. Hingston crossed my path on several occasions. In the Forties, when so many writers were struggling, he belonged to the Jerrold set, and was given some literary work by Mr. Lloyd. This was not forgotten when, years after, Mr. Lloyd went to ask Douglas Jerrold's aid. A visit to America was followed by Hingston returning as the agent of Artemus Ward. Later he figured as the lessee and manager of the Opera Comique. For the opening he bought a new farce from John Oxenford, the *Times* critic. During an interval the manager mingled freely with the audience, and several of us enjoyed his hospitality. Suddenly a voice cried, "Ah, Hingston, at your old game, trying to nobble the Press!" "Yes," replied the manager, "and I've squared three of them for tenpence." The amount was likely to be correct, as the theatre people bought drinks at a lower rate than the public. It is absurd to suppose that such an incident had any effect on what was written, but the free-and-easy method did much to lighten labour and make the evening pass pleasantly.

THE JOURNALISTIC CALLING.

Many pressmen in the fierce competition of to-day are prone to think that their predecessors had an easier and more rosy time. Things were different, of course, but we had to make the most of our opportunities and push ahead against all manner of opposition. Just before I was born the King of the Belgians sent a letter to the English Court in which he said:—

"One must not mind what newspapers say. Their power is a fiction of the worst description, and their efforts marked by the worst faith and the greatest untruths. If all editors of the papers in the countries where the liberty of the Press exists were to be assembled, we should have a *crew* to which you would *not* confide a dog that you would value, still less your honour and reputation."

In the Forties, when care was needed to escape imprisonment, the *Glasgow National* devoted a column to the troubles of journalists, summing up with this advice:—

"Reader! have you yet fixed upon a profession? If not, never once think of becoming an editor. Beg, take a pedlar's pack, keep lodgers, take up a school, set up a mangle, take in washing. For humanity's sake, and especially for your own, do anything rather than become a newspaper editor."

Speaking on behalf of the Press Fund in 1867, Mr. Gladstone, after pointing out that journalism "offered few prizes," went on to say:—

"This is a profession fed from time to time by the ardent and unsparing efforts of our youth for the discharge of duties to which I believe no man, except in the perfection of mental and physical faculties, is really equal."

Soon after I was entrusted with the direction of the paper, the Rev. J. Foster announced that he would preach a sermon on *Lloyd's News* in a Nonconformist pulpit at the East End. It was a general condemnation of newspaper reading, the extravagance of which will be understood by a couple of sentences:—

"The general body of working people may be divided into two classes—those who go to church and those who read *Lloyd's News*."

"In the better land, to which I hope all here present are journeying, there will be no *Lloyd's* paper, because there will be no sin, nor sorrow, nor trouble."

As to age, I recall that when Blanchard Jerrold applied for a post at the Great Exhibition of 1851 he was met with the reply, "We are sorry to refuse, as we know that your knowledge of French would enable you to discharge the duties admirably, but when we look at your youthful appearance, we dare not make the appointment."

On the contrary, I looked older than my years, and had no difficulty in mixing with men.

A little incident will throw light on the question of qualification. I found myself one of a Press party invited to the exhibition of a method for providing real ice for skaters all the year round. This was described with an elaborate amount of scientific detail. Seated beside me at the succeeding lunch was Murphy, an old and esteemed reporter of the *Daily News*. To him the confession was quietly made, "I can't think what I am going to make of this, for I don't understand it a bit." "My young friend," said Murphy, "if you are only going to write about things you understand you won't go far on the Press."

The beginner who is apt to be worried about "style" can fall back upon Matthew Arnold's advice: "Have something to say and say it as clearly as you can; that is the only secret of style."

De Blowitz, the famous *Times* correspondent, said truly of journalism, "A man's success is in proportion to the trouble he takes."

During my stay in Denver, Colorado, I met a jovial Irishman, editor and proprietor of the *Rocky Mountain Times.* "We don't make much money," said he, "but we've lots of fun."

If the following passage, quoted from a copy of the *Printers' Circular*, Philadelphia, of 1882, is correct, it shows that the American scare headlines were designed for a less worthy purpose than was supposed:—

"The professor of journalism who periodically tells us all about newspapers, has failed to notice a comparatively modern and a very important feature of the newspaper, namely, the headlines. This is a department of the paper which has steadily conquered for itself an influence which every newspaper manager—sometimes inadequately—recognises. It often happens that the ingenious artist in this department is really editing the paper. He can convey an impression which the writers of ponderous leaders are endeavouring to avoid. He can create a doubt or awaken suspicion by a single artfully-chosen word, or sow broadcast an opinion which it may take columns of writing to show is unfounded. Suggestions that are buried in the body of the articles may attract no attention, but the flaming headline takes the eye at once, and its diagnosis of the matter which it criticises may be very wide of the mark without the average reader applying any correction. The headline largely regulates the emphasis that is given to the report of current events. Small matters in this way may be magnified and mere conjectures invested with nearly the dignity of facts."

No other calling affords so much variety and opens up such possibilities. It leads alike to high

RETIREMENT AND REFLECTION.

places in the service of the State and to the Bankruptcy Court. Some win their way to eminence in Parliament, others acquire titles; a few remain content with comfortable fortunes. The many labour on with more or less satisfaction; even for them journalism has its fascination.

My part is set forth in these pages. Ruskin's teaching early impressed itself on my mind. "Give a man a block of stone," said he, "and let him carve his whole soul into it." It was not a stone, but a newspaper that was placed in my charge, and into this I put the whole aim and purpose of my life.

* * * * *

Joseph Hatton sounded a deep note when he wrote, "What stories of struggle and self-sacrifice there are awaiting the revivifying touch of the romancer who shall take hold of the personal history of Fleet Street and tell them in their integrity—many of them tragedies of drink."

True! alas, too true! But who will dare to be the judge? At the last, when the final roll is called, will those we deem successful, or the weaker brethren, whom we call failures, receive the Crown of Life?

AUTHOR'S ADIEU

At this stage I pause to express my heartfelt gratitude to the benign Providence which has enabled me to buffet through the world for threescore and twelve years. There has been plenty of hard work, but with enough variety to enable me to say truly that I have had a good time. Retirement has not meant idleness, and despite many grievous losses — the latest good kind-hearted Arthur Lloyd — I rejoice in being surrounded by troops of friends. Of the four sons and five daughters who form my family, the eldest son is a worker on *Lloyd's*; the second is running a paper in Western Australia; the youngest (who served as chief of the Army X-Ray department during the first year of the Boer war) is again in South Africa; while a daughter has married and settled in British Columbia.

"That's something towards Empire building," a friend whispers slyly; "more than can be said of a celibate priest, who only talks of other people's duties." Children I know are essential for the full happiness and joy of home; but let me tell those preachers without knowledge that the upbringing of a large family makes a vast addition to the cares and responsibilities of working parents.

Shakspere reminds me that :—

"Perseverance
Keeps honour bright; to have done, is to hang
Quite out of fashion, like a rusty mail
In monumental mockery."

After all is said, " 'Tis a very good world that we live in"; any number of good fellows are left, and I devoutly hope to be able to persevere in their midst for some little time longer.

In connection with this volume I have to cordially thank the proprietors of the *Illustrated London News* for permission to copy the admirable engravings of past events. Two of my fellow-journalists, Edward Salmon and W. F. Aitken, have kindly read the proofs; and my son Frederick has furnished blocks for the illustrations.

To the Pressmen of to-day I offer most cordial greetings. Those who have glanced at these pages will appreciate the changed conditions under which newspapers are produced. It is my sincere wish that the workers, who are now so much better equipped, may find increased opportunities for progress and advancement, with all that tends to make life pleasant.

INDEX.

à BECKETT, Arthur, 110.
   ,,   Gilbert, 134.
Abel, 262.
Aberdeen, Lord, 218.
   ,,   Lady, 218, 290.
Abraham, 262.
Ada, the Betrayed, 88.
Adam, 262.
Addington, 271.
Admiralty, 274, 292.
Advertisements, on copper coins, 43; tax on, 45; abolition of tax, 47.
Africa, 138, 198, 235, 236.
Agricultural Hall, 151.
Ainsworth, 250.
Aird, Sir John, 268, 269.
Albert, Prince: visit to Cambridge, 3; made Chancellor of University, 6; at Great Exhibition, 20; attacks on, 27; death of, 74.
Albery, James, 112.
Albion, the old, 105, 106.
Alden, W. L., 212.
Aldershot, 150.
Alexander, Mrs., 258.
Alexandra Palace, 185.
Alexandria, 161, 296.
Algeçiras, 236, 299.
Algeria, 293, 348.
Algiers, 293, 294.
Alhambra, Granada, 236.
Allan, Bridge of, 141.
Allen, Grant, 195.
   ,,   Mr., 87, 97.
Alma, Battle of, 42.
Alsatia, 87.
America, 79, 112, 113, 133, 185, 212, 253, 257, 265, 320, 324, 325, 359.
Americans, 188, 213, 253.
American War, 72.

Anderson, David, 135, 178.
Answers, 205.
   ,,   to correspondents, 228.
Antonio Gardens, Malta, 236.
Antony, 157.
Applegath machine, 51.
Archer, Tom, 110, 135.
"Arizona," s.s., 212, 213.
Armenians, 281.
Armstrong, Mr., 182.
   ,,   Mrs., 181.
   ,,   Eliza, 179, 183.
Arthur's seat, 140.
Arthur Street Mystery, 166.
Ashburnham Grounds, Cremorne, 97.
Ashley's Hotel, 109.
Asquith, Rt. Hon. H. H., 178.
Assouan, 280.
Assyrians, 262.
Astarte, 293.
Athenæum, 89, 91, 211.
Athens, 135, 265.
Atkins, city policeman, 218.
Atlantic, 212.
Australia, 41, 206, 210, 212, 276.

BAAL, Temple of, 262.
Baalbec, 135, 262.
Bacon, 242.
Baldwin, parachutist, 186.
Baker, Arthur Clements, 241.
   ,,   James, 342.
Ball, Mr., 45.
Bancroft, Sir S., 150.
   ,,   Lady, 59.
Banff, Canada, 222.
Banks, George L., 253.
Bannockburn, battlefield, 141.
Bantry, 173.
Baradas, 157.
Barking Road, 68.
Barnes, 147.

Barnes, E. C., 155.
Barnum, 193.
Barr, Robert, 212.
Barrett, Michael, 94.
" Wilson, 213, 214, 254, 255.
Barrie, J. M., 209.
Barrow-in-Furness, Bishop of, 211.
Barry, L. M., 188.
Barthélémy, 49.
Bartholomew Fair, 69.
Bartlett, Ashmead, 152.
" William Lehmann, 152.
Bateman, Colonel, 111, 112, 113, 115, 317.
" Mrs., 114, 115.
" Isabel, 112, 115, 117.
Bath and Wells, Bishop of, 211.
Battenberg, Prince Henry of, 281, 234, 290.
Bauer, Harold, 334.
Bayliss, F. W., 304.
Bay of Biscay, 297.
Beaconsfield, Lord, 206, 208.
Beadle "Mooney," the, 68.
Beales, Edmond, 87.
Beck, Adolf, 308.
Bedford, Bishop of, 211.
" Paul, 81.
Belfast, 301.
Belgians, King of the, 199, 360.
Bell, C. F. Moberly, 344.
Bellew, The Rev. Mr., 100.
Bellingham, 248.
Belmore, George, 113.
Bending, Edward, 273.
Benham, Dr. R. Fitzroy, 341.
Ben Ledi, 141.
Ben Lomond, 140.
Bennett, Sir John, 192.
Benson, Dr., 210, 211.
" Mr., magistrate, 126.
Bentley, Messrs., 144.
Bentley's Printing Office, 120.
Berberines, 281.
Beresford, Lord Charles, 187.
" Lady Charles, 188.
Berlin, 270, 342, 343.
Berlin Congress, 343.
Berners Street, Commercial Road, 183.
Bertram, Charles, 273, 336.
Besant, Walter, 201.
Bethany, 259.

Bethlehem, 259.
Bethsaida, 259.
Beverley, Bishop of, 211.
Beyrout, 265.
Bibl, Dr. Rudolf, 323.
Biggar, Joseph, M.P., 189.
Bigge, Lieut.-Col., Sir A. J., 232, 233, 234.
Birmingham, 158.
Bishopsgate Police Station, 184.
Bishop's Income, 227.
Biskra, 293.
Bismarck, Prince, 269.
Black, William, 199, 200, 331.
Blackfriars Bridge, 69, 118.
" Road, 112.
"Black Spirits and White," 211
Blanchard, E. L., 66, 88, 91.
" Laman, 88.
" Sydney, 118, 119.
Blondin, 242, 243.
"Bloody Sunday," the Czar's, 179.
Bloomsbury Chapel, 100.
Boatrace, Oxford and Cambridge, 31, 152.
Bocognano, 302.
Bolt Court, 36.
Bolt in Tun, 35.
Bom Jesus, 348.
Bonaparte, 154, 302, 322.
Bond, 148.
Boon, John, 332.
Booth, Bramwell, 180, 182, 183.
Bordighera, 301.
Borthwick, Hon. Oliver, 163.
Bosnia, 335.
Botzen, 323.
Boucicault, 105.
Boulogne, 57, 307.
Bouverie Street, 128.
Bow, 121.
Bow Street, 109, 178, 182.
Boyle, Robert W., 127, 129.
Bradbury, Mr., 62.
Braddon, Miss, 66, 203.
Bradshaw, Mr. W. F., 332.
Bradshaw's Guide, 35.
Braga, 348.
Brand, Deane, 273.
Brander, Pass of, 141.
Brassey, Lord, 211.
Bread, price of, 84.
Breakneck Steps, 58.
Brereton, Austin, 316.

INDEX.

Bribery at Election, 23.
Bridewell Police Station, 130.
Bright, John, 72, 96, 140, 164, 170.
Brighton, 290.
Bristol Hotel, London, 239.
British Empire, 171.
Brixton, 321.
Broadmoor, 247.
Brock's Fireworks, 156.
Brompton, 171.
Brooke, G. V., 114.
Brooklyn, 213.
Brooks, Captain, 212, 213.
Brough, L., 59, 65.
  ,, Brothers, 134.
Brown, Dr. Gordon, 184.
Browne, Dr. Lennox, 268.
  ,, Tom, 355.
Browning, Mrs. Barrett, 302.
Bruxelles, Palais de, 199.
Bryan, Mr., 219.
  ,, Alfred, 241, 273, 352.
Buckland, Frank, 138.
Buckstone, 105, 358.
Bude, 268.
Bulloch, J. M., 316.
Bunsen, Madame, 6.
Burdett, Angela Georgina, 152, 153, 154.
  ,, Sir Francis, 153.
Burgin, G. B., 212.
Burke, Mr., 156.
  ,, Richard, 93.
Burleigh, Bennet, 149, 178.
  ,, Street, 320.
Burnand, 134.
Burnham, Lord, 36, 78, 332, 333, 343.
Burns, John, 178.
  ,, Robert, 25, 141, 355.
Burton, Sir Richard, 57.
Bussaco, 348.
Butler, Richard, 321, 332.
Byron, Lord, 35, 134, 299, 348.
  ,, H. J., 105.

CADIZ, 299.
Cain, 262.
Caine, Hall, 250, 251, 337.
Cairo, 280, 283, 285, 296.
Calais, 137.
Calcraft, 50, 94.
Calgary, 221, 222.
Caliph Haroun Al Raschid, 262.

Calvary, 258.
Calvert, Mrs., 317.
Calvinia, South Africa, 326.
Camberwell Grove, 68.
Cambridge, 4, 41, 155, 191, 270; fire at St. Michael's Church, 11; county gaol, 13; Parker's Piece, 22; Pickerel Inn, 24; election of, 1852...23; University, 133.
Cambridge, Duke of, 150, 289, 350.
Camden Place, 124.
Campbell, Herbert, 273.
Canada, 221, 257.
Canadian Pacific Railway, 221.
Canary Islands, 296.
Cannes, 301.
Canterbury, 44, 270.
  ,, Archbishop of, 210, 211, 271.
Cantwell, Dr., 146.
Capernaum, 259.
"Cap'n Davy's Honeymoon," 251.
Carden, Sir Robert, 116.
Cardinal's Ring, 209.
Carlyle, 4, 207, 221, 248.
Carpenter, Mr., 45.
Carrington, Lord, 107, 208.
Carron Wharf, Whitechapel, 245.
Carthage, 293.
Casa Blanca, 296.
Catling, Arthur, 212.
  ,, Edward (author's father), 1, 5, 6, 24.
  ,, James, 334.
  ,, Mr. and Mrs. Thomas, 304.
  ,, Mr. and Mrs. T. T., 304.
  ,, Thomas, born, 1; first saw Queen, 3; escaped drowning, 5; first visit to theatre, 7; games, 7; chased by an elephant, 8; at an execution, 12; school days, 13, 14, 15; start on *Cambridge Chronicle*, 17; at Great Exhibition, 21; first peep behind the scenes, 21; playwriting, 22; at election of 1852...23; fourteenth birthday, 25; St. Augustine's College missed, 27; leaving home, 30; early days in London, 31; work on *Lloyd's*, 32; reading

Byron, 35; a new apprenticeship, 42; at Working Men's College, 48; execution at Newgate, 49; Spurgeon panic, 60; first sub-editing, 65; starting a literary fund, 66; a police reward, 70; join the London Society of Compositors, 71; on amateur stage, 71; war makes long hours, 72; Prince Consort's death, 74; teaching law to a judge, 81; buying a house, 82; from composing to sub-editing, 84; theatrical notices, 89; Milton's *Areopagitica*, 100; journey to Paris, 102; entrance into clubland, 109; join Savage Club, 110; at the Lyceum, 114; meeting with T. P. O'Connor, 118; office fire, 121; Napoleon III. lying in state, 124; Wainwright in court, 125; smoke with a murderer, 131; meeting with Captain Webb, 137; visit to channel tunnel, 137; stroking a gorilla, 139; visit to Scotland, 140; reviewing for *Daily Chronicle*, 143, 144; meet Bennet Burleigh, 149; first interview with Irving, 154; work for *Morning Post*, 162; death of Douglas Jerrold, 164; Mr. Lloyd's confidence, 166; my opinion on Gordon, 168; Home Rule troubles, 168, 169; visit Mr. Froude, 171; trip to Ireland, 173; at an eviction, 174; the Armstrong case, 179; "Why I am a Liberal," 189; meet Barnum at Olympia, 193; ask Gladstone to write an article, 195; his consent, 197; Stanley's refusal, 199; win a libel case, 203; talk with Lord Rowton, 207; call on the Archbishop of Canterbury, 210; start for America, 212, 213, 214; meet President Cleveland, 215; opening of Chicago Exhibition, 217; visit Salt Lake City, 220; return through Canada, 221; Niagara Falls, 223; Henry Pettitt, 224; the million circulation, 231; permission to reproduce Queen's letter, 232; health gives way, 234; start for Gibraltar, 235; at a bull-fight, 236; visit the Holy Land, 258; wedding in Tiberias, 260; Richon le Zion, 264; travel with Mr. Sankey, 265; meet Mr. Gladstone, 267; mistaken identity, 268; Masonic honours, 271; Edward Terry as Grand Treasurer, 274; consecration of Rahere Lodge, 275; lunch with Swinburne, 277; with George Sanger at Windsor, 279; start for Egypt, 280; convicts flogged, 281; in Khartoum, 285; back to London, 286; Paris Exhibition, 287; serve on a City Committee, 288; one man among 2,000 women, 290; Algeria and the Sahara, 293; Coronation of Edward VII., 294; Morocco and the Canary Islands, 296; contempt of court, 297; holiday in Southern Spain, 299; Corsica, 302; fifty years' work on *Lloyd's*, 302; entertained by brother Savages, 305; assisting a martyr of the law, 309; loss of a great friend, 313; first meeting with Henry Irving, 314; great reception in Austria, 322; presented to H. I. H. Prince Ferdinand, 322; tracing long-lost relatives, 324; retire from *Lloyd's*, 328; appreciations from friends, 329; farewell dinner, 332; Easter in Rome, 334; Bosnia and Herzegovina, 335; illness and recovery, 340; meet Dr. Benham, 341; a delegate in Berlin, 342; received by Prince Von Buelow, 343; edit the "Press Album," 344; the Midnight Sun, 344; in the depths of a Cornish mine, 346; tour through Portugal, 347.

Cave, J. A., 358.
,, of the Winds, 223, 224.
Cavendish, Lord Frederick, 156, 157.
Centenary of Sunday Schools, 150.
Central News, 332.

INDEX.

Chamberlain, Joseph, 158, 159, 170, 210.
Chambers' Encyclopædia, 54.
„ McCall, 273.
„ W. and R., 205.
Chancery Lane, 121.
Channel Tunnel, 137.
Chapman & Hall, Messrs., 98.
Chapple, Dr. W. A., 347.
Charing Cross, 287.
Chatham Island, New Zealand, 325.
Chatterton, 105.
Chelmsford, 171.
„ Lord, 78.
Cheltnam, C. S., 105.
Cheshire Cheese, 136.
Chicago, 212, 216, 217, 266.
Chinamen, 221.
Chingford, 155.
Chippendale, 318.
Chislehurst, 122, 124.
Church, W. E., 212, 276, 331, 351.
„ Missionary House, 67.
Cicero, 133.
Cintra, 348.
City Road, 68.
„ Tragedy, 164.
Clarke, Sir Edward, 230.
Clerkenwell, 68, 93, 341.
Cleveland, President, 215, 216, 218.
„ Mrs., 218.
Clifford, Walter, 273.
Clifton House, 222.
Clive, Franklin, 273.
"Clovernook," 62.
Clowes, William, 204, 205.
Clubs: Cobden, 158; Reunion, 228; Savage, 109, 110, 210, 228, 239, 303, 304, 307, 354; Urban, 228, 351; Whitefriars, 228, 331; Lotus, 213; Reform, 269.
Coates, John, 334.
Cobden, Richard, 133, 158.
Cogers, The, 156.
Coimbra, 348.
Coining Half Farthings, 5.
Coleman, John, 351.
Collins, Mr. and Mrs., 129.
Comet of 1854...34.
Commissioner of Police, Chief, 179.

Committee, Lord Mayor and Sheriffs', 288.
Commons, House of, 118, 158, 167, 169, 171, 188, 189.
Condobalin, New South Wales, 326.
Conquest, George, 226.
Constantine, 293.
Constantinople, 265.
Contempt of Court in a murder case, 297.
Cook (Murder), 58.
Cook's Office, 280.
Cooke, R., 187.
„ T. P., 64.
Cooper, Fenimore, 212.
Copperfield, Master, 42.
Coram Street, 249.
Cordova, 299.
Cork, 173.
Cornwall, 219, 268, 346, 348.
Corporation Lane, 93.
Correctors of the Press, 206.
Corsica, 302.
Costoleri, Signor, 334.
Coutts, the banker, 153.
Covent Garden, 109, 110, 354.
Cowes, 292.
Cowper Street School, 133.
Cranworth, Lord, 78, 79.
Cremorne Gardens, 97.
Crichton-Browne, Sir James, 341, 351.
Crimea, 42, 55, 64, 312.
Criterion, 305.
Cromer, Lord, 168.
Cronje, 283.
Crosby Hall, 71.
Crossfield Road, Hampstead, 202.
Crosswell, Dr., 44.
Crown Court, 37, 62, 187.
Cruikshank, George, 146.
Cruikshanks, C., 351.
Crystal Palace, 242.
„ „ Gardens, 20, 69.
Cuba, 265, 269.
Cumberland, Stuart, 337.
Cumming, Dr., 33, 62, 73.
Cunningham, Thomas, 42.
Curtis, George Byron, 118, 303.
Custance, Harry (Jockey), 71, 72.
Customs, The, 144, 287.
Czar, 179.

B B 2

Daily Chronicle, 52, 128, 143, 144, 162, 188, 201, 209, 269, 332, 350.
Daily Telegraph, 52, 65, 135, 141, 250, 332, 333.
Dagonet, 287.
Dallas, Mr., 142.
Dalmally, 140, 141.
Damascus, 135, 262.
Dardanelles, 265.
David, 262.
Davies, Ben, 273.
   „   D. Ffrangcon, 334.
Day, Alice, 125.
   „   Mr. Justice, 246, 247.
Dead Sea, 259.
De Blowitz, 362.
Delahay Street, 162.
Delane, John, 202, 203.
Dellagana, the Brothers, 76, 79.
Denman, Mr. Justice, 82, 148, 248.
Denmark, Crown Prince of, 275.
Denver, 219, 362.
Denvil, Henry Gaskill, 34.
Deptford, 44.
Derby, Bishop of, 211.
   „   Day, 161.
Devonshire, Duke of, 20.
Dibbs, Mr. George, 210.
Dickens, Charles, 17, 49, 62, 64, 66, 68, 98, 99, 100, 102, 119, 120, 155, 250.
Dickson, Mr., 163.
Dick Turpin, 38.
Dido, 293.
Dieppe, 103.
Dilke, Ashton, 136.
Dispatch, 36, 45, 122.
Divorce Court, 142.
Dixon, Hepworth, 62.
Dobbs, Hannah, 149, 150.
Dogberry, 120.
Dog Tax, 19.
Dolcoath Mine, 346.
Donald, Canada, 222.
   „   Robert, 332.
   „   Ross of Heimra, 201.
Donne, W. B., 105.
Dons, 190.
Doran, Alban, 351.
Doughty, A., 110.
Douglass, John, 91, 101, 357.
Dover, 226, 267.
   „   Admiralty Pier, 137.

Dover, Bishop of, 211.
Drew, Theodore, 273.
Drury Lane, 35.
   „   „   Lodge, 239, 273, 275.
Dryden, 91.
Dublin, 117, 133, 153, 173, 175.
Duncombe, T. S., 97.
Dunn, Nicol, 316.
Dunphie, Charles, 162.
Duval, Claude, 38.
Dyer, Sir Christopher, 301.

Earley, William, 162.
Edinburgh, 140, 167.
Edinburgh Daily Review, 170.
Editors of *Lloyd's*, 45.
Edmonton, Canada, 221.
   „   London, 327.
Edward VII., 294, 295, 296.
Edwards, George Spencer, 316, 321.
   „   Hamilton, 301.
Egley, Maw, 351.
Egypt, 135, 161, 167, 276, 279, 283, 287.
Egyptian Hall, 69.
Ela, the Outcast, 38.
Elizabeth, Queen, 186, 279.
Ely, Bishop of, 211.
Emperor, German, 177, 270.
Encyclopædia Britannica, 77.
Enfield, 44.
England, 272, 323, 347.
Englishmen, 177.
Ennis, 145.
Epping Forest opened, 156.
Epsom, 161.
   „   Racecourse, 71.
Escott, T. H. S., 164.
Europe, 345.
Euston Square Murder, 148.
Evans, Howard, 164, 212.
Evans's Entertainment, 36.
   „   Hotel, 305.
Everett, George, 274.
Exchange Telegraph Co., 332.
Executions: Barthélémy, 49; Bellingham, 248; Palmer, 59; double, at Cambridge, 13; Wiggins, 94.
Exeter Hall, 60, 187.
Exhibitions: Chicago, 216; The Great, 20, 45, 361; Paris, 287.
Exmouth Street, 68.

INDEX.

Fairs: Bartholomew, 69; Camberwell, 69; Greenwich, 32, 69.
Falconer, 81, 105.
Fanfaronade, 59.
Farjeon, B. L., 201.
Farringdon Street, 58, 68.
Fashoda, 285, 286.
"Father of the Chapel," 41.
Fawcett, 291.
Fenn, G. Manville, 201.
Ferdinand, Prince, of Austria, 323.
Fernandez, James, 105, 273, 307.
Ferretti, Mastaï, 272.
Finigan, J. Lysaght, 145.
Fire at *Lloyd's* Office, 121.
Fisher, J. R., 144, 342.
Fleet Club, 121.
   „ Street, 35, 36, 41, 53, 55, 104, 108, 126, 128, 129, 135, 146, 156, 164, 173, 186, 218, 249, 250, 280, 292, 302, 331, 333, 351, 363.
Fletcher, A. E., 144.
Florence, 334.
Follett, Sir William, 248.
Forbes, Archibald, 164.
Fort National, 293.
Fortunes of Nigel, 37.
Foster, Rev. J., 360.
Founding of *Lloyd's News*, 43.
France, 76, 101, 161, 280.
Francis, 136.
   „ Joseph, Emperor, Austria, 324
Frankfort, 343.
Frederick, Prince, Germany, 176.
French, 287.
   „ Revolution, 248.
   „ Sydney, 136.
Freeman, Mrs., 121.
Freemasonry, Notes on, 271, 272, 275.
Freemasons' Hall, 287.
   „ Tavern, 268.
Free Trade, 133, 158, 190.
Frost, Thomas, 49.
Froude, James, 170, 171.
"Furmenty," 8.
Furniss, Harry, 352.

"Galignani's Messenger," Song, 69.
Galilee, 259.
Ganthony, R., 273.

Ganz, W., 273.
Gardiner, A. G., 332.
Garrick Street, 336.
Gayhurst, 107.
Geary Brothers, 118, 119.
Ged, 76.
George III., 240, 291.
   „ IV., 294, 296.
   „ V., 308, 348.
Gerardy, Jean, 334.
German Emperor, 177, 270.
Germany, 76, 101, 342.
Gibbon, Charles, 331.
Gibraltar, 235, 236, 296, 299.
Gilbert, Sir W. S., 134, 241.
Gladstone, W. E., 96, 156, 166, 167, 168, 169, 170, 171, 172, 195, 196, 197, 215, 267, 360.
Gladstone, Mrs., 150, 170.
Glaisher, Mr., 2.
Glasgow, 141, 142, 301.
Glencroe, Pass of, 140.
Glenesk, Lord, 163, 332.
Glengariff, 173.
Glenny, George, 65, 162.
Glyn, Miss, 90, 142.
Gnatbrain, Buckstone as, 64.
Goat Island, 223.
Goddard, Dr. Leonard, 341.
Godfrey, Lieut. Dan, 273.
Godson, Dr., 275.
Goldsmith, Oliver, 37, 58.
Gordon, General, 166, 167, 286.
   „ Hotel, 110, 305.
   „ Miss, 258.
Gorst, Sir John, 149, 150, 270.
Goschen, 170.
Gould, Sir F. Carruthers, 332.
Goulston Street, 185.
Government and Trafalgar Square meetings, 179.
Graham, Cunninghame, 178.
   „ Leopold, 70.
Granada, 236, 299.
Grand Lodge, 273, 274.
Grant, Baron, 118.
Grantham, Justice, 309.
Granville, Lord, 101, 156.
Gravelotte, Jean François (Blondin), 243.
Gray's Inn Road, 178.
Great Britain, 196.
Great Exhibition, 20, 45, 361.
Greeks, 281.
Green, Alderman Frank, 288.

Green Arbour Court, 58.
Green, balloonist, 69.
Greenwich, 34, 158.
Grenadier Guards, Band of, 273.
Grossmith, George, 109, 306.
,, Weedon, 109.
Grosvenor, Lord Robert, 56.
Guildhall, 21, 191, 289.
Gwynne, Mr., 286.

HACKER, Matilda, 148.
Haldane, Right Hon. R. B., as bail, 178.
Hales, H., reporter, 181, 182, 247.
Hall, Rev. Newman, 142, 143.
,, Mrs., 143.
,, Sam., 36.
,, Sydney, 306.
Halliday, Andrew, 105, 357.
Hamburg, 342.
,, America Line, 342.
Hamilton, Lord George, 274.
Hamlet, 213.
Hammerfest, 344.
Hance, Alfred H., 127, 304, 334, 351.
,, Mrs., 304.
Handel Festival, 69.
Hanging Sword Alley, 37, 68.
Hannibal, 293.
Harmsworth, Alfred C., 205, 206, 332, 344.
Harris, Augustus, 150, 236, 238, 240, 273, 307.
,, Lady, 240.
,, Walter, 218.
Harte, Bret, 202.
Hartington, Lord, 170.
Harworth, Captain, 97.
Hatton, Joseph, 253, 363.
,, Sir Christopher, 186.
Hawarden, 267.
Haweis, Rev. Mr., 164.
Haxell's Hotel, 305.
Hayle, Cornwall, 314.
Heaton, Henniker, M.P., 199, 270, 333.
Hebron, 259.
Heenan, prizefighter, 71.
Henderson, Dalgety, 287.
Herbert, Miss, 90.
Herbertstown, 173.
Herman, Henry, 201, 212, 214.
Hersee, Henry, 109.
Hervé, Louis, 273.

Herzegovina, 335.
High Beach, 155.
,, Courts, 297.
Hilmy, Prince Ilbrahim, 239.
Hind, Mr., 34.
Hingston, E. P., 359.
Hockey in the Hole, 68.
Hodder, George, 95, 97.
Hoe & Co., 213.
,, Machine, 53.
,, Richard, 51, 53, 74, 77, 78, 80.
Hogan, Mary Ann, 174.
Holborn, 68, 132, 325.
,, Hill, 58.
,, Viaduct, 118.
Holland, Hon. Sydney, 244.
Hollingshead, John, 95, 105, 107.
Holloway, 230.
Holy Land, 258.
,, Sepulchre, Church of, 258, 259.
Home Office, 233, 234, 309.
,, Rule, 168, 169, 171, 176.
,, Secretary, 181, 231, 232, 245, 309.
Hood, Tom, 58, 110, 134, 317, 331.
,, Tom, the younger, 135, 136.
Hooper, Mr., 22.
Hope, Beresford, 28.
Hornsey, 68.
Horrovitz, Dr., 269.
Horse Shoe Fall, 223.
Hospital Fund, Prince of Wales's, 243.
Hospitals : St. Bartholomew's, 82, 243, 275 ; Poplar, 243 ; Queen's Jubilee, Kensington, 342 ; Royal South London Ophthalmic, 350.
Hôtel des Anglais, Mentone, 301.
Hours and Holidays of Bank Clerks, 144.
House of Commons, 352.
,, ,, Lords, 72.
Howell, G., 187.
Hugo, Victor, 122.
Hummums, 354.
Humphry, Mrs., 322.
,, Miss Pearl, 322.
"Hungry Forties," 4.
Hustings, 22.
Huxley, 301.

INDEX. 375

Hyde Park, 56, 87, 162.
Hyères, 301.

IAGO, 157.
Icilius, 237.
Ilford Cemetery, 246.
Illustrated London News, 34, 55.
Impalement, The, 35.
Imperial Federation, 211.
   „   Penny Post, 270.
Income Tax, 34, 187.
India, 100, 279.
Indian Princes, 296.
Ingoldsby, 50.
Institute of Journalists, 332.
Inverary, 140.
Inversnaid, 140.
Ireland, 117, 147, 156, 167, 168, 171, 172, 173.
Irving, Henry, 90, 105, 112 ; his salary, 113, 114 ; in the "Bells," 113 ; hundredth performance of "Hamlet," 114 ; parting from Mrs. Bateman, 117 ; his article for the Jubilee Number of *Lloyd's*, 211 ; my last interview with, 154, 155 ; 211, 213, 306, 314, 316, 317, 318, 319, 320 ; entertained by pressmen, 321.
Irving, Washington, 8.
Isaacs, L. H., 187, 188.
Isaiah, 263.
Isleworth, 131.
Islington, 311.
Italy, 235, 258.

JACKSON, Mr., 320.
   „   Phipps, 144.
Jacobite rising, 76.
Jacobs, conjurer, 336.
Jacques, reporter, 183.
Jaffa, 258.
Jagelman, James, 331.
James, David, 105, 358.
Jarrett, Rebecca, 183.
Javal, P. Cremieux, 273.
Jeffries, Miss, 213.
Jelf, Sir A. R., 203.
Jermy, Mr., 9.
Jerome, Jerome K., 212.
Jerrold, Douglas, 37, 45, 46, 47, 56, 57, 61, 62, 64, 66, 80, 88, 134, 145, 164, 177, 255, 272, 359.
Jerrold, Tom, 255.

Jerrold, Walter, 344.
   „   William Blanchard, 62, 89, 96, 128, 160, 161, 361.
Jerusalem, 258, 259, 263.
Jews, 262.
Jingle, 113.
Johnson, Dr., 36, 310.
   „   and Nelson Lee, 44.
   „   Tavern, 36.
   „   W. S., 319.
Jones, A. Kennedy, 344.
   „   Henry Arthur, 214.
Jordan, 259.
Josephus, 262.
Journalists, British International Association of, 342.
Judea, 264.
Judges and Contempt, 298.
Jupiter, Temple of, 262.

KATRINE, Loch, 140.
Kean, Charles, 59, 113, 153, 154, 321.
   „   Edmund, 114, 154, 157.
   „   Mrs., 321.
Keeley, Mrs., 322.
   „   Miss M., 64.
Kegan Paul, 144.
Kelvin, Lord, 301.
Kendal, Mrs., 64.
Kensington, 42, 342.
   „   South, 163.
Kent, 44, 226, 270.
Kershaw, Mr., 156.
Khalifa, 284, 286.
Khartoum, 167, 280, 283, 284, 285, 287.
Khedive, 285.
Kift, J., 273.
Kilburn, 47.
Killarney, 173.
"King Arthur," poem, 119.
King, Lovett, 273.
   „   Yeend, 333.
King's College, London, 48.
   „   Cross, 319.
Kings and Key, 35.
Kipling, Rudyard, 201, 202, 250, 251.
Kiralfy, Imre, 193.
Kirby, 186.
   „   Great Hall of, 186.
Kitchener, Lord, 238, 275, 283, 284.
Knight Bruce, Lord Justice, 78.

INDEX.

Knight, Charles, 62.
„ Joseph, 320, 331.
Knock Long Station, Ireland, 173.
Koening, 77.

Lambeth Palace, 150, 210, 271.
Land Purchase Scheme, 169.
Langtry, Mrs., 213.
Larkin, Miss, 358.
Latey, John Lash, 97.
Lathom, Earl of, 275.
Lawrence, Sir Joseph, 288.
Lawson, The Hon. Harry, 332, 344.
Lea Bridge Road, 68.
Leadenhall Institute, 71.
Lebanon, 262.
Ledger, Edward, 105.
Lee, Nelson, 44, 357.
Le Hay, John, 273.
Leigh, H. S., 305.
Leith, 140.
„ Hill, 102.
Lemon, Mark, 62.
Le Sage, John M., 332.
Letchworth, Sir E., 272.
Levanter, 235.
Levy, Jonas, 228.
Lewis, George, 116.
Liberal, 168, 189, 190.
Licensing Act of 1872, 107.
Lichfield, Bishop of, 211.
"Light That Failed, The," 202.
Lillie Bridge, 151.
Limerick, 173.
Lincoln, R., 188.
Linn's Fish Shop, 41.
Linton, Sir James, 333.
„ Mrs. Lynn, 201.
Lisbon, 348.
Litton, Miss Marie, 358.
Lloyd, Mr. Arthur, 304, 332.
„ Mrs. Arthur, 304.
„ Mr. Edward, 39, 40, 43, 44, 45, 46, 47, 52, 53, 61, 78, 86, 87, 91, 92, 98, 124, 126, 127, 143, 144, 152, 160, 161, 162, 164, 166, 169, 194, 195, 198, 203, 294, 359.
„ Mr. Frank, 198, 200, 304, 329, 332, 333, 339, 344.

Lloyd, Mrs. Frank, 304.
„ Mr. Harry, 304, 332.
„ Mr. Herbert, 276.
Lloyd's, 32, 36, 44, 46, 47, 48, 56, 65, 72, 79, 85, 87, 89, 97, 104, 117, 118, 131, 132, 139, 140, 143, 152, 153, 162, 164, 168, 170, 171, 179, 180, 181, 183, 194, 196, 200, 202, 203, 207, 211, 231, 234, 243, 246, 270, 272, 292, 300, 302, 303, 304, 313, 319, 325, 327, 328, 329, 330, 331; started unstamped at a penny, 43; first stamped number twopence, 45; down to a penny, 73; Jubilee Number, 210; a million circulation, 241.
Lloyd's Paper Mill, 139.
Londesborough, Earl of, 273.
London, 150, 271, 288, 289, 312, 314, 316, 322, 326, 338, 343, 345.
London Bridge, 57, 125.
Longfellow, 67.
Lords, House of, 207.
Loveday, Henry, 321.
Lovell, John, 136.
Lowe, Robert, 104.
Lucy, Sir Henry, 110, 169.
Lueger, Dr., 322.
Luna Island, 223.
Luxor, 280.
Lyons, Joseph, 334.
Lytton, Lord, 64, 88, 119, 120.

Maccabe, 243.
Macduff, 157.
Macedonians, 262.
M'Hardy, Professor Malcolm, 350.
McKendrick, Mr., 235.
Mackenzie, H. H. Morell, 273.
McNaghten, trial of, 248.
Macready, 113, 157, 158.
Macsycophant, Sir Pertinax, 146.
Madge, W. T., 332.
Magazines: *Cassell's*, 66, *Cornhill*, 66; *Fortnightly*, 164; *London Journal*, 66; *Nineteenth Century*, 195.
Mahdi, 286.
Mahomet, 262.
Malaga, 299.
Mallaka, 262.

INDEX. 377

Malta, 235, 236, 296.
Mamillius, Ellen Terry as, 59.
"Manchester Man, The," 253.
Manning, Cardinal, 208.
Mannings, The, 49.
Mansfield, Chief Justice, 248.
Mansion House, 209.
Maple, Blundell, 187, 188.
Margate, 312, 314, 357.
Marlborough College, 317.
Marshall, Frank, 321.
Marston, Henry, 157, 158.
Martin, Sir Theodore, 27.
Maskelyne, Mr., 337.
Massena, General, 349.
Matabele War, 350.
Match Tax, 104.
Mathews, Charles, 356.
Mathias, 113.
Matthews, J. H., 274.
Maurice, Rev. F. D., 48, 49.
May, Phil, 354, 355.
Maybrick, Mrs., 300.
Mayhew, Athol, 358.
,, Horace, 62, 88.
Mazagan, 296.
Mead, Mr., 149.
,, Alfred, 331.
Mecca, 357.
,, Kaaba of, 299.
Medea, 116.
Mediterranean, 235, 240, 258, 280, 299, 302.
Melanesia, 172.
Mellon, Harriet, 153.
Melville's Macbeth, 7.
Mentone, 269, 301.
Meran, 323.
Meritt, Paul, 226.
Merriman, Mr., 302.
Merry, Mr., 71, 72.
,, Tom, 355.
Midlothian, 167, 170.
Miljacka River, 335.
Millward, Charles, 110, 305.
Milnes, Monckton, 62.
Milton, 100.
Mitre Square, 183, 184.
,, Tragedy, 184.
Mogador, 296.
Montague, H. J., 105.
Mont Blanc, 340.
Monte D'Oro, 302.
Mont Estoril, 348.
Montmartre, 104.

Moody, Mr., 265.
Moore, Alfred, 273.
,, John, 332.
Morgan, Alderman Vaughan, 288.
Morley, Lord, 169, 171.
Mormons, 219, 220.
Morrell, Mr., 56.
Morris, Clara, 74.
Morton, A. C., 347.
,, Charles, 68, 303.
Mostar, 335.
Mourey, Madame, 183.
Muddock, J. E., 304.
Mudford, Mr., 96, 118.
Murphy, Mr., 361.
Murray, David Christie, 337, 338, 339.
,, John, 344.
Music Halls: Bedford, 70; Canterbury, 69, 304; Deacons, 97; Palace, 304.
Mutual Building Association of New York, 196.

NAPLES, 258.
Napoleon III., 56, 122, 124, 128, 293.
,, Prince Louis, 153, 154.
Natal, 270.
National Sunday League, 56.
Nazareth, 260.
"Newcomes, The," 37.
Newgate, 49, 147, 148, 230.
Newhaven, 103.
New Jersey, 213.
New "Pilgrim's Progress," 135.
New River, 68.
New South Wales, 210, 270.
Newspapers: *Athenæum*, 41, 206, 211, 351; *Cambridge Chronicle*, 17, 26; *Clerkenwell News*, 52, 126, 127, 144; *Daily Chronicle*, 52, 128, 143, 144, 162, 188, 201, 209, 269, 332, 350; *Daily Graphic*, 202, 270, 332; *Daily Mail*, 332; *Daily News*, 95, 169, 332, 361; *Daily Telegraph*, 52, 65, 135, 141, 250, 332, 333; *Dispatch*, 36, 45, 122; *Echo*, 118; *Edinburgh Daily Review*, 170; *Evening Standard*, 108; *Family Herald*, 22; *Field*, 332; *Figaro*, 110; *Fun*, 115, 132, 135, 136; *Glas-

gow National, 360; *Hornet*, 110, 311; *Illustrated London News*, 97, 269; *Islington Gazette*, 311; *Judy*, 351; *La Patrie*, 52; *Le Matin*, 288; *Lloyd's*, see under Lloyd's; *Moonshine*, 241, 351; *Morning Advertiser*, 32, 36; *Morning Leader*, 332; *Morning Post*, 87, 162, 163, 332; *News of the World*, 111, 332; *Northern Whig*, 144; *One and All*, 255; *Pall Mall Gazette*, 180, 183; *People*, 332; *Police News*, 149; *Porcupine*, 305; *Printers' Circular, Philadelphia*, 362; *Punch*, 35, 46, 352; *Referee*, 135, 136, 234, 255, 287, 332; *Rocky Mountain Times*, 362; *Salt Lake Herald*, 220; *Standard*, 96, 108, 117, 118, 143, 303, 332; *Sunday Times*, 36; *The Hour*, 127; *The Penny Pickwick*, 98; *Times*, 6, 24, 42, 51, 58, 62, 77, 79, 119, 190, 192, 202, 270, 297, 334, 359, 362; *Times of India*, 118; *Tribune*, 332; *Truth*, 110; *Westminster Gazette*, 303.
New York, 51, 53, 80, 113, 117, 196, 213, 215, 219.
New Zealand, 327, 347.
Niagara, 137, 222, 242.
Nice, 269, 301, 302.
Nicholls, Harry, 273, 333.
Nicholson, Baron, 109.
Nicoll, Sir William Robertson, 273, 332.
Nile, 279, 282, 283, 284.
„ Expedition, 168.
Noah, 262.
North Cape, 344.
North, Colonel, 186.
Northcliffe, Lord, 205, 206, 332, 344.
Northcott, John, 111, 212, 273, 313, 321.
Norton, Dr. John, 245.
Norway, 270, 345.
Norwood, 321.
„ Cemetery, 62.

O'BRIEN, William, 176.
Occidental Hotel, 109.

O'Connor, T. P., 333.
Odell, E. J., 105, 273.
Ogden, H. M., 188.
Ogleby, Sir John, 146.
O'Grady, The, 174, 175.
Old Bailey, 49, 133, 147, 150, 182, 229.
Old Broad Street, 316.
Oliphant, Mrs., 201.
Oliver, Miss K., 64.
Olives, Mount of, 259.
Olympia, 193.
Omdurman, 283, 284, 286.
Ophelia, 213.
Opium den in Australia, 212.
Ouida, 201, 252, 253.
Oxenford, John, 359.
Oxford, Trial of, 248.
„ University, 133.

PAARDEBURG, 283.
Page, Dr. F. Byrd, 334.
Paget, Lord Alfred, 105.
Pain, Barry, 212.
Palace Yard, 170.
Palermo, 272.
Palestine, 135.
Palmer, William, 58.
Pangloss, Dr., 157.
Paper Duties repealed, 72, 73.
Papier maché stereos, 76.
Paris, 39, 52, 102, 104, 128, 288.
Park Lane, 87.
Parke, Ernest, 332, 344.
Parkinson, J. C., 150, 273.
Parliament, 163, 170, 181, 296.
„ Acts of, 187.
Parnell, J. H., 145.
Patent Office, 53.
Patterson, Mr., 172.
Pattison, Mr. F. W., 144.
Pavilion, Brighton, 290.
Paxton, Sir Joseph, 20, 255.
Payn, James, 201, 253, 269.
Peace, Charles, 147.
„ Sir Walter, 270.
Peacock, Ed. E., 303, 332.
Pearcy, Mrs., 203.
Pearson, Arthur, 332, 344.
Peele's Coffee House, 35.
"Peerage for the People," 45.
Penniket, 36.
Penny Post introduced, 249.
Penrose, Mr., 220.

INDEX.

Perdita, Marie Wilton as, 59.
Persians, 262.
Perth, W. A., 246.
Peterborough, Bishop of, 211.
Pettitt, Henry, 224, 225, 226.
Phelps, 64, 66, 145, 146, 157, 213, 321.
Phené, Dr., 351.
Philadelphia, 215.
Philpotts, Eden, 212.
Photography — sun portraits, 19.
Piccadilly, 322.
Pickburn, 127.
Pickersgill, Mr., 187.
Pickled Egg Walk, 68.
Pickwick, 82, 98, 99, 112.
Pieman, Tossing a, 19.
Pimlico, 129.
  ,,   Murder, 132.
Plays :—*A Life of Pleasure*, 224 ; *A Message from Mars*, 358 ; *A Rapid Thaw*, 90 ; *A Valentine*, 81 ; *A Winter's Tale*, 59 ; *A Woman's Revenge*, 224 ; *Belphegor*, 59 ; *Black Ey'd Susan*, 64 ; *Bluebeard*, 237 ; *Bonnie Dundee*, 81 ; *Caste*, 90 ; *Charles the First*, 113 ; *Clari, the Maid of Milan*, 34 ; *Dora*, 90 ; *Fair Maid of Perth*, 357 ; *Fanchette*, 112 ; *George de Barnwell*, 81 ; *Hamlet*, 113, 114, 117, 213 ; *Henry V.*, 237 ; *Human Nature*, 238 ; *Lady Audley's Secret*, 81 ; *Macbeth*, 7, 71, 115, 157 ; *Madame Sans Gêne*, 318 ; *Manfred*, 84 ; *Merchant of Venice*, 319 ; *Mont Blanc*, 69 ; *One Touch of Nature*, 81 ; *Othello*, 318 ; *Our Boys*, 358 ; *Overland Mail*, 358 ; *Pericles*, 47 ; *Pink Dominos*, 237 ; *Richelieu*, 120 ; *Romeo and Juliet*, 242 ; *Sign of the Cross*, 255 ; *The Bells*, 112, 318 ; *The Great City*, 90 ; *The Grey Mare*, 81 ; *The Housekeeper*, 64 ; *The Rent Day*, 64 ; *The Silver King*, 214; *The World*, 237 ; *Two Roses*, 112, 317 ; *Virginius*, 237 ; *Walker, London*, 209.
Plough Monday, 8.
Plunkett, Captain, 174, 175.
Plymouth, 145.
Poland, Sir H. B., 125, 183.
Police News, 149.
Polytechnic, The Old, 71.
Pompeii, 258.
Pope Pio Nono, 272.
Poplar Hospital, 244.
Portsmouth, 292.
Portuguese, 347.
Potter, T. B., 159.
Pounds, Courtice, 273.
Powell, Baden, 350.
Powis, Lord, 6.
Press Association, 136, 332.
  ,,   Fund, 360,
  ,,   Gallery, 169.
Preston, Henry, 325.
Prevention of Cruelty to Animals Act, 204.
Primrose Hill, 68.
Prince Von Buelow, 343.
Prince, murderer, 247.
Princess Royal, 176.
Printing revolutionised, 50.
Prior, Melton, 306.
Prisoner as machinist, 18.
Proctor, John, 351.
Protection, 133.
Proverbs, Book of, 25.
Pryor, S. J., 332.
Psalms, 92.
Puddle Dock, 68.
Punch, 35, 46, 352.
Purkess, Mr., 149.
Putney Hill, 276.

" Q," 201, 250.
Queen's Bench, 203.
  ,,   Jubilee Hospital, 342.

RADCLIFFE, John, 273.
Rahere Lodge, 275.
Railways: introduction of, 5 ; open carriages, 32 ; Canadian Pacific, 221 ; London, Chatham and Dover, 189 ; London and Brighton, 228 ; Great Eastern 316 ; South Eastern, 57 ; tariff war in America, 219 ; earliest mountain railway, 324.
Rayleigh, Mr., 156.

Rea, J. U., 65, 85, 86.
Reade, Charles, 90, 121.
Red Lion Square, 48.
Reece, Robert, 105, 134.
Reeves, Sims, 64.
Regent's Park, 256, 319.
Regent Street, 335.
Reichstag, Berlin, 342.
Rendel, Mr., 195.
Reseler, Dr., 343.
Reuter's Agency, 73, 312, 332.
Richard III., 279.
Richardson, 37.
   „   Sir Benjamin Ward, 341.
Richelieu, 146.
Richford, U.S.A., 325.
Richmond, 154.
   „   Park, 97.
Richon le Zion, 263.
Richter, Jean Paul, 66.
Riddell, George A., 332.
Ridley, Sir Matthew White, 231.
"Rights and Responsibilities of Labour," 198.
Rignold, George, 237.
Ripon, Bishop of, 211.
   „   Marquis of, 272.
Ripper atrocities, 183.
Ristori, Madame, 116.
Riva, 323.
Riviera, 302, 340.
Robbins, E., 332.
Roberts, Lord, 275.
Robertson of Brighton, 49.
   „   Forbes, 321.
   „   Stuart, 331.
   „   Tom, 155.
Rochdale, 133.
Rochester, Bishop of, 211, 350.
   „   Row Police Station, 130, 131.
Rockies, The, 222.
Rolfe, Baron, 11.
Roman Catholic, 208.
Romano's, 355.
Romans, 80, 262, 348.
Rome, 135, 258, 334.
Ronald, Landon, 333.
Ronda, Spain, 236, 299.
Rosebery, Lord, 133.
Ross, 36.
Rothschild, Baron, 263.
Roumania, Queen of, 202.
Rovereto, 323.

Rowton, Lord, 206, 207, 208.
   „   House, 207, 208.
Royal Academy, 192, 333, 344.
   „   Humane Society, 137.
   „   Standard, 215.
Rugby, 133, 271.
Rush murders, 9.
Ruskin, 49.
Russell, Clark, 201.
   „   Sir Edward, 311.
   „   W. H., 64.
Russia, 55.
   „   War with, 33.
Russians, 263.
Ryan, Father, 176.
Rymer, Mr., 39.

SADLER'S WELLS, 47, 89, 96.
Saffron Hill, 68.
Sahara, 293.
St. Alban's, Duke of, 153.
St. Bartholomew's Hospital, 82, 243, 275.
St. Bride's, 35, 41, 67.
   „   Institute, 330.
St. Cloud, 103.
St. Denis, Gate of, 103.
St. Dunstan's Church, 186.
St. George's Day, 214.
   „   Hanover Square, 142.
   „   Road, Southwark, 327.
St. James's Great Hall, 100.
   „   Square, 195, 197.
St. John's College, Cambridge, 270.
   „   Gate, 120.
St. Margaret's Hall, Canterbury, 270.
St. Martin's Hall, 72.
St. Paul's Cathedral, 108, 244.
St. Petersburg, 179, 312.
St. Sepulchre's Church, 50.
Sala, George Augustus, 74, 95, 206.
Salamon, Gordon, 333.
Sala's Journal, 206.
Salisbury, Lord, 335.
   „   Square, 32, 38, 67, 121, 132, 183, 202.
Salomons, Sir Julian, 270.
Salt Lake City, 219.
Salvation Army, 180.
Salvationists, 180.
Salzburg, 323.

INDEX. 381

Samos, 266.
Sampson, Henry, 116, 135, 136, 137.
" Mrs., 116.
Sand, Georges, 112.
Sandringham, 107.
Sands, 8.
San Francisco, 133, 220.
Sanger, Lord George, 279.
Sankey, Ira D., 265.
San Remo, 268.
Saracens, 262.
Sardou, 225.
Sargent, John S., 333.
Saskatchewan River, 222.
Savage Club Lodge, 273, 274.
Savages, 155, 303, 355.
Savoy, 239, 306.
Sawyer, William, 331.
Sayers, prizefighter, 71.
Scallywag, The, 195.
Schartau, Mr., 273.
Schweitzer, Herr George, 343.
Scotland, 140, 157, 347.
" Yard, 93, 177.
Scott, Hope, 172.
" Mrs., 325.
" Sir Walter, 37, 119, 318, 338, 357.
Scribblers' Club, 109, 110.
Scripp League, 188.
Seacoal Lane, 58.
Seaforth Highlanders, 284, 285.
Seaman, Edward T., 321.
Sedan, 125.
"Self-Help," by Samuel Smiles, 205.
Selwyn, Rev. William, 172.
Semmering, 323.
Senior, William, 332.
Serajevo, 335.
Sermon on the Mount, 259.
Seville, 299.
Shakspere, 47, 92, 113, 119, 122, 242, 262, 318, 341.
Sharon, 263.
Sharp, Mr., 144.
Sharpe, jockey, 72.
Shoreditch, 125.
Shorter, Clement, 316, 332.
Sidi Okba, 293.
Sims, George R., 116, 136, 212, 255, 287, 306, 330.
Sinclair, Archdeacon, 292.
Singer, Herr W., 343.

Sirdar, 286.
Sittingbourne, 139.
Skelmersdale, Lord, 275.
Skinner, Mr., 144.
Sly, Christopher, 146.
Smiles, Samuel, 205.
Smith, Albert, 64, 69.
" George Barnett, 164.
" Joseph, 220.
" Major Henry, 184.
" Sir Donald, 245.
Smyrna, 264.
Snow-hill, 68.
Soden, J. E., 306.
Sodor and Man, Bishop of, 211.
Soho Square, 128.
Somerset House, 144.
Sothern, actor, 81.
Soudan, 167.
Soudanese, 281, 283, 284, 285.
South Africa, 246, 276, 283, 350.
Southampton, 269.
" Street, 355.
Southwark, Bishop of, 211.
" Police Court, 125.
Southwell, Bishop of, 211.
Spain, Southern, 101; 235, 236, 299.
Spaniards, 294.
Spencer, Herbert, 256.
" J. E., 301.
Spielmann, M. H., 344.
Spurgeon, Arthur, 332.
" C. H., 60, 61, 211.
Spurgeon's Tabernacle, 96.
Stafford, Execution at, 59.
Stamp Duty, 52, 79.
Stanley, Dean, 258.
" H. M., 198, 199.
Stead, W. T., 179, 180, 182, 183.
Stephen, King, 243.
Stephenson, Sir A. K., 182.
Stereotyping, 76.
Sterry, Ashby, 331.
Stevens, B. F., 351.
Stewart, Mr., 301.
Stirling Castle, 141.
Stirlingshire, 347.
Stockmar, Baron, 27.
Stoker, Bram, 154, 321, 333.
Storm of 1843, 2.
Strand, The, 110, 177, 178, 250, 305, 355.
Stratton Street, 316.
Suffield, Lord, 208.

Sullivan, Barry, 331.
Sun Building Society, 132.
  „ Temple of the, 262.
Sunday Schools Centenary, 150.
Sunderland, 327.
Surface, Charles, 311.
Surrey, 352.
  „ Gardens, 60.
Sutherland, 347.
Swinburne, 122, 276.
Switzerland, 340.
Syllabub, 8.
Syracuse, 236.
Syria, 262, 265.
Syrians, 281.

TALFOURD, 134.
Talmage, Dr., 213.
Tangier, 236, 296.
Taunay, Mons. Victor, 288, 343.
Tavistock Hotel, Covent Garden, 188.
Tax on Advertisements, 45.
Taylor, Rev. Dr., 270.
Teazle, Lady, 311.
Telegraph Co., Electric and International, 74.
Temple Bar, 108.
  „ Dr., 271.
  „ The, 35.
Tennyson, Lord, 66, 138.
Terra del Fuego, 225.
Terriss, William, 247.
Terry, Edward, 273, 274.
  „ Ellen, 59, 117, 213.
  „ Kate, 90.
Thackeray, W. M., 37, 62, 64, 66, 91, 119, 249, 250.
Thames, The, 58, 68, 140, 147, 247.
Theatres: Adelphi, 64, 81, 90, 224, 225; Court, 163; Covent Garden, 34, 81; Criterion, 237; Drury Lane, 35, 62, 64, 81, 90, 116, 224, 237, 238, 314, 354, 357; Gaiety, 95, 107; Grecian, 226; Haymarket, 64, 81, 105, 322, 337; Lyceum, 111, 112, 317, 319; New Olympic, 214; Opera Comique, 359; Princess's, 59, 90, 146, 321; Prince of Wales's, 90; Royalty, 237; Sadler's Wells, 47, 68, 97, 146, 213, 321; St.

James's, 81, 90; Surrey, 350; The Standard, 34, 91, 101, 357; Vaudeville, 105, 317.
Thiers, Mons., 104.
Thormanby, Derby winner, 72.
Thomas, Arthur, 346.
  „ G. Stole, 332.
  „ Henwood, 144.
  „ W. L., 270.
Thompson, Miss, 147.
Thomson, John, 122.
  „ William, 301.
Thorn, Geoffrey, 273.
Thorndike, 273.
Thorne, Thomas, 105.
Three Kings Court, 86.
Thurgood, Mr., 121.
Tiberias, 260.
Tindal, Chief Justice, 248.
Tinder-box, 4.
Tinsley, William, 106, 319.
Tipstaff, The, 298.
Toll-gates, 228.
Tomatoes, 20.
Tom Thumb, 8.
Toole, J. L., 59, 81, 105, 116, 209, 273, 316, 319.
Toronto, 326.
Tory, 190.
Townley, Charles, 110, 306, 311.
Trafalgar Square, 177, 179.
Transvaal, 284.
Trappist Monastery of Staovéli, 294.
Treadaway, Fdk., 129, 130, 131.
Treasury, The, 182.
  „ The Washington, 216.
Tree, Ellen, 53, 154.
Treloar, Sir William, 135, 332.
Trent, 323.
Trinity College, Dublin, 133.
  „ Church, New York, 215.
Truscott, Sir Francis, 306.
Tudor Street, 68.
Tunis, 293.
Tupper, Sir Charles, 221.
Turk, 262.
Turkey, 335.
Turner, Lord Justice, 78.
  „ Godfrey, 331.
  „ Neil, 330.
Turtles, 74, 77, 80.
Twain, Mark, 134, 135, 278.
Twist, Oliver, 68.
Tynan, 156, 157.

INDEX.

Union Bank, 298.
,, Jack, 215, 220.
Upton, Frederick, 334.
Urban, Sylvanus, 351.
Utah, U.S.A., 219.
Uxbridge Road Station, 268.
Uz, 262.

Van Amburg, 8.
Vancouver, 221.
Vancouver Island, 220.
Van Horne, W. C., 221.
Vauxhall, 207.
,, Gardens, 69.
Venice, 135, 258, 334.
Venus, Temple of, 262.
Versailles, 103.
Verulam, 326.
Vesuvius, 258.
Vezin, Herman, 358.
Victoria House, 218.
,, Queen, 232, 233, 234, 240, 244, 248, 292; visit by road to Cambridge, 2; visit by rail to Cambridge, 6; speech, 19; visit to City, July 9th, 1851...20; extract from Prince Consort's letter, 27; grief at Prince Consort's death, 76; present at thanksgiving service at St. Paul's, 108; opened Epping Forest, 155; Jubilee, 176; thanksgiving service, Westminster Abbey, 176; birthday celebrations in Vancouver Island, 220; letter on death of Prince Henry of Battenberg reproduced in *Lloyd's*, 231; Diamond Jubilee, 243; witnessed Sanger's circus at Windsor, 279; passing of, 291; cost of Coronation, 295.
Vienna, 269, 322, 343.
Vine, Sir Somers, 307.
Vizetelly, Jas., 249.
Vizzavona, 302.
Von Moltke, 343.
Von Rheinhaben, 343.
Von Schoen, 343.
Von Veltheim, Madame, 246.
,, ,, Moritz, 246, 247.
Voules, Horace, 118.

Wady Halfa, 280, 281, 283.

Wainwright, Henry, 125, 126.
,, Thomas, 125, 126.
Wakefield, Bishop of, 211, 226.
Wales, 43, 226.
,, Prince of, 80, 107, 108, 150, 191, 210, 241, 242, 243, 272, 275, 306.
,, Princess of, 150.
Wallack, Lester, 153.
Walpole, Horace, 151.
Walter, Mr., 270.
,, Arthur, 342.
"Wandering Jew, The," 39.
Wandsworth Prison, 340.
Ward, Artemus, 134, 155, 359.
Warming-pan, 4.
Warner, Charles, 105.
,, William Robert, 133.
Warren, Sir Charles, 177, 185.
,, Rev. Walpole, 215.
Warwick, 210.
Washington, 215.
,, Portrait of, 215.
Water Lane, 68.
Waterloo Bridge, 178.
Watkin, Sir Edward, 137.
Watling Street, 226.
Watson, Aaron, 304.
Watts-Dunton, T., 276.
Webb, Captain, 137.
Webster, Benjamin, 81, 105, 356.
,, Kate, 147.
Weldon-Stone, 186.
Wellington, Duke of, 46, 55, 349.
,, Duchess of, 153, 154.
,, Monument, 192.
,, Street, 178.
Welsh rabbit, 36.
West End, 172.
Westminster, 162, 209, 245.
,, Abbey, 67, 176, 177, 295.
,, Aquarium, 138.
,, Bridge, 158.
,, Hall, 295.
Weston, The Walker, 151.
Weyman, Stanley, 201.
Wheatsheaf Yard, 32.
Wheeler, Mr., 325.
Whisky for medicinal use, 216, 217.
Whitechapel, 140.
,, Tragedy, 125.
Whitefriars Club, 228, 331.
Whitehead, Lord Mayor, 209.

White House, Washington, 215, 216.
Wiesbaden, 343.
Wiggins executed, 94.
Wilde, Oscar, 229, 230, 231.
William IV., 295.
Williams, Charles, 108, 212, 286.
Willis, Dr., 235.
„ Mr., 143.
Willis's Rooms, 154, 306.
Wills, Mr., 113.
„ „ Justice, 229.
Wilmot, Charles, 109.
Wilson, Dr. Andrew, 162, 212.
„ J. Farlow, 332.
Wilton, Miss, 59, 81.
Winchester, 133.
Winchilsea, Lord, 186, 187.
Window Tax, 20.
Windsor, 234, 279.
Windsor Castle, 74, 75, 76, 232, 233.
Wingate, Lady, 286.
Winnipeg, 222.
Winter, John Strange (Mrs. Stannard), 256.
Wisconsin, 328.
Wiseman, Cardinal, 67.
Wombwell's Show, 7.
Wood, Walter, 117.
Woolacott, J. E., 332.
Woolman, 121.
Worcester, Bishop of, 211.
Working Men's College, 48.
Wright, George, 77.
„ Willie, 273.
Wyndham, Sir Charles, 308.

YORK, 146.

ZANGWILL, L., 212.

www.ingramcontent.com/pod-product-compliance
Lightning Source LLC
Chambersburg PA
CBHW062125160426
43191CB00013B/2195